THE
TREASURE
OF
EARTHEN
VESSELS

Brian H. Childs and David W. Waanders, editors

THE TREASURE OF EARTHEN VESSELS

Explorations in Theological Anthropology

In Honor of James N. Lapsley

Westminster John Knox Press
Louisville, Kentucky

Scripture quotations from the New Revised Standard Version of the Bible are copyright © 1989 by the Division of Christian Education of the National Coun-cil of the Churches of Christ in the U.S.A., and are used by permission.

Book design by Susan E. Jackson

Cover design by Frank Peronne

First edition

Published by Westminster John Knox Press
Louisville, Kentucky

This book is printed on acid-free paper that meets the American National Standards Institute Z39.48 standard. ∞

PRINTED IN THE UNITED STATES OF AMERICA

94 95 96 97 98 99 00 01 02 03 04—10 9 8 7 6 5 4 3 2 1

Library of Congress Cataloging-in-Publication Data

The treasure of earthen vessels : explorations in theological anthropology
   in honor of James N. Lapsley / Brian H. Childs, David W. Waanders,
   editors. — 1st ed.
       p.   cm.
   Includes bibliographical references.
   ISBN 0-664-25493-4 (alk. paper)
   1. Man (Christian theology).   2. Lapsley, James N.   I. Lapsley, James N.
II. Childs, Brian H.   III. Waanders, David W.
BT701.2.T72   1994
233—dc20
                                                                    94-524

Contents

A Personal Tribute to
James N. Lapsley

Liston O. Mills

One of the more unfortunate aspects of the academic life is that appreciation is often unspoken or, if spoken, is couched in terms of intellectual achievement. What is ignored or neglected are the threads of commitment, friendship, pain, loyalty, and courage that go into the shaping of a life. I was pleased, then, to learn that this volume honoring Jim Lapsley was to include a personal word. And I was gratified when requested to speak that word.

If memory serves, I met Jim in Washington, D.C., in 1964 at a meeting of the Association of Seminary Professors in the Practical Fields. It was the first such meeting both for us and for several others who were getting started as teachers. It was a great time to be a pastoral theologian even though most of us were not absolutely sure what that was. We felt that we had an important contribution to make both to theological education and to the church, and we wanted to ensure that the values we prized found expression. After an evening session, several new professors retreated for refreshments and conversation. In retrospect, I realize that many of the characteristics we have come to appreciate in Jim were apparent in that meeting.

It was clear, for example, that he had a deep commitment to the values he perceived in pastoral care as well as an equally deep commitment to the Christian tradition. Over the years these commitments became explicit. His work at The Menninger Foundation and his ongoing clinical experience convinced him that something valuable was to be learned by "grubbing in the root systems of human life" and that it was important to use a variety of behavioral science theories in this enterprise. But he was, and is, convinced that whatever understandings we glean must be placed in relation to what we envision as central in the theological tradition. His real quest was to understand what it meant to be human in today's world. Eventually, this quest came to focus in the concepts of salvation and health and their relation, and was grounded in the conviction that the most pressing deficiency in pastoral care was its lack of adequate theological anthropology.

Obviously, this orientation to pastoral theology involved unusual analytical ability and critical judgment that over time included increasing awareness of what he described as the "convolutions of culture." He realized, earlier than most, that the therapeutic had indeed triumphed and attended the results for church and ministry. During the 1970s he published articles and editorials arguing that, despite its contributions, pastors must be critical and discriminating in their appropriation of dynamic psychology. He pointed to our need for a sexual ethic that would deal fairly and justly with the homosexual community. He noted the cultural change from a guilt to a shame culture and suggested the implications this might have for our orientation to counseling theory. He decried our silence about death. Finally, he advocated lay pastoral care long before it became fashionable.

These judgments reflect his view of the church as a potentially healing and redemptive community consisting of persons whose lives have been touched by the gospel. He entered the fray as a theologian and a minister, and sought to estimate the value of such sacred cows as sensitivity training, premarital counseling, and client-centered therapy. He has always been willing to show himself and to submit his ideas for critical reflection while encouraging others to do the same. The fruits of his emphases have been obvious both in his students and in his colleagues. The former benefited from his clarity, his perspective, and his person. The latter demonstrated their confidence in him by electing him Dean of the Faculty at Princeton Theological Seminary in 1985.

The values that are reflected in these endeavors have been present in his work with colleagues in pastoral care. His concern for the field is genuine and intense. He has consistently participated in our efforts for self-understanding and definition. He served on the editorial committee of the *Journal of Pastoral Care* and has consistently supported clinical pastoral education as a mode of learning. He has also served as Chair, succeeding Seward Hiltner, of the editorial committee of *Pastoral Psychology*.

His concern for the field has not been restricted, however, to its definitions, methods, and ideas. I recall a conversation in the Philadelphia airport in the late 1970s during which he began to reflect on the isolation experienced by teachers of pastoral care. No professional or academic setting addressed the issues peculiar to these individuals. Though it was in labor for nearly a decade, the Society for Pastoral Theology was conceived that day. The impetus for it was our need for a forum for mutual sharing among peers about the pedagogical, theological, and pastoral problems endemic to our work.

The qualities I have described have served us well. Chuck Gerkin once described Jim as an "old Calvinist" possessed of a "healthy skepticism." He was right. Jim's Calvinist roots manifested themselves not in rigid orthodoxies but in what, in my judgment, is a legitimate suspicion of plans, schemes, and programs that do not acknowledge the soft underbelly of our common life. His skepticism has more than once called us to attention when we were, as we so often are, tempted by this or that fad, cliché, or latest miracle cure. Like many Presbyterians, he manifests a capacity for planning and organization, an affinity for policy and procedure, and an attention to detail that has frequently saved us from ourselves.

These are some of the ways in which we are indebted to Jim Lapsley. But some of us owe him a larger debt in that we have known him not simply as colleague or teacher but as friend. With him the term that comes to mind is fidelity. I have seen it in his devotion to his late wife, Brenda Weakley Lapsley, particularly in their endurance of her long and tortuous illness. I have seen it in his devotion to and pride in his children, Joe, a musician, and Jacqueline, a student at Princeton Theological Seminary. I have seen it in his frequent trips to Tennessee to attend an aging and ailing mother to ensure that she received proper care. And I, along with many others—students, colleagues, neighbors—have known it firsthand. What Jim brings to persons is not effusiveness or glad-handedness. He brings instead a wry humor and unfailing candor. I recall writing him after an illness and describing my new regimen of diet and exercise. His response was that he hoped I would not become "intolerably ascetic." He gives to others measured judgment and a capacity to hear and understand. Most of all, he brings a lack of alarm and a smile in the presence of human foibles—a subtle playfulness that precludes taking himself or others too seriously, especially when they don't deserve it.

When I last saw Jim, he and his wife Helen had attended a reunion at his college, Rhodes, and then returned to his home church, First Presbyterian of Clarksville, Tennessee, as guests for a celebration. It was clear that his retirement and his marriage to Helen, a gracious and intelligent woman, had made the move to Sun City symbolic of a promising future. He spoke earnestly of his new study and how good it was not to be distracted from primary interests. When they left, I recalled some words I had written about him years before: "[He] served as my confidant, guide, and most important, friend. I sought his counsel on all major decisions and many minor ones, and more than once, I handed him my frustrations. He always responded with understanding and good sense; no one can ask for more."

Acknowledgments

We first acknowledge our indebtedness to Jim Lapsley, who has been our teacher and mentor and over the years our colleague and friend. This collection of essays reflects Jim's influence on the field of pastoral theology in that each of the contributors has been either a former student or closely associated colleague of his. He has made a lasting impression on all of us.

We want to thank Thomas W. Gillespie, President of Princeton Theological Seminary, for his financial and moral support of this project, which honors his former professor and Dean. President Gillespie's support not only honors Jim Lapsley, it also furthers the conversation in the field of pastoral theology about the ministry of the church.

The authors of these essays deserve our special thanks. Their timely responses to deadlines and their encouragement of this project have reinforced our sense of colleagueship and our regard for Jim.

Harold Twiss of Westminster John Knox Press has offered gracious encouragement and sound editorial skill. We are grateful for both.

Our respective institutions have supported us through this project. At Columbia Theological Seminary, Academic Dean James Hudnut-Beumler has encouraged this project as has Dean Richard Weis at New Brunswick Theological Seminary. Our faculty colleagues have also been helpful in pointing to resources. We would also like to thank Columbia Seminary student assistant Elizabeth

Morgan for preparing the manuscript for the typist. Our typist, Rita Johnston, is an editor as well, and we thank her for her efforts.

Our families have supported us and loved us in spite of occasional absences. Our thanks to them is ongoing.

Brian H. Childs
David W. Waanders

1
Introduction

DAVID W. WAANDERS

When Brian Childs and I were discussing our interest in coediting a book of essays in honor of Jim Lapsley, the Christian anthropology theme presented itself readily. Theological understandings of human life and experience have been among Jim Lapsley's primary scholarly interests for well over twenty years, beginning with his book *The Concept of Willing*.[1] The book grew out of a conference at Princeton Theological Seminary in 1963 that brought together a number of theologians and physicians. Lapsley's concluding essay, "Willing and Selfhood," represents one of his earliest efforts at exploring theological understandings of the self.

The anthropology theme was addressed more broadly and explicitly in Lapsley's *Salvation and Health* in 1972.[2] In it Lapsley described what he termed a crisis in the church's understanding of human life and experience in that the church lacked a dynamic psychological understanding of human beings. Thus the church's theological understanding was not adequate for a contemporary analysis of human life, nor sufficient for developing a theory of care for ministry to persons in the contemporary context.

Since the publication of *Salvation and Health*, Lapsley has focused his discussion of Christian anthropology upon the concept of self wherein he has continued to weave together a dynamic psychological understanding, using the thought of Heinz Kohut in particular, with a broader theological understanding of human beings and human experience. His essays "The 'Self,' Its Vicissitudes and Possibilities: An Essay in Theological Anthropology" and "Spirit and

1

Self" address the problem of developing a theological anthropology using conceptual understandings drawn from depth psychology.[3] More recently, in his book *Renewal in Late Life through Pastoral Counseling*, Lapsley develops a "model of human being" in which he relates concepts of "spirit" and "self."[4]

In our view, Jim Lapsley's efforts in *Salvation and Health* to develop an understanding of human experience that has theological integrity and that incorporates depth-level analyses of "human being" have not reached as wide a hearing as these efforts deserve. The need for a thoroughly developed theological anthropology remains of critical importance to the church. Our current context of cultural diversity, the need for more clear understandings of the relationship between women and men and their differences, the climate of violence in our communities and around the world, the ways by which power is used and abused, and the increasingly complex ethical choices that present themselves to us as we seek to understand what it means to be human at this time in history—*all* these beg for an understanding of human life and existence that is informed by sound theological thinking and is describable in language that reflects sociocultural awareness and psychological understanding.

It has been these kinds of concerns that suggested that the focus of this book be upon Christian anthropology. Each of the contributors has been either a former student or colleague of Jim Lapsley, and each has had an interest in the ministry of care and has contributed to the development of pastoral theology. When we invited people to contribute an essay to this volume, we asked them to address some aspect of theological anthropology. In organizing this book around the theme of anthropology, the book serves, in a way, as a symposium, although the contributors, with the exception of Lapsley, have not had the opportunity to see what each of the others has written prior to publication.

In order to set the stage for the broad scope that the chapters in this book cover, some historical perspective is called for. When Augustine observed that human hearts are restless until they find their rest in God, he was pointing to the inability of humans to understand themselves fully, apart from their relationship with God. Theologians have traditionally framed the doctrinal understanding of human beings in relational terms, that is, the divine/ human relationship.

This relational sense has also influenced the theological under-standing of the purpose, or *telos*, of human life. The Westminster Shorter Catechism, for example, in its first question asks: "What is the chief end of [humankind]?" And the answer: ". . . to glorify God, and to enjoy [God] forever."[5]

Historically, Protestant theological formulations have held that human beings cannot understand themselves completely without some revelatory influence that comes to them from beyond them-selves. For Luther and Calvin, human sinfulness was understood to distort human perception; and if persons were to know themselves, they must see themselves through the lenses of a divine perspective (that is, scripture). Karl Barth, in recent years, is perhaps the most widely known theologian to espouse this kind of position.

Stemming from Friederich Schleiermacher's exploration of hu-man experience as the starting place of theological inquiry[6] and from theologians who have followed in his wake, the human sci-ences have been used increasingly in the development of theologi-cal anthropology. Wolfhart Pannenberg, in his monumental study of anthropology, has used biology, psychology, sociology, and cul-tural anthropology in developing his theological understanding of human beings.[7]

Along with the use of understandings of human beings that have come from the human sciences have come some fundamental shifts in theological assumptions about human beings that stand in sharp contrast to traditional viewpoints such as those of Calvin, Luther, and Barth. Pannenberg, for example, takes Barth to task for begin-ning his theological discussion with God without providing a ra-tional justification for his position, and in so doing says that Barth "unwittingly adopted the most extreme form of theological sub-jectivism." Pannenberg believes that theology must have a rational justification and that "in the modern age anthropology has become not only in fact but also with objective necessity the terrain on which theologians must base their claim of universal validity for what they say."[8] This view assumes that theological inquiry, of necessity, begins with human experience.

Shifting our attention to pastoral care, E. Brooks Holifield adds another perspective to this discussion when he observes that in American Protestantism, from the colonial period to the end of the 1960s, there has been a "movement from an ideal of otherworldly salvation to an implicit ethic of self-realization." He goes on, more pointedly, to note changing attitudes toward the "self" from "an ideal of self-denial to one of self-love, from self-love to self-culture, from self-culture to self-mastery, from self-mastery to self-realization within a trustworthy culture, and finally to a later form of self-realization counterpoised against cultural mores and social institutes."[9]

Whereas theologians like Pannenberg have made the case that beginning with a focus upon human beings is an essential point of departure for theology, Holifield, in examining patterns of pastoral care in America, cautions against a ministry and a theology implicit in that ministry which focus *only* upon human experience and the self. His point is that when the agenda for pastoral care is directed by psychological and humanistic values rather than a theological understanding of human *telos*, then pastoral care is impoverished, if not left without purpose altogether.

Jim Lapsley's work reflects a connection with traditional theological perspectives on anthropology while maintaining links to more modern approaches in that he has grasped the issues that have been most central in the theological tradition and has reworked them in ways that have integrity within the current context of the human sciences.

Lapsley's discussion of salvation is a case in point. Central to the theological tradition of Western Christendom, from the time of Augustine right on through the Reformation, has been the problem of sin and guilt. Humans were seen to be in need of rescue through salvation from their sinful and guilty condition in order to be restored to a forgiven relationship with God. Lapsley's discussion of salvation reflects his sense of what has been central to anthropology in the theological tradition; but then in the way that he links salvation and health, using insights from process theology, he redirects the focus of salvation from the past toward the present and future. Lapsley's subsequent work in describing the self in relation to spirit reflects a similar concern to maintain continuity with the broad theological tradition while pressing for a more dynamic psychological understanding of human beings that he hopes will enhance pastoral practice.

The following is a brief description of each of the chapters of this volume.

Rodney J. Hunter (Chap. 2—Participation in the Life of God: Revisioning Lapsley's Salvation-Health Model) provides a thorough and very helpful summary of Lapsley's book *Salvation and Health* and then focuses his discussion on a critique of Lapsley's salvation/health model, noting three areas of the model that need further development. Hunter calls for an expansion of the "participation" concept of the model in order to include the *receptive* dimensions of participation: a more "systemic" understanding of human beings that accounts for the impacts of society and family upon health and salvation; and a theoretical understanding of evil that understands the structure of evil and evil as a "force" in human experience.

John B. Cobb, Jr., (Chap. 3—Salvation and Health: A Pluralistic Perspective) asks how salvation and health are related and then notes a number of ways by which these terms can be defined and related. He pays particular attention to the pastoral counseling context in describing various ways of defining health. He then describes five definitions of salvation at work in the Christian community today. Cobb also stretches our understandings of these themes by bringing a multicultural perspective to bear upon them.

Charles V. Gerkin (Chap. 4—Projective Identification and the Image of God: Reflections on Object Relations Theory and the Psychology of Religion) contributes to the developmental understanding of anthropology with his discussion of the origin of the God image in infancy. Using object relations theorists, he looks at how the child develops a separate sense of self and how this process is related to a person's images of God. From a therapeutic perspective he wonders about three types of God image—how they are formed and how they continue to influence persons in later life: God as the fulfiller of all wishes; God as one who rejects persons, making them feel guilt or shame; and God who is ideal, perfect, leaving humans with a sense of mystery but also haunted, at times, by God's absence.

James G. Emerson, Jr., (Chap. 5—K'ung Fu-tze, Meet Jim Lapsley), with his teaching experience at the Taiwan Theological College and Seminary and at other theological schools in Asia, brings a cross-cultural perspective to our consideration of anthropological themes. Emerson poses an imaginary conversation between Jim Lapsley and Confucius (or K'ung Fu-tze in Chinese transliteration) and then develops in particular the themes of selfhood, shame, and actualization of the good by comparing Chinese and Western understandings of these themes.

Donald Capps (Chap. 6—The Soul as the "Coreness" of the Self) turns his attention to Lapsley's most recent work, where "spirit" and "self" are developed (*Renewal in Late Life through Pastoral Counseling*). Capps takes issue with Lapsley's discussion of self as the core of the person and offers the concept of soul, which can account for the "coreness" of the self and help "to explain the embodiment of self and spirit." He then uses James Hillman's distinction between soul and spirit to develop the understanding of soul in relation to organs of the body, particularly the liver. Capps explores ancient understandings of soul and of melancholia as soul-sickness and concludes with a section on soul-recovery in relation to the digestive system.

Brian H. Childs (Chap. 7—Whose Participation and Whose Humanity? Medicine's Challenge to Theological Anthropology), a coeditor of this book, begins with a helpful commentary on several aspects of Lapsley's salvation and health model with particular emphasis on the levels of health and salvatory participation. Childs then challenges Lapsley's model by exploring how persons in "boundary situations" contribute to an understanding of anthropology. Drawing upon his experience in bioethics, Childs discusses the "boundary situations" of neonates who are severely impaired neurologically and older persons who, through disease or trauma, are organically alive but have no conscious interaction with others. Using some adaptations of narrative theology, Childs shows how persons in boundary situations can participate in the stories of wider communities and that by considering what their existence means, theological anthropology is further developed in a more communal direction.

Don S. Browning (Chap. 8—Immanence and Transcendence in Pastoral Care and Preaching), in considering the relation between pastoral care and preaching, describes the tension between the theological perspectives of Karl Barth and his son Markus Barth on the one hand and Carl Rogers and his influence on the pastoral counseling movement on the other hand. He revisits his own work, *Atonement and Psychotherapy*, and that of Thomas Oden, *Kerygma and Counseling*, and notes how both he and Oden attempted to integrate the thought of Barth and of Rogers.[10] Browning then uses a theory of hermeneutics to draw preaching and pastoral care together as differing kinds of conversation, and shows how preaching and pastoral care not only enhance one another but also how each of these pastoral activities can participate in the other.

Emma J. Justes (Chap. 9—We Belong Together: Toward an Inclusive Anthropology) makes a case for including the voices of people who have been underrepresented in the shaping of theological anthropology: namely, women, people of color, and people of varied languages and cultures. Reflecting on how perceived differences tend to divide persons along the lines of such factors as gender, race, class, culture, or sexual orientation, Justes calls for more inclusiveness and for perceptions that bring people together. Drawing upon feminist insights as well as cross-cultural understandings gained from her sabbatical in South Africa, Justes offers an education model that features affiliative and communal approaches to learning.

James E. Loder (Chap. 10—Incisions from a Two-Edged Sword: The Incarnation and the Soul/Spirit Relationship) addresses the relationship of soul and spirit using an interpretation of the text in Hebrews 4:12–13 as a way of focusing the discussion. Loder establishes an incarnational model (Christ as Word of God) as the standard by which the relation between soul and spirit will be measured and also uses the notion of complementarity to describe incarnation. He draws upon Pannenberg to develop an understanding of human spirit and Holy Spirit, and concludes by tracing the intricate relationships of Holy Spirit to human spirit and the relation of spirit and soul in human experience.

Freda A. Gardner (Chap. 11—Another Look at the Elderly) contributes a developmental perspective to theological anthropology. Noting numerous negative attitudes in the culture toward the elderly, she calls for a realistic view of older persons that sees their potentials as well as their limitations. Gardner identifies four themes faced by older people that need understanding: the reality of death, the myth/sin of independence, body and gender in perception of self and others, and discipleship and ministry. She concludes with some very helpful observations about ministry with older people, and she shares some resources for enhancing the ministry to the elderly.

John H. Patton (Chap. 12—Forgiveness, Lost Contracts, and Pastoral Theology) presents a further development of his work on forgiveness, with particular attention here to forgiveness as it pertains to victims of violence and sexual abuse. Patton revises his understanding of forgiveness within the context of violence and abuse, noting that when survivors are pressed to forgive their abusers, this may contribute to their revictimization. Forgiveness occurs when, through positive self-esteem, the person who had been a victim of abuse no longer builds identity around something that happened in the past. "Forgiveness" is putting to better use the energy once consumed by rage and resentment and moving on with life.

Herbert Anderson (Chap. 13—The Recovery of Soul) explores the concept of soul in something of a phenomenological way by observing the many ways in which "soul" is understood: at one time poetically, at another paradoxically, at times mystically, and then from a pastoral care perspective. Anderson states his aims: (1) to recover the meaning and use of soul for our time; (2) to examine how the recovery of soul might enhance our theology and anthropology; and (3) to explore some of the implications of a recovery of soul for pastoral care. He concludes the essay with some implications for pastoral care.

Christie Cozad Neuger (Chap. 14—Gender: Women and Identity) examines the cultural factors that have shaped concepts of identity. She observes that historically women have not been given the right, the access, or the credibility to influence the ways in which culture forms human identity. Neuger cites the work of several feminist writers whose anthropological work addresses the issue of women's identity formation. In concluding her essay by noting God's mirroring/reflecting qualities as influencing women's identity, Neuger calls for the development of new images of God that reflect authentic female experience and identity and thereby strengthen the self.

James N. Lapsley (Chap. 15—Responses, Arguments, Musings, and Further Directions), in his inimitable style, reflects on each of the constructive essays of this book and concludes with some thoughts about further direction for theological anthropology.

NOTES

1. James N. Lapsley, ed., *The Concept of Willing* (Nashville: Abingdon Press, 1967).

2. James N. Lapsley, *Salvation and Health: The Interlocking Processes of Life* (Philadelphia: Westminster Press, 1972).

3. James N. Lapsley, "The 'Self,' Its Vicissitudes and Possibilities: An Essay in Theological Anthropology," *Pastoral Psychology* 35, no. 1 (Fall 1986): 23–45; and idem, "Spirit and Self," *Pastoral Psychology* 38, no. 3 (Spring 1990): 135–46.

4. James N. Lapsley, *Renewal in Late Life through Pastoral Counseling* (New York: Paulist Press, 1992).

5. From The Confession of Faith of the Presbyterian Church (U.S.A.), rev. ed., 14th printing (Richmond: The Board of Education of the Presbyterian Church in the United States, 1965).

6. Friederich Schleiermacher, *The Christian Faith* (Edinburgh: T. & T. Clark, 1928), 1960.

7. Wolfhart Pannenberg, *Anthropology in Theological Perspective*, trans. Matthew J. O'Connell (Philadelphia: Westminster Press, 1985).

8. Ibid., 16.

9. E. Brooks Holifield, *A History of Pastoral Care in America: From Salvation to Self-Realization* (Nashville: Abingdon Press, 1983), 11, 12.

10. Don S. Browning, *Atonement and Psychotherapy* (Philadelphia: Westminster Press, 1966); and Thomas Oden, *Kerygma and Counseling* (Philadelphia: Westminster Press, 1966).

2

Participation in the Life of God:
Revisioning Lapsley's Salvation-Health Model

RODNEY J. HUNTER

It is now over twenty years since James Lapsley published his slim volume *Salvation and Health: The Interlocking Processes of Life*, a book that unfortunately seems to have attracted little serious attention despite its significant attempt to deal with what is arguably still the most pressing problem in pastoral theology; namely, how to understand psychological and other forms of health theologically, from the standpoint of the Christian gospel.[1] The problem is basic and pressing because nothing so thoroughly characterizes modern pastoral theology—meaning roughly twentieth-century pastoral care and counseling and their related theories—as the overwhelming adoption of secular psychological categories. Especially since the Second World War, psychological and psychiatric modes of thought and practice have come almost fully to define human well-being in a comprehensive and inclusive way within much of mainline ministry and within pastoral theological theory in particular, despite efforts by various pastoral theorists to give a theological account of the field.[2] These efforts have not been superficial, but neither have they been especially effective or persuasive. The problem, Lapsley contended a quarter of a century ago, is the lack of concrete, empirically meaningful theological theory of human beings—a theological anthropology—that would integrally relate psychological and theological concerns. Pastoral caregivers need to know why and how what they do psychologically has meaning theologically, and this can occur only if they function with an understanding of human beings that draws these two perspectives together with a single unified conception. *Salvation and Health* was Lapsley's primary, though somewhat sketchy, attempt to get such a theory going in the field, and it remains one of the most original and potentially useful and important attempts of its kind.

By the same token, *Salvation and Health* is a problematic proposal. Hampered in some measure by conceptual underdevelopment, Lapsley's brief manner of presentation, and especially by the unfamiliarity of many readers with his Whiteheadian process conceptuality, the book has lacked a significant readership or the history of dialogue and debate that, I am persuaded, it still deserves. Hence, my effort in this essay is to revisit this book with an eye for critical appropriation and development of its major thesis. Although *Salvation and Health* is not entirely adequate to today's theoretical needs, it offers a helpful starting place for developing a much-needed theological anthropology for ministry.

My thesis is that Lapsley's proposal concerning the relation of salvation and health, as interlocking life processes, needs to be further developed along three lines: toward (1) greater recognition of the passive as well as active modes of "participation" (a key term in his theory), thus a more significant role for irredeemable suffering and seemingly unforgivable sin, and hence for grace; (2) the inclusion of systemic as well as individual modes of agency in the process model, hence the possibility of transindividual forms of saving and destructive activity in the world; and (3) a concept of evil as an active, conditioning, or influencing force in the world of human and transhuman affairs, hence a more realistic or pessimistic understanding of the human predicament in terms of violence and victimization, and what is involved in being saved from it, than Lapsley's Whiteheadian model provides.

LAPSLEY'S SALVATION AND HEALTH MODEL

It would be presumptuous to try to reduce to a few pages what required an entire book for Lapsley to expound, all the more so because I have already referred to his publication, despite its length, as "somewhat sketchy." Therefore, I will offer here a brief overview of its most fundamental concepts, with the hope that interested readers will be led back to the source for a more adequate and nuanced presentation.

Lapsley is convinced, to begin with, that a concern for health, broadly conceived as both physical and psychological, is a recurring and often integral theme in biblical faith and Christian history. Salvation, however variously understood in scripture and tradition, usually bears some relation to human vitality and welfare in more or less ordinary empirical and historical forms—which may be called "health" for present purposes (in addition to other forms of historical welfare like peace and justice in human society). But there is no clear consensus in scripture or tradition as to *how* they are related (or even in extreme instances *whether* they are). To construct a contemporary answer to this question, Lapsley extrapolates a notion from the various meanings of salvation in the Bible; namely, that salvation in (and possibly beyond) the world seems always to be tantamount to participating in God's life-giving life. To be saved is to participate in the life of God. To be lost is, in some sense, to obstruct or to be left out; it is *not* to participate. Salvation is, therefore, not primarily a question of eschatology—whether we live beyond death—though this may be included in some form; it is primarily about living in the power of God's vitality, freedom, and love in this world, and possibly beyond it as well.[3]

This kind of participation means, in the process theology scheme, receiving, creating, and giving "value" to other persons, society, and the cosmos as a whole, and to God, through the adventure of living. In process terms, every moment of existence, for everything that exists—human, subhuman, animate, inanimate—is an event, an "experience" of sorts, in which some degree of subjective satisfaction or "value" is created. The effects of these satisfactions then become available to subsequent events of experience for *their* satisfactions. Thus the world is a gigantic complex of myriad happenings large and small, all contributing their subjective value achievements to subsequent happenings. In this grand conception, not only do all existing beings continually contribute to one another, but all contribute to the ongoing experiencing of God, and God indeed contributes the divine experience back again into the world. Thus, for Lapsley as for all process thinkers, "participation" is a rich and complex concept pointing to a truly cosmic as well as social, historical, and interpersonal process.

To participate in the life of *God*, however, means, more explicitly, to be generative of those particular values that God, in the divine goodness and wisdom, cherishes, saves, and returns to the world. Other values, other sorts of participation, get dropped from the divine process, as it were, in God's ongoing work of judgment. Thus, to be "saved" is to participate in the value-creating and value-saving work of God that Whiteheadians call "everlasting"— within, yet not limited by, time as we experience it.

In practical and pastoral terms, saving participation means achieving those kinds of satisfactions that contribute most richly and fully to the life of others interpersonally. One of the attractive features of the process theology for pastoral care and counseling is that it recognizes and honors with eternity or "everlastingness" the elusive, intangible ways in which ordinary people in ordinary experience generate such values as love, care, truth, and justice. Process theology also finds, within these ordinary experiences, the gentle but persistent and persuasive "lure" of God toward the creation of such values. Thus God is intimately present in every life at every moment, however profoundly distorted or evil its actual choices may prove to be.

To this sublime conception of salvation, then, Lapsley brings the question of health. What is health, and how is it related to participation? After surveying the complexities and relativities involved in this notoriously difficult question, he concludes, or rather proposes, that "*health generically refers to the relatively active potential for appropriate functioning which any individual possesses at any given time.* [Italics added] It is, then, the *enabling* factor that is present to some degree in everyone, not something that either is, or is not, present."[4] The idea, in other words, is that one must have a degree of "active potential for appropriate functioning" in order to participate in the world-historical process. Health is that potential. It enables one to participate. (The theologically important reciprocal question, whether participating may in some sense engender or enable health, is one that Lapsley seems to recognize but does not develop—a point to which I will return.) The "relatively active potential to participate" is obviously variable, not only from day to day and hour to hour over the life span of individuals, but adults generally exhibit greater potential to participate, and they can participate on a broader and more significant range of interactions than can children.

These variations in potential for functioning are in turn the product, says Lapsley, of the interaction between two basic life processes. The first is homeostasis, or what he terms "maintenance" processes, meaning all the ways in which living organisms stabilize themselves and maintain consistent modes of functioning (such as body temperature in higher animals). In humans, he says, the most important psychological forms of homeostasis involve maintaining a more or less steady sense of identity (being the same person through varying circumstances and relationships) and self-esteem (feeling basically positive about oneself despite rejections, criticism, and other forms of emotional threat broadly summarized as guilt and shame). The other critical life process is development, meaning growth into greater structural and functional complexity. Adults are more complex psychologically than children, and some adults more than others. (Complexity, I assume, equates broadly with flexibility of adaption to circumstances and creative problem-solving capacities.) These two life processes, maintenance and development, interact reciprocally, each affecting the other: some achieved equilibrium is necessary for development, and development in turn establishes new forms of equilibrium (e.g., in adolescent identity formation). Between them, maintenance and development make participation possible—that is, they establish the relative degree of potential for functioning in the social and cosmic-historical process.

Given the general structure—the genius, if I may put it that way—of Lapsley's theory then appears in the way he is able to combine these basic factors to create a finely differentiated set of possible interactions between health, the potential for functioning, and salvation, participation in the life and saving work of God. Where maintenance functions are not well established (e.g., in psychotic disorders) or where there has been little development (e.g., in young children), the potential for participating in the divine life with the world is accordingly diminished, though saving participation is still possible because some potential for appropriate functioning exists, however limited. Lapsley arranges these possibilities hierarchically as Levels I and II.

Of greater complexity and interest, however, are those "levels" of participation in which a high degree of achieved homeostasis and development is present; thus also a broader range of participation in the world and God is possible, but in which one's energies are nonetheless invested to a large degree in the tasks of maintenance (Level III) or development (Level IV) despite the significant participation that may be underway. This internal demand on one's energies undermines and limits outward participation. Level III participators, for example, who Lapsley says comprise most adults most of the time, include people whose work, family, and social activities may be generating important values for others and for God, but whose inner motivations are marked by compensatory needs to maintain identity or self-esteem (e.g., a person who marries in the unconscious hope of compensating for personal deficiencies). These inner forces of maintenance restrict the creativity and flexibility of the individual's social and cosmic functioning, hence limiting the *range* of values they can create for others and for God. At the same time these compensatory, restricting influences do not entirely negate the value of what they contribute to others (their "participation").

Developmental processes, however, can limit wider participation in life (Level IV), as when young persons unconsciously commit themselves to marital partners or careers (e.g., in psychology or ministry) in order to "grow up." Such motivations are by no means necessarily negative in their effects and may, in fact, be essential and very positive forms of participation (Lapsley considers this type of qualified participation—Level IV—of higher worth than the purely compensatory, Level III type). Still, it is important to recognize that the participation involved in such persons is inwardly shaped and limited by developmental factors whose consequences eventually appear in the *style* and *content* of their participating.

There are persons, however, whose homeostatic and developmental tasks have been sufficiently completed so that they no longer require major diversions of energy from participation. These people (Level V) are relatively free from inner compulsions and growth needs and are able to give themselves more or less fully to their chosen interactions with the world (work, family, society, culture, religion, etc.). Their participation is, therefore, more objectively in tune with the needs, the limits, and the possibilities of the wider world, and they are more able to make truly significant, even "everlasting" contributions to the life of God as well. Moreover, inner maintenance and developmental needs can diminish altogether, to the point where participation is almost entirely "for participation's sake," free of the distorting effects of inner needs (Level VI), hence "transpropriate" or self-transcending in nature. For the most part, these are truly extraordinary individuals, often religious, social, or cultural innovators, though I gather it is not essential to the concept of Level VI that such individuals have recognized or historically significant influence.[5]

Armed with this complex conception of the meaning and inter-relation of salvation and health, Lapsley is able to deduce a number of practical directives for ministry in general and pastoral care and counseling in particular. To whatever extent one is able to perceive the state of the salvation-health relationship in particular persons at particular times, recognizing the kind of possibilities and limitations they may have enables one to minister more realistically and creatively. For instance, it could be pastorally important to recognize the inner, compensatory dynamics and limitations of folks like the typically older, "pillar of the church" individuals who may make great contributions of time, energy, and resources but function with a limited, rigid range of social and cultural understandings; whereas younger, active "pillars" may have broader vision and range but prove less durably committed over time, a function of the way their changing developmental needs shape their church involvement. Such insight also enables the pastor to appreciate the potential for positive, "eternal" significance in whatever participation is present, and to participate more consciously and intentionally with God in shaping the kinds of "lures" that may draw such persons more fully into saving participation with God, whatever their "level" of participatory functioning.[6] The scheme, in other words, purports to show precisely how specific psychological dynamics relate to the ultimate ends and purposes of life—how they are important and influential but not of ultimate or decisive importance. In spite of its cosmic conceptuality and process metaphysics, it is therefore a pastoral *theology*, and moreover, one that tends to be eminently practical in the church's mission and ministry.

CRITICAL INTERLUDE

Most pastors and theological students with whom I have discussed this mode, however, are put off by several of its features and implications. The one that strikes most of them first is its hierarchical structure (levels of participation) that, if not an invitation to pastoral elitism and condescension, may nonetheless seem inconsistent with the Christian belief that all persons are in some basic sense equal before God. The very idea of a hierarchy is much out of fashion today, especially among feminists, as a mode of thinking that inevitably entails oppressive class, race, or gender distinctions. The concern is well founded, and perhaps it would have been better for Lapsley to have cast his theory in the nonhierarchical imagery of concentric circles, with the "higher" levels interpreted as wider, more inclusive modes of participation.[7] But even a change of image would not entirely dispense with the concern, which is that the theory does in fact envision something like discernible quantitative and/or qualitative differences in the way individuals participate in that which is of ultimate importance: God and the world-historical process in their ongoing interactions.

In his defense, Lapsley can surely point to abundant empirical evidence of such differences: some people at least appear to live qualitatively "larger" or "richer" lives than others—lives that are richer in intangible values of all kinds, such as love, kindness, truthfulness, integrity, creativity, care, and so on. However, problems appear when we explore the psychological and other sources of such value-generating lives and relate those "nontheological" factors to judgments of potential spiritual significance. If some people live more fully in and with the life of God than do others, is their health—the interaction of maintenance and developmental processes in their lives—a necessary "enabling factor" for such spiritual participation? If so, the psychologically strong participate more fully or significantly in God's life with the world and are in that sense spiritually privileged. Or, on the contrary, is participation in the life of God fundamentally unrelated to such historical and psychological potentials? To hold this position is effectively to deny a significant connection between salvation and health, a point Lapsley—I feel rightly—judges to be empirically and theologically wrong if not also morally and professionally irresponsible. Thus, if *some* relation is held to exist between saving participation and health factors, something like Lapsley's "health as enabling factor" concept seems unavoidable, and it becomes necessary to face the perhaps uncomfortable consequence that there are significant differences in the spiritual capabilities of persons—perhaps more accurately, between persons at particular times in their lives, because these potentials and modes of participation are variable.

Thus the argument that the theory invites elitist class distinctions seems to require a more nuanced reading: one must distinguish between making any distinctions between people whatsoever, and making invidious, condescending, stereotyping, or otherwise dehumanizing distinctions. Obviously, it is solely the former that Lapsley intends. Whether one *can* make distinctions of this kind without becoming entangled in oppressive thought forms is another matter. This issue is far from resolved in pastoral theology and other disciplines like psychotherapy, where the social dynamics and implications of all attempts to categorize human beings, for diagnostic and valuative purposes, however well intentioned, are sometimes regarded as inherently objectionable on moral, religious, or therapeutic grounds. I cannot go further into the matter here. For the present, however, I will simply state my own judgment that there is no *logical* reason why making distinctions regarding participation in divine saving process needs to lead to oppressive consequences.[8] I also question whether it is even possible to eliminate such categorizing. Moreover, the recognition of such differences can *facilitate* therapeutic and moral action, whereas, conversely, being aware of important differences in capacities of persons is surely necessary for preventing unreasonable expectations and various forms of exploitation and abuse. Not to be aware of categories, or supposing that one does not make significant judgments about others, is arguably the surest road to the most profound and destructive forms of exploitation.

What kind of confidence, therefore, can or should one have in making "spiritual" judgments about other persons (or even about oneself)? Is Lapsley's attempt to erect a general theory of psychospiritual interaction a moral and theological presumption, an overreaching of what it is possible for human beings to know? This is the other major criticism his theory usually stirs up, and it is an important one. Although most of my students are willing to concede that there "is something" to the insights behind Lapsley's hierarchy (if not conceived hierarchically), many of them regard the whole enterprise as a dangerous attempt to categorize people theologically; therefore, they dismiss it out of hand.

Is this a fair charge? Certainly, *any* theory that presupposes the possibility of knowing the deepest truths about another human being would be theologically and epistemologically presumptuous. "The true saints have not such a spirit of discerning that they can certainly determine who are godly and who are not."[9] On the other hand, there is no reason to assume that Lapsley's categories or any other valuative categories in pastoral theology require such a claim. Like clinical assessments of all kinds, they ought to function tentatively and heuristically as pointers to what may be the case—as partial indicators, not as absolute, unambiguous final judgments. Furthermore, upon reflection, it is apparent that no theologically serious ministry, lay or clerical, simple or sophisticated, can be performed without *some* concepts about "the human condition" and ultimate norms of human welfare and fulfillment. Indeed, all human actions, including all forms of ministry, are shaped by cognitive and valuative "maps" of the world of some sort, often implicit and assumed without critical reflection. The danger comes only when we confuse our fallible and approximate "maps" with the real, complex, and profoundly mysterious "territory" of lived human experience and the presence of God within it.

Thus the issue is not *whether* we will employ descriptive and valuative categories in ministry, but whether or not the categories we employ are relatively well developed and appropriate to faith and to the mysteries of life. Lapsley's theory, precisely because of its insightful power to disclose and distinguish psychological and "spiritual" (i.e., divinely participative) dynamics, however approximate and fallible and in need of revision its categories may be, confronts us with this basic, if uncomfortable, truth. In ministry, we have no choice but to perceive and assess the "spiritual state" of others and ourselves empirically as best we can, recognizing that we can never do so completely or infallibly, and may be most grievously mistaken when we think we are not profoundly right. In fact, we make valuative and psychological judgments all the time, whether we acknowledge it or not and whether we take critical responsibility for our "maps" or not. Thus we owe it to those to whom and with whom we minister to construct the best conceptual tools we can and to use them faithfully and responsibly, though always using them like all theories with a saving sense of their ultimate fallibility, ambiguity, and inadequacy, and with a deeper trust in the movement of the Spirit that blows where it will, opening us beyond ourselves and all our categories to a world that God is yet creating and redeeming, that eye hath not seen nor ear heard.

REVISIONING THE MODEL

Equally important for evaluating and rethinking the Lapsley model as these criticisms are, three other issues related to the content of the theory itself need to be examined.

The Concept of Participation

Although it is not hard to grasp the concepts of maintenance and development, the third factor in health—participation—is less obvious in meaning and, in my view, somewhat inadequately conceived in Lapsley's theory. Broadly speaking, participation means being part of something larger than oneself and implies interacting successfully with that larger reality or environment, from parent-child relationships to the largest human communities and cultures. Whereas the aim of maintenance is the steady state and the aim of development is increased complexity, what does participation aim at in Lapsley's theory? What is it "about"?

One would suppose that it is about *exchange*—the giving and receiving of physical, emotional, intellectual, and spiritual values, the trading of "goods" and "services," in a sense. But stating the idea in the language of economics is somewhat misleading, because in process metaphysics that which is most truly given and received in the cosmic order—the "values" that the consummation of human experiences bequeath to others and to themselves in subsequent moments—is intangible and spiritual. Speaking of persons living, working, or playing together in a significant participation such as marriage, Lapsley stresses that "something of their lives does actually flow into the others from a process point of view. They give of themselves to the lives of those with whom they participate, and to some extent literally become a part of them."[10]

Nevertheless, Lapsley's concept of participation seems to stress only one side of the exchange principle, the "giving" side. Although Lapsley seems to assume that receiving as well as giving is involved in participating, receiving gets less attention and seems theoretically less important. Health as an enabling factor for salvation enables us mainly to create and *give*, to generate value for the sake of others and ourselves. In creating and giving, our lives flow out into the lives of others and, most significantly, into God. In God the values we have created, insofar as they can be harmonized with God's will, are saved "everlastingly" and poured back into the world to enrich human life and the cosmos anew.

Theologically, the great attractiveness and importance of this concept is that it states clearly that we do not live simply in and for ourselves, but that salvation—meaning filled life with God—has to do with living with and for each other. It is a profoundly social concept of salvation, which Lapsley stresses over against (I think) the popular culture's individualism, which is especially evident in its dominant psychologies that have so deeply influenced ministry. Health (or psychological strength and maturity), though valuable to the person, is not an end in itself; it is rather the base from which truly valuable existence can be lived in the form of contributions to the larger human and cosmic order. We are saved to the degree that we participate by contributing everlastingly to the whole reality—human, cosmic, and divine. The end and fulfillment of life lies in enriching the whole of things through participating in their "creative advance" (Whitehead).

There is another aspect to this, however, that Lapsley seems not to value or develop as fully, which is the "receiving" aspect. To participate means also to receive, to allow oneself to be enriched by others and by God, even and perhaps especially in extreme situations where giving, in the sense of generating value-enriching experiences to others, is not in fact possible, such as genuinely meaningless, unredeemed, and irredeemable suffering. Deep spiritual values and even "triumphs" do sometimes arise from intense or prolonged, "meaningless" suffering, but surely there are vast oceans of human and nonhuman suffering from which no proportionate redeeming value is generated or can be generated. In this dark mystery of negativity, is there any possibility of "participating in God"? Is "saving" participation possible when we have nothing to give—when we are utterly without health or when we suffer beyond any conceivable moral justification—when we are "dead"? Is it not the case that the most profound and, in the long run, most important form of "participating in the life of God" takes precisely this agonized and negative form of mutual, empty, impotent, and meaningless suffering?[11]

This idea can be elaborated in a variety of less extreme instances. Marriages, for example, as a form of participation, encounter their crucial turning points not where spouses are giving deeply or constructively to one another, but where the relationship suffers its limits, where hardship isolates or moral failure estranges the partners. There, a receptive, accepting form of participation seems necessary in the form of a faithful, accepting presence and forgiving spirit if the relationship is either to continue or to be healed. These forms of participation involve a degree of significant mutual giving, but they also involve an even deeper willingness simply to be present and to "receive" from the other—essentially, to suffer with and for the other. The concept of receiving points to all the ways in which we participate not by offering our strengths but by making ourselves open and vulnerable, not by what we do or what we are able to give but by who we are and what we are willing to receive. Biblically and theologically, this means living in grace and by grace. It does not negate the importance and value, perhaps even the eternal value, of what we may contribute to others and even to God. But it holds that the full meaning and measure of participation includes a profound receptivity, a valuing of being as well as doing, and a willingness to suffer with and for each other even when no redeeming values can be found.[12]

If the concept of participation is developed in this direction, adjustments need to be made in the concepts of health and salvation. Health can no longer be defined entirely as an enabling factor. More precisely, health becomes an enabling factor only for the active, creating, and giving or contributing aspect of participation. But participation in the divine life is not limited to active contribution to it. Salvation is not entirely based upon or limited by the health available to one at any given time. Also included in the divine life, as participants of sorts, are those who cannot contribute, who suffer the limitation or destruction of their vital capacities—in short, the victims, the dying, and the dead, and all others to whatever extent they share in the helplessness and weakness of death. "They also serve who only stand and wait," as Milton profoundly discovered through his own suffering. What they "give" is not what they create and contribute actively, but what they *are*, and their participation is in the form of presence rather than creation or achievement.

Here another problem arises. How can such a notion of participation avoid the monstrous prospect of implying a theodicy, a justifying of meaningless, impotent, or violent suffering as somehow part of a greater good? If even the dying and the dead participate in God, is their experience of suffering not thereby oddly made right—"justified"? The answer to this depends, I think, on whether or not it is assumed that participation in divine life means that God makes or finds meaning and justification in meaningless, absurd suffering. The alternative is to suppose that these experiences are also in some sense or to some degree equally meaningless and absurd for God, and that God's participation in human suffering means God's own sharing of that suffering too, without making it right or being able to make it right in any sense. In that case, participation means simply "being there." Period. And perhaps that is enough, as pastoral experience not infrequently attests. Perhaps relationship itself is "what it's all about." "For I am convinced that neither death, nor life . . . nor height, nor depth, nor anything else in all creation, will be able to separate us from the love of God in Christ Jesus our Lord" (Rom. 8:38–39).

The Concept of Society

One of the strengths of Lapsley's model is, as noted, its deeply social character. Every human life literally flows into every other life, and all lives flow from and into God. There are no totally isolated individuals. We all create and cocreate one another through our unique life experiences. Yet here is also a sense in which this process model retains a kind of individualism at its core, despite the interflow of individual experiences. This feature is rooted in Whitehead's notion that only the individual "actual occasion" is real—actual occasions being the basic unit of reality, the simplest possible kind of subjective, experiencing "happening." Human beings, like other high-grade living entities, are in this system complex "societies" of occasions having a "dominant occasion" (roughly, the mind or personality) that synthesizes myriad subordinate occasions. Dominant occasions, like all occasions, have "subjective immediacy"; they exist as subjective events. But superordinate human societies—families, communities, nations, and the like—do not have "subjective immediacy." They exist as societies or interactive systems of events without the organizing functions of an internally synthesizing dominant occasion like the human mind. They have no "soul," though they may have central coordinating *institutions* (such as government) or other organizing functions.

Though it seems intuitively correct that large social organizations do not have the exact equivalent of a mind or soul, my question is whether this way of conceiving higher social systems is entirely adequate to the remarkable, quasi-independent power that transindividual social systems seem to have as agents in their own right in relation to individual human beings. Contemporary pastoral theory, in particular, has been much impressed with the so-called systems view of human families and personality. In this way of thinking, which has garnered considerable clinical and empirical support and is widely integrated into contemporary pastoral counseling, social systems like the family have a life of their own that includes but transcends its individual members. As in all systems theories, "the whole is greater than the sum of its parts." This is not to say that the family (for instance) has its own "subjective immediacy" (mind or consciousness), but that it functions in quasi-autonomous, transindividual systemic ways.

All social systems in fact exhibit such features. Institutions and business corporations, for instance, are remarkable for their enduring functional and cultural features even though individual personalities come and go; and they are notorious for their power to maintain homeostasis and resist fundamental, structural change. Indeed, if attempts to change organizations or institutions are to succeed in achieving more than superficial change, they require systems ways of thinking and forms of intervention based on systems principles like circular causation, feedback, and homeostasis. Such concepts have been extensively used in family theory and therapeutic interventions related to violence and victimizing, whose cyclical patterns exhibit systemic features that usually make individualistic therapeutic interventions fruitless by themselves.

I am not personally able to judge whether process metaphysics is able to make sense of this sort of phenomena without modification, though I believe it can, for there are many common ideas in the two conceptualities.[13] In any case, systems thinking is important in any human relations discipline or profession today and needs to be taken seriously by pastoral theology and theories relating health and salvation.[14]

Applied to Lapsley's basic model, systems thinking may suggest some interesting and important revisions. Basically, systems thinking would emphasize the extent to which individual free choosing is constrained and oriented by systemic processes larger than and inclusive of the choices made by individual dominant occasions (persons). Process thought fully recognizes the role of past events in determining the range of relevant possibilities open to any actual occasion at a given time; and, because a system is simply a type of occasion (lacking a dominant occasion), systems theory would seem to fit comfortably into the process scheme at this point. What it contributes is not a conceptual change in process thought, but a matter of emphasis on the quasi-independence of macro systems vis-à-vis individuals, recognizing the very significant degree to which individual free actions (choices) are systematically constrained and oriented in particular ways, often unrecognized by the participants.

Because the macro system functions as a society with a degree of autonomy, it is necessary to say that the larger system to some degree holds, carries, or possesses its component individuals within itself, limiting their options to the kinds of possibilities that accord with the larger system's functional needs. We are members of systems such as families, organizations, institutions, nations, and traditions; but they also possess, drive, and direct us in accord with their own systemic principles of homeostasis and development. Such larger systems have their own internal dynamics and histories which, though they include, draw upon, and depend upon the energies and choices of us who are their members, also transcend and control the range of possibilities that we as individual agents can, in fact, exercise. To varying degrees we participate in them as *their* agents, doing their bidding in countless, mostly subtle and unrecognized ways, hour by hour, day by day, year by year. In varying degrees but always to a significant extent, we are the carriers of these macro systemic needs and organizational principles, and, over time, we are the bearers of their traditions and cultures. This is perhaps a difficult concept for Americans in particular to comprehend, schooled as we are in a fierce individualism concerning our own sense of free agency in the world. But a rational analysis of the total picture of human society shows clearly that we are, on the whole, at least as much guided and constrained by macro systems as we are freely choosing agents within those systems, and probably far more so, even when we pride ourselves on nonconformist individuality.

If so, what does this mean for the health-and-salvation question, and how might it affect Lapsley's model? It seems that it would have two basic implications. First, it would emphasize more than Lapsley does the role of systemic participation in health, specifically in the establishing of maintenance and the stimulation of development. It is well known that even biomedical functions are profoundly affected by social (or systemic) interaction and participation, not only in infants and children but in persons of all ages. Our ability to achieve and maintain necessary equilibria, such as identity and self-esteem, is not achieved entirely from within; it depends also on the quality of one's social relationships. These include other persons as well as larger systems of relationship such as family, community, nation, economic systems, and so on, all of which provide resources for and partially govern individual psychological functioning. Thus health depends critically on healthy families and communities as well as on healthy individual choices. This makes Lapsley's variable of participation more than an outgrowth of accrued internal maintenance and development. Participation is also partly an enabling and limiting principle.

Salvation must similarly be reconceived with greater emphasis given to participation in this systemic sense (in addition to the counterbalancing emphasis on participation as receptivity noted in the previous section). To be saved in this sense, and to this degree, is to be relocated from destructive to constructive macro systemic participation. "He has rescued us from the power of darkness and transferred us into the kingdom of his beloved Son, in whom we have redemption, the forgiveness of sins" (Col. 1:13–14). For me to be saved, to participate in the saving work of God, is, therefore, not simply to be making individual choices that generate the kinds of values that God saves but to be a participant in a transindividual system (the "kingdom of God") that limits and shapes the range of possibilities of my individual choices and actions. I am a "member of the body of Christ," "hid with Christ in God," not a spiritual lone ranger. I am one who receives as well as gives, whose very will and heart are shaped by him of whose "body" I am a part, the Christ, the divine social systemic reality in the world.

Ministry in this view, including pastoral care and counseling, is called to focus more explicitly on the macro systemic aspects of the human condition and the divine saving work. The pastoral task is not only to aid individuals in the subtle decision making about their lives; it is also to help individuals become a part of constructive, healthy, and saving systems—families, communities, and uniquely, church systems. It matters to *what* and to *whom* we belong, in which streams we are swimming, with which persons we live, in which organizations and institutions we work, and in which rituals, traditions, and meaning and value systems we operate. A major concern of ministry is to help form those communities and to help individuals become a part of them. There is nothing in Lapsley's model that would necessarily deny any of this, but the concept of transindividual, semiautonomous systems needs to be worked into it explicitly, and emphasis should be placed more heavily on social and systemic participation and its practical consequences for ministry than is envisioned in *Salvation and Health*.

The Concept of Evil

The question of whether process thought can give an account of evil that is adequate to its experiential profundity and destructiveness has been the focus of a fair amount of recent work among process and other theologians.[15] The problem arises with Lapsley also, despite his clear efforts to give an adequate place to sin and evil in theological anthropology. His major point is surely important: as persons advance in their capacity to participate in the human and transhuman world with God (as they become more complexly developed and more homeostatically balanced, thus having more energy free for giving and receiving beyond themselves), they become, in essence, more free to create either good values *or* evil ones. Individuals, who are highly developed psychologically, are not necessarily more moral in their choices and actions.[16] Lapsley cites Robert E. Lee as a particularly fascinating instance of an individual who, by all accounts, was psychologically healthy and mature to an extraordinary degree but was also tragically self-restricted by an essentially provincial value system of home and hearth. As a result of this value system (not as a psychological weakness), Lee sided with the Confederacy, lending his enormous talents to a fundamentally evil cause, ultimately resulting in more suffering and destruction for both sides than might otherwise have been the case.

Evil, in the Whiteheadian understanding, is bad choosing; that is, making choices that actualize values obstructive or contrary to the will of God, to the harmonizing of value in which God is ceaselessly engaged. However, if the systemic revision of the human situation sketched out in the preceding discussion is introduced into the process model of the world, it becomes possible to conceptualize a transindividual organization of evil in the world—"principalities and powers of this age" that work together, systemically, to obstruct and destroy human and cosmic harmony—and to attribute a certain degree of moral agency or force to the systems of transindividual evil. Something like a principle of "the demonic" that operates, like all systems, with a degree of autonomy and limited control over its component individuals might be conjectured. Such a transindividual concept of evil has in fact recently been proposed by process theologian David Ray Griffin.[17] In Griffin's still somewhat undeveloped proposal, the demonic is a by-product of the human history of evil choices; it is not coeternal with God and the world. Though it has evolved out of human history, it has acquired a quasi-independence and power of its own that tyrannizes and victimizes human society by drawing individual and social systems into its destructive sphere of influence.

A systemic conception of evil seems appropriate to the way much evil actually occurs in the modern world, especially if evil is conceived along biblical lines as essentially violence and victimization. Studies in family violence have shown the cyclical and systemic nature of this phenomenon, which seems to "possess" both perpetrator and victim. Similar systemic features also appear in public histories of violence, such as those of Northern Ireland, the Balkans, and the Middle East. In such situations, the ongoing cycle of violence seems larger than can be decisively contained or controlled by individuals, institutions, or governments. In all of these cases, the systemic character of the evil, its quasi-independence, lends it the appearance, and to some degree the reality, of being a force in its own right. Griffin's proposal is helpful in establishing the plausibility of demonic evil understood as a semiautonomous agent or force while denying its primal rootedness in the order of things as such. As a derivation reality, the demonic is an emergent though no less real an agent of violence in the world.

The provocative theories of René Girard come to mind in this connection as a possibly helpful supplement to the process scheme.[18] Girard has developed an insightful theory of violence that reaches well beyond his own field of literary criticism into cultural anthropology, sociology, and psychology. In his view, human beings are not violent innately—there is no death or aggressive "instinct" à la Freud, nor is violence simply a learned or conditioned behavior. It is rather a potential given in the basic nature of human motivation or "desire" which, in Girard's conception, is also social in nature. Though our desires spring in some sense from within ourselves as individuals, biologically and emotionally, they are always profoundly shaped by what *other* people desire. We are creatures of imitation; and when the imitative aspect of desire gets the upper hand, it distorts desire into social rivalry, conflict, and violence. Such rivalry constitutes a sort of system, a mutual entrapment in a rivalrous process. Because all human desiring is imitative (or mimetic), human society is continually threatened with the potential for violence and must devise social institutions for preventing, containing, or modifying it. The fundamental arrangement of this sort, on which, according to Girard, all human societies were originally constructed, is scapegoating or sacrifice (a concept familiar to family systems therapists). Humans caught in potentially dangerous rivalries discover that their adversarial, murderous tendencies can be deflected onto a third party, the "surrogate victim." Moreover, the victim can be blamed for the problem while simultaneously being transfigured as a savior from the problem—as a god. In this conception, human social organization arose from sacrifice and its accompanying deceptions and misrepresentations, and has preserved itself into modern times through rationalized versions of this fundamental mechanism, long after most public sacrificial cults have disappeared, at least by that name, from religion and politics.[19] The compulsions of the moral order, external and internal (the superego), the continuing importance of public myths of gods and heroes and of ritual reenactments of sacrifice (such as wars, capital punishment, interpersonal scapegoating, and blame shifting) perpetuate the dynamics of these primal mechanisms in our time.

I cite Girard here as one possible way of filling in the picture of how evil is organized and how it functions as something like an active agency or force in human life and not merely as a consequence of individual choices or as a deprivation of the good. Whether via Girard or other sources, getting clear about the way evil is organized in transindividual, systemic ways—thereby exerting a force or power in some sense of its own—is, I think, an important part of the picture of the world that pastoral theology must take seriously into account in its attempts to conceptualize the relation of health and salvation. For one thing, it points to the need to recover, in systems theory form, the idea of demonic possession and, in some appropriately related form, the ministry of exorcism. This suggestion understands exorcism in a broad sense as meaning being freed from the decisively controlling power of evil macro systems—as being transferred, in some basic respect, from the "power of darkness" into the "kingdom of his beloved Son." I say "in some basic respect" because, theologically and biblically, it is, I believe, of great importance when considering this topic also to consider the "wheat and the tares" problem—the fact that evil and good are ambiguously and inseparably intertwined in this cosmic-historical order, and can be sifted out and the tares brought to judgment only eschatologically (Matt. 13:24–30).

Dramatic stories of total demonic possession and total exorcism are in this light not the best models for understanding the phenomenon of the demonic (systemic violence) or for enacting ministries of liberation and exorcism. More to the point is the possibility of challenging the systemic evil that enwraps and engulfs all our lives in those ways and places where we may be able to do so, such as cultures of violence in terms of race, gender, class oppression, or materialistic greed and acquisitiveness. Such liberations as are achieved, presumably always partial, ambiguous, and temporary, may still stand as proleptic signs of eschatological deliverance.[20]

In terms of ministry, especially care and counseling, this means working selectively and systemically at the systems that dominate our lives and the lives of those for whom we have special caring responsibilities, a task integral to the promotion of healthy and "salvific" participation in the life and redemptive work of God. Specifically, it means forming communities of consciousness concerning these matters—the church, basically but not exclusively—and encouraging persons (beginning with ourselves) to "come out," at least selectively, from participation in systemic evil—including all its explicit and implicit forms of scapegoating and misattributions of violence—and to enter into the "community of the redeemed." This is needful not only for the sake of our immediate functional capacities—our health, vitality, and maturity—but for the sake of our ultimate participation in the life of God.

Both care and counseling, in this view, must become more community oriented. In particular, the model that currently defines specialized pastoral counseling as a form of psychotherapy (pastoral psychotherapy) needs to be expanded to include specific ways of relating counselees to redemptive communities, and must bring the experiences and dynamics of participation in those communities more directly into the therapeutic work and relationship of the counseling. Even everyday expressions of pastoral care in the church need to incorporate much more fully and regularly those institutional forms, rituals, sacred meanings, and other community-forming processes that draw our attention to those larger communal and sacred realities in which we live and move and have our being, and that warn us against those similarly encompassing and seemingly all-powerful realities that enslave and distort even our well-intended actions and most heartfelt desires.

> For our struggle is not against enemies of blood and flesh, but against the rulers, against the authorities, against the cosmic powers of this present darkness, against the spiritual forces of evil in the heavenly places. Therefore take up the whole armor of God, so that you may be able to withstand on that evil day, and having done everything, to stand firm (Eph. 6:12–13).

CONCLUSION

To sum up, both pastoral theology and ministry today still need a useful, empirical model explaining how salvation, understood as the mode of our ultimate relation to God, is related to those more tangible and immediate expressions of vitality we call health, strength, and maturity. Lapsley's theory gives us a strong start in this direction, especially its social and historically meaningful interpretation of salvation and its empirically insightful ways of relating basic health processes to saving forms of participation in the life of God. At the same time, I have suggested ways I believe his theory needs to be further developed. If his concept of participation is deepened to encompass noncreative, impotent suffering, his concept of society is expanded to include the semiautonomous power of social systems, and his doctrine of evil is developed to include the demonic as a force of systemic, organized violence, we will have a more detailed, profound, and ultimately practical map, one able to give greater theological meaning and direction, in empirically concrete ways, to the spiritual art of ministry.

NOTES

1. James N. Lapsley, *Salvation and Health: The Interlocking Processes of Life* (Philadelphia: Westminster Press, 1972). See also by James N. Lapsley, "Practical Theology and Pastoral Care: An Essay in Pastoral Theology," in *Practical Theology: The Emerging Field in Theology, Church, and World*, ed. Don S. Browning (New York:

Harper & Row, 1982), 167–86; "The 'Self,' Its Vicissitudes and Possibilities: An Essay in Theological Anthropology," *Pastoral Psychology* 35, no. 1 (Fall 1986): 23–45; and "Spirit and Self," *Pastoral Psychology* 38, no. 3 (Spring 1990): 135–46. In these more recent writings, Lapsley broadens his psychology from the mechanistic systems concepts of Loevinger's psychoanalytic ego psychology to include Kohut's more humanistic and theologically useful concept of self, and develops the concept of participation by introducing the theological notion of spirit, human and divine, into his anthropology. Spirit for Lapsley is a theologically appropriate way of conceptualizing the intensity and directionality of the human being, with the directionality conceived as having three aspects: toward self, others, and culture. Though these are important additions to the original theory, they do not directly impinge upon the concerns raised in this essay.

2. See, for example, Edward Thornton, *Theology and Pastoral Counseling* (Englewood Cliffs, N.J.: Prentice-Hall, 1964); Daniel Day Williams, *The Minister and the Care of Souls* (New York: Harper & Row, 1961); Wayne E. Oates, *Protestant Pastoral Counseling* (Philadelphia: Westminster Press, 1962); Gordon E. Jackson, *Pastoral Care and Process Theology* (Washington, D.C.: University Press of America, 1981); Howard John Clinebell, *Basic Types of Pastoral Care and Counseling*, rev. and enlarged ed. (Nashville: Abingdon Press, 1984); Eduard Thurneysen, *A Theology of Pastoral Care* (Philadelphia: Westminster Press, 1962).

3. In *Salvation and Health* Lapsley seems to subscribe to Whitehead's notion of objective immortality in which only the memory of one's personhood is cherished and saved in the life of God, not one's subjective existence as a living being. This point is secondary to his argument and should not be allowed to detract from the main point concerning participation as the key to the meaning of salvation. I see no reason, however, given his theory as a whole, why Lapsley could not adopt David Griffin's more recent argument in favor of subjective immortality within the Whiteheadian scheme. See David Ray Griffin, *Evil Revisited: Responses and Reconsiderations* (Albany: State University of New York Press, 1991), 36f.

4. Lapsley, *Salvation and Health*, 71.

5. Despite fundamental differences, interesting similarities exist between Lapsley's theory and James Fowler's theory of faith development. See James Fowler, *Stages of Faith: The Psychology of Human*

Development and the Quest for Meaning (San Francisco: Harper & Row, 1981), and subsequent writings, especially *Faith Development and Pastoral Care* (Philadelphia: Fortress Press, 1986). Fowler's theory is based on the cognitive structural developmental theory of Piaget and Kohlberg and posits an invariant sequence of development from stage to stage, though it includes psychodynamic features drawn from Erik Erikson and others.

6. Religious leadership conceived as helping the church envision possibilities—the "luring" of people into fuller life with God—takes two forms. The primary form is helping God lure people toward the most saving kind of participation of which they are capable—making choices that most fully conform to the will of God with whatever participational capacity may be available. Second, there is the lure toward more full and rich *modes* of participation—development toward greater vitality or health. Both are important, though in Lapsley's view the enhancement of health seems to be subordinate, ultimately, to creative participation in the divine life with whatever health one has at the moment.

7. The imagery of concentric circles nicely expresses degrees of *quantitative* inclusiveness—some people make more wide-ranging social and spiritual contributions to the world-historical process, beyond serving their own needs, than do others. But it does not help in depicting the *qualitative* dimension of participation—that some people's contributions, though not socially wide ranging, may be more rich, intensive, and valuable than those of others having a wider sphere of influence. Unfortunately, Lapsley does not sort out this important quantity/quality question, which is laden with theological significance.

8. The concept of hierarchy seems to be essential in theories of social and biological systems. Living systems exhibit multiple subsystems of control and communication arranged hierarchically in degrees of inclusiveness: the circulatory system functions as a part of the total body system, families function as part of larger communities, etc.

9. Jonathan Edwards, *Religious Affections*, ed. John E. Smith (New Haven: Yale University Press, 1959), 419.

10. Lapsley, *Salvation and Health*, 90.

11. The process view holds that not only does our suffering participate in the life of God; God also participates with us in our suffering, which means that God must in some sense be capable of

suffering. See Paul S. Fiddes, *The Creative Suffering of God* (Oxford: Clarendon Press, 1988). Larry Graham, in a major recent work on pastoral theory, *Care of Persons, Care of Worlds: A Psychosystems Approach to Pastoral Care and Counseling* (Nashville: Abingdon Press, 1992), also calls for recovering the receptive dimension of human action to balance much recent emphasis on its active or "agential" aspect, though Graham does not emphasize the theological meaning of mute, meaningless suffering.

12. This idea must not be confused with masochistic, self-punitive suffering or other forms of violence inflicted or permitted against oneself (as in spouse abuse and other dependent victimizations). To be open to experience, receptive of the gifts of others, and accepting of the realities of life, including the reality of evil and suffering, is to be fundamentally and holistically life affirming. To be self-punitive, or a participant in a cycle of self-denigrating abuse and violence (however much the victim may appear to be innocent and forgiving), has nothing to do with the tragic, necessary acceptance and moral protest of evil; it is instead a way of being passively in complicity with evil, perpetuating the suffering it inflicts.

13. See James E. Huchingson, "Organization and Process: Systems Philosophy and Whiteheadian Metaphysics," *Process Studies* 11, no. 4 (Winter 1981): 226–41.

14. Larry Graham's recent *Care of Persons, Care of Worlds* offers a major rethinking of pastoral care and counseling in systems theory (as well as process theological) terms. Graham shares my opinion that Lapsley's theory is implicitly individualistic despite the thoroughgoing social character of its process metaphysics.

15. See Griffin, *Evil Revisited*.

16. Lapsley suggests, however, that there may be a tilt or tendency toward moral goodness in more highly developed persons, though such inclinations are not inevitable. (See his *Salvation and Health*, 90.)

17. See Griffin, *Evil Revisited*, 31–34.

18. See René Girard, *Violence and the Sacred* (Baltimore and London: Johns Hopkins University Press, 1977); and Robert G. Hamerton-Kelly, *Sacred Violence: Paul's Hermeneutic of the Cross* (Minneapolis: Fortress Press, 1992), which contains an excellent summary and bibliography of Girard's work (pp. 13–39).

19. It is not clear whether Girard believes that the primitive

sacrificial systems continue to function "in the depths" of modern society, beneath its rationalizing successor institutions like law and religion, or whether they are superseded by modernity's rationalizations.

20. Lapsley wants to add a note of eschatological finality to the Whiteheadian system. He regards Pannenberg's theology, similar in many ways to Whitehead though Hegelian in conceptuality, as offering such a possibility (pp. 55–56), but he does not develop or use the idea further in *Salvation and Health*. A similar but not identical attempt to render process thought amenable to eschatological finality is envisioned by David Griffin, *Evil Revisited*, 37f.

3
Salvation and Health: A Pluralistic Perspective

JOHN B. COBB, JR.

How are "health" and "salvation" related? This question has been asked most frequently and with greatest urgency by pastoral counselors. They have been quite sure that counseling is helpful in restoring or attaining some form of health, but they have been perplexed as to how that relates to the theologically understood mission of the church. Salvation has stood for the goal of that mission.

No one has worked with greater subtlety on this question than James Lapsley. He defined both health and salvation with precision and then showed the complex relations between the processes they identify. He described the two terms as interlocking.

I share much of Lapsley's perspective and find convincing much of what he wrote. However, my approach differs from his in one respect. Although he recognizes that there has been diversity in the usage of both terms, he writes as if his task is to identify their correct usage. From my point of view, there is no one "correct" usage of such terms.

At this point, the opposite extreme from Lapsley's approach would be to say that either term can mean whatever a writer stipulates it to mean. That is not false. Writers *can* announce that they are defining terms in eccentric ways, and interested readers, if there are any, must then recall these definitions each time those terms appear.

The general situation is somewhere between these extremes. Words have some range of uses with vague boundaries and limits.

These change over time. Most of the words used by a writer participate in this indeterminateness of meaning. They have to be understood from their contexts in the writing. Often, in order to make
an argument, the writer defines certain terms with greater precision. The definitions offered normally lift up meanings already
present in the ordinary hearing of the words while excluding, for
the purpose at hand, others. Of course, each definition makes use
of words that are not themselves defined; therefore, vagueness and
ambiguity remain.

This procedure is just that followed by Lapsley. Hence, my differences with him are not on this point. The question, then, is
one's attitude toward one's definitions. Does one think of them as
"correct"? Or does one think of them as stipulative within the
range of ordinary meanings? The latter approach, as opposed to the
former, allows one to consider a variety of fruitful stipulations.

What practical difference does this make? The usual approach,
the one followed by Lapsley, at least makes a clear recommenda-
tion as to how the terms *should* be used. In this case, Lapsley proposed particular understandings of health and of salvation as
normative for pastoral counselors and, indeed, for church people
generally. He then explains how health and salvation are related.
This in turn has clear implications for the counseling work of
pastors and how it is to be related to their total ministries.

If, instead, one views any definition of health and salvation as
being to a large extent stipulative, and if one recognizes that no
one stipulation is necessarily better than others in all times and
places, then one will also understand that the whole situation is
fluid and that the role of counseling in the work of the church is
dependent on the context.

HEALTH AND SALVATION AS GOALS OF PASTORAL COUNSELING

There is an understandable fear of the kind of relativism that
follows from this emphasis on the stipulative element in definitions. One may agree that health and salvation are, indeed, words
with many meanings, but one may then seek greater specificity
through an intermediate step. One may acknowledge that the real
question is not about these terms as such, but about the relation of
the goal of pastoral counseling to the overall purpose of the church
and its ministry. One may then stipulate that among the many

possible uses of the terms, for this discussion health identifies the former and salvation the latter. Once that stipulation is made, one may argue, the task is to determine the correct definitions of these terms; that is, to identify the proper goals of counseling, on the one hand, and of the church as a whole, on the other.

This has the advantage of shifting from a debate about how to use words to a discussion of activities and communities. But if the desire is to avoid relativity, the gain is somewhat illusory. Consider pastoral counseling. It is not a fixed entity that is inherently designated by the term *pastoral counseling*. Pastors are related to parishioners in many ways, and it is useful to sort these relationships out. These are likely to include situations of advising, consoling, referring to others for particular types of assistance, exhorting, supporting, listening, and so forth. It is possible to group some aspects of these together under the rubric "counseling," but it is certainly not necessary to do so. Most of the church, through most of its history, has gotten along without doing this. And if it *is* done, there is no one correct selection from the total range of pastoral care that *is* counseling.

In the United States in the twentieth century, however, a major part of pastoral care *was* organized under the rubric "counseling." A particular range of personal problems, generally thought of as psychological ones, came to the fore in the church's life as ones to which pastors should give special attention. Usually they were dealt with in one-to-one conversations. Seminaries gave separate emphasis to preparing pastors to be truly helpful to their parishioners in these settings. What went on seemed so important that some pastors specialized in this form of ministry. It was found that this special ministry could be carried out by persons other than the parishioners' pastor. It was also found that pastors with these skills could help persons not otherwise related to the church. Special pastoral counseling centers were established. It was discovered, in fact, that one did not have to be a pastor at all in order to work effectively in these centers.

This development, peculiar to particular churches at particular times and places, raised acutely the question about the relation of the goals of pastoral counseling to the goals of the church—of health and salvation, in this sense. And to this question there were certainly better and worse answers. Lapsley's answer was among the best.

Yet institutional structures and the activities that go on within them are fluid. Parishioners brought varied concerns to their pastors and to the pastoral counseling centers. Pastors and professional pastoral counselors had diverse purposes. The very discussion of health and salvation affected these purposes. It tended to make explicit the extent to which pastoral counseling had become an extension of the secular counseling movement, which in turn was under the influence of particular schools of psychology. Awareness of that relation changed attitudes toward pastoral counseling among both counselors and other church people. Meanwhile, the self-understanding of secular counseling was changing, as were the dominant forms of psychology and their relations to other styles of thought.

This is not the place to trace the recent history of pastoral counseling in the United States, but a few developments can be noted. Much of this counseling has shifted from the medical model, where the goal centers on health, to the growth model. *Health* can be used here, too, but its meaning is much less clear. Often the related term *wholeness* is preferred. If pastoral counseling aims at helping parishioners grow, then the question of what is the ultimate end of life is directly raised. The term *salvation* may answer this question. Helping parishioners grow, then, may become more a matter of traditional spiritual direction than of psychological healing.

In addition, from within the pastoral counseling movement have come criticisms of the individualistic one-to-one approach. One objection is that people are so bound up with one another that the problems of the parishioner cannot be solved without changes in the family system in which she or he is involved. Another is that working with individuals to help them adjust to, or grow in, an evil society may be giving support to that society and ultimately damaging the individuals. Feminists, above all, have pointed out how most of the counseling profession, including its pastoral practitioners, have, in fact, supported patriarchy and pressured women to conform.

Critical developments within pastoral counseling have greatly reduced its autonomy in relation to the church's self-understanding in general. One can no longer contrast the purpose of the counseling ministry and the purpose of the church's ministry generally. Even in this society, in which the counseling specialization arose and flourished with a focus on psychological health, the purposes once segregated under the rubric of "counseling" are interacting with all aspects of ministry, and the general goal of ministry is hotly disputed.

The point of this excursus is to say that the stipulative or arbitrary element in the definition of health cannot be overcome by identifying it as the goal of a particular ministry. Ministry is diverse, and its boundaries in relation to the whole ministry of the church are fluid. But *health* remains an often-used term, referring to what is sought in some aspects of ministry, and those aspects continue to be prominent in one-to-one conversations between pastors and troubled parishioners. It is still appropriate, however, to reflect on some of the alternative meanings of that "term" even though no one meaning is correct.

The Various Definitions of Health

Given the freedom to stipulate meanings within a range of usage, one could still stipulate that health will mean whatever those persons who call themselves pastoral counselors make their goal. However, this would lead to eccentric conclusions and would be an awkward way of discussing the real and important question of how counseling relates to other pastoral activities. It is more fruitful to consider how health is generally understood.

The primary and clearest use of this word has to do with the human body. Health identifies a bodily condition that is universally desired. It is, on the one hand, the absence of sickness and, on the other, a positive feeling of energy or vitality or physical well-being. Of course, in ordinary usage, one may *feel* healthy without being so, for one may have a disease that has not yet affected one's feelings. But complications of this sort are not important for present purposes.

Health does not identify the only desideratum with respect to bodily condition. A healthy man may be distressed that he is not well-coordinated or strong. A healthy woman might be willing to sacrifice some of her good health for beauty.

Other complexities about physical health exist, and its meaning therefore remains vague. There are cultural differences. What health means at different stages of life also changes somewhat. But for most practical purposes, these variations are not especially important. The stipulative element in defining bodily health is minor.

Nevertheless, health, as it has functioned in pastoral counseling, has not referred primarily to physical health. Few people in our society come to their pastors to deal with bacterial infections or a malfunctioning liver. The health that is under consideration here is psychological.

It would be possible to stipulate that health applies only to the body. Other terms would then be needed to refer to what is now called "mental health." There might be some advantage in the rethinking that would be involved in changing terminology.

Nevertheless, there would be difficulties, too. The psyche and the soma are so intimately connected that, even when no physical cause can be identified, the soma may not be healthy. Psychological disturbances express themselves in bodily ones. Other emotional states promote bodily healing. It is at least natural, almost inevitable, to think that psychological states also are healthy and unhealthy.

It could be stipulated that psychological health is defined by its promotion of physical health. Once again there would be some advantages in this delineation. Some psychological states sometimes cause obvious bodily disorders, whereas at other times they do not. Yet they are disturbing and lead to self-damaging behavior. It is again natural, almost inevitable, to think of them as unhealthy. If the meaning of health is extended in this way, then there arises the difficult question of its definition.

One way of proceeding here is to emphasize the analogies between the psychological condition and the bodily one. Just as there are aches and pains and fevers that are symptoms of bodily disease, so there are self-defeating attitudes and anxieties that are recognized as symptoms of psychological disorders. Freedom from such disorders can be identified as "health."

There are severe limitations in this approach, however. Whereas people in general know when they are sick physically, they may believe the problem lies elsewhere when they suffer from psychological "disorders." They are likely to believe that it is the actions of others or just bad luck that causes their repeated failures rather than anything about themselves. Their inability to see accurately what is going on may be another disorder, but not one that they are likely to acknowledge.

This means that whereas for medical doctors the problem of defining health is a minor one, for counselors it is of crucial importance. They must decide whether the person who has problems is healthy. If so, then the solution of the problems, if possible at all, lies in gaining new information, learning new stratagems, or changing the behavior of others. If not, then at least part of the solution will lie in gaining psychological health.

If the counselor decides that lack of such health is a source of the problems, she or he must persuade the counselee of this. They can then work together to attain healing. Healing in this case will be gaining freedom from those feelings, attitudes, and patterns of behavior that contribute to the problems. Health could then be defined as that psychological condition that does not generate problems for the counselee or worsen those caused by the objective situation and by other people.

Clearly, psychological health defined in this way is far more relative to context than is bodily health. Emotions, attitudes, and patterns of behavior that generate avoidable problems at one stage of life, or in one cultural context, do not generate such problems in all stages and contexts. No judgment about an objectively desirable psychological state is involved.

There are definite advantages in defining psychological health in some such way as this. But again, there are problems. The word *health* has strongly normative connotations. No one wants to be unhealthy. But the net effect of seeking health, as thus defined, is to adjust to objectively given conditions. In a segregationist society, too strong a commitment to interact with all human beings in an unbiased way causes avoidable problems. In a patriarchal society, a woman's passion to be taken seriously as an equal partner with men causes problems she can avoid by reconciling herself to the subordinate position she is allotted. Are these feelings unhealthy?

One solution is to stipulate that the term *health* will be used only descriptively and not normatively. If a counselee desires health as defined, the counselor will assist. If a counselee does not want health as defined, the counselor will assist the counselee in attaining some other goal. Health is only one possible goal of counseling.

Such a solution is less possible for a pastoral counselor than for others. As pastor, one is not value free. Although assisting others to attain their life goals may be an inherently appropriate pastoral activity, the pastor cannot be indifferent to what those goals are. If the pastor judges that the attainment of those goals will be destructive to oneself or to others, she or he cannot proceed to assist without more ado.

A pastor may still decide to restrict the meaning of health in this way and then specify that as pastor she or he distinguishes health from Christian virtue or morality. Somewhat as physical health is one desideratum among others for the body, so the pastor may regard psychological health as one such desideratum. The pastor will then explain to the parishioner that, although psychological health is generally desirable, there are other considerations, such as morality, that sometimes override it.

There is an alternative strategy. The stipulation of the meaning of health may be governed more by its normative character than by its analogy to bodily health. One may then say that what seems to be healthy may not be truly so. True health involves the willingness to pay a high price for the sake of justice and liberation, even when one does not directly benefit from them. If this move is made, health will become identical with the pastor's ideal for human life. It will no longer be in any distinctive sense, psychological health.

Even when health is defined as broader than psychological, it may still be stipulated to refer only to individual persons. But that limitation may also be transcended. Because the true health of a person cannot be separated from the type of society and world she or he should strive to attain, that kind of society and world can also be called "health." People do indeed speak of a healthy society and a healthy world in this way.

Although many stipulations of meaning are possible for the word *health*, I am suggesting that three are of particular importance and use, and that the choice between them will largely determine how health is related to salvation. The first option is to define health in terms of a psychologically workable content. I have suggested freedom from emotions, attitudes, and patterns of behavior that cause avoidable problems. But of course, many other definitions of this sort are possible.

The second option is to define health as the ideal for personal life in general. This leaves wide open the question of what is ideal. All religious traditions, and many secular ones, offer answers to that question.

The third option is to define health still more broadly as the ideal for human society and the wider world. Here again, there are many competing ideals. This definition leaves open the material content.

The Various Definitions of Salvation

The freedom of stipulation is even larger in the definition of salvation. This is especially true if one goes to the closely related word *save*. One saves money. One's furniture is saved from a fire. A loan saves one from bankruptcy. A general saves a nation from defeat. A lawyer's skillful defense saves a young man from prison. A lifeguard saves a swimmer from drowning.

In the Bible, "save" has a similarly wide range of uses. But in the context of the present question, most of these are only indirectly relevant. Yet it is not irrelevant to point out that in the Bible these secular uses are not sharply separated from religious ones. God saves both individuals and the whole people of Israel from diverse evils in the ongoing course of personal life and history.

The word *salvation* more strongly focuses attention on religious matters. Here the condition to which we are saved has a more general, inclusive, or ultimate character. If we are saved from death in this sense, it is not so that death will strike us in another way. It means, instead, that the death that will surely come sooner or later loses its "sting."

We will return to the important point that in the Bible this sharp distinction between secular and religious meanings of save and salvation is largely absent. First we will pursue the consequences of adopting the distinction as Christian theology generally has. When we limit ourselves to religious salvation, how is this understood? From what and to what are we saved?

One classical formulation is that we are saved from sin, death, and the devil. Salvation from sin meant for some, especially in the early church, that people actually stopped sinning. The difficulty in reconciling this with experienced Christian life led to many modifications. Luther concluded that the Christian remains always a sinner, while at the same time always justified. That is, freedom from sin meant freedom from enslavement to sin and from the alienation from God that is its ordinary result.

Freedom from death has generally meant freedom from the finality of death and, accordingly, from the fear of death. For the believer there is, beyond death, everlasting life with Christ. Hence, death is a passage to blessedness, which in turn eliminates the terror of dying.

In the past two centuries, many Christians have ceased to find convincing a picture of a blessed everlasting continuation of individual existence. Accordingly, salvation from death has been focused on the second element in classical Christian thinking; that is, freedom from the fear of death. It is argued that we are freed from such fear not by the assurance that there is continuing life after death but because of the quality of our relationship to God here and now, or the assurance that in God the value of our lives is saved.

Freedom from the devil has meant that the power or powers of evil no longer control us either in this life or beyond. Those powers are still manifest in the world, but through Christ it has become possible for us to live under the power of God instead. At death, we will escape the devil's power once and for all. Although the notion of a single dominant personalized evil power has faded from Christian consciousness, the awareness that much that happens in this world expresses entrenched powers of evil has not. That in Christ it is possible to order our lives to God instead of to these powers is as important a belief today as ever.

For example, patriarchy is an entrenched system with enormous power both objectively in institutions and social practice and subjectively in the feelings and attitudes of both women and men. In Christ it becomes possible both to see patriarchy for what it is and to order our lives around a God who transcends and judges it. Thus we are freed from the power of this entrenched evil in principle, although it still has great capacity to do us harm both outwardly and inwardly.

What salvation frees us from is clearer than what it frees us to. This was long obscured by the widespread conviction through most of Christian history that the fullness of salvation was life with Christ in heaven. Disputes about just what it meant to live in freedom from sin, death, and the devil were intense. But these debates were relativized by the assumption that all Christians agreed that the ultimate goal was the attainment of heaven after this life had passed. In the great majority of cases, this understanding of salvation was intensified by a vivid sense of the alternative—

hell. To gain eternal blessedness and avoid everlasting torture was self-evidently of supreme importance.

The Enlightenment did not oppose the ideas of heaven and hell. It did, however, connect them less equivocally with the quality of moral life lived here and now, so that it spoke more of rewards and punishments rather than of faith and election. But it was as crucially important to Immanuel Kant as to traditional Christians to live in such a way that one would be rewarded rather than punished after death.

Sometimes questions as to the relation of health and salvation are asked as if the meaning of salvation retained the unique specificity that I have described. Obviously it does not. Beginning in the Romantic period, there was a revulsion against this focus on what happens after death and a redefinition of the goal of Christianity and, therefore, of salvation in terms of the quality of life prior to death. Of course, many Christians still understand salvation as meaning heaven vs. hell. Of these, some live from that understanding. Others abandon all talk of salvation. We are free to stipulate this definition and live with these consequences.

Schleiermacher inaugurated a new period in Christian thought that brought salvation down from heaven to earth. His meaning was no less "religious." He defined salvation in terms of the dominance of God-consciousness in experience. This began a tradition that understood salvation in terms of personal experience. This might, as with Schleiermacher, focus on the experience of God and have mystical tendencies. It could, however, focus on the forgiveness of sins, or overcoming the fear of death, or freedom from the control of evil powers.

Once salvation was understood in this-worldly terms, other possibilities arose. Most important was a recovery of the idea of the kingdom of God, so central to Jesus' message. This kingdom could be understood as a world in which God's will is done, and which could receive its content from the passion for social justice and righteousness of the Hebrew prophets. The heart of Christian faith became for some the assurance that the course of history will end in this kind of fulfillment.

The shift from otherworldly to this-worldly definitions of salvation has reopened the door to softening the boundary between the secular and religious. One might see God's salvific activity at work in movements of liberation from oppression and the ending of wars without assuming that the resultant freedom and peace will endure forever. One can claim this as a prophetic, instead of an apocalyptic, view of salvation. One can then speak of physical and psychological healing as expressions of God's salvific work as well as gaining civil rights for minorities. Today one may be particularly concerned with the salvation of the world from nuclear and ecological catastrophes. The breadth of biblical language can be recovered.

The initial impulse to redefine salvation in this-worldly terms was partly from those who were skeptical about the reality of life after death. But others, who have shared in this refocusing, believe that physical death is not the end. Indeed, this belief in life after death may be quite important to them. The difference is that they seek salvation in this world and leave to God what may happen after death. Usually, they reject the notion of eternal torment for unbelievers.

In summary, there are five definitions of salvation at work in the Christian community today. First, many subscribe to the otherworldly thought that identifies salvation as from hell to heaven. Second, there are those who identify salvation with a particular mode of actual Christian experience. Third, some define salvation as God's incorporation of our lives into the divine life either at the end of time or continuously through time. Fourth, others see salvation as a future consummation of history in freedom and justice in which all somehow participate. And fifth, still others understand salvation as the continuing work of God in history bringing about justice and peace and the integrity of creation.

SALVATION IN GLOBAL PERSPECTIVE

This discussion of salvation has been confined to its meanings among Christians. These overlap with the uses of the work in Jewish and Muslim circles, but they ignore the Indian and Chinese religious families.

A global perspective, therefore, raises a different issue. Should salvation mean the ultimate goal of life, however defined? This is a sixth possibility, which dramatically extends the implications of the term. Hindu Moksha and Buddhist enlightenment are then also forms of salvation. One could also speak of the classless society of Marxism as a form of salvation, and perhaps of Hitler's

thousand-year Reich free of Jews! The ideals held by leading psychotherapeutic thinkers for human existence would also qualify.

This sixth definition allows for comparative studies of various
religious and secular doctrines of salvation. This is a strength. On
the other hand, it proves difficult to free "salvation" sufficiently
from connotations derived from its Western use for it to serve well
in such comparisons. To call Buddhist enlightenment "salvation"
can be misleading and can block certain lines of inquiry.

For example, if we limit "salvation" to the range of meanings it
has acquired in Christianity, then we can ask how it is related to
that different phenomenon, Buddhist enlightenment. If we define
salvation in otherworldly terms, we may conclude that enlightenment is irrelevant to salvation but valuable for mundane purposes.
If we define salvation as God's ongoing saving work in the world,
we may decide that enlightenment is one form that salvation can
take or a contribution to the realization of some expressions of
salvation. In short, Christians may appropriate enlightenment as a
positive contribution in some way complementary to what they
have learned in their own traditions.

On the other hand, when Buddhist enlightenment is viewed as
one form of salvation, very different from Christian salvation, then
it appears incompatible. In order to affirm Christian salvation in
any of its definitions, one must reject the sharply opposed Buddhist
view of salvation. They cannot both be *the* goal of human life. The
difference made by the selection of definitions, thus, can be of great
historical importance.

Of course, still other consequences are possible. One could judge
that no one idea of salvation suffices, that we need to work toward
a new definition that incorporates elements from the others. This is
the syncretist approach. Its weakness is that none of the traditions
find themselves adequately represented in it, so that it lacks roots
and rarely survives. It is better that new formulations of the end or
goal of life emerge organically out of individual traditions as they
experience one another in new ways.

VARIED WAYS OF RELATING HEALTH AND SALVATION

Confronted by an array of possible definitions, or types of definition of both health and salvation, we can describe their relation in a
variety of ways. One selection of definitions makes them virtually

identical. If health is the ideal condition, and Christians define that ideal condition, and salvation is that for which God is working in the world, then Christians would intend to describe health as equivalent to salvation. Our ideal should be God's aim.

If this is the health at which the pastoral counselor aims, then the compartmentalization of counseling will be reduced. This does not mean that parishioners will not bring deeply personal and urgent problems that need to be discussed in a one-to-one context. It also does not mean that psychological understanding will cease to be relevant to the response. But the pastor's overall concern will be how to guide the life of the church so that it can serve God's purposes in the whole of things. The one-on-one counseling activities will then be considered in that context.

Guiding parishioners into cooperative activity in responding to the great issues of the day will not be alien to the one-to-one conversations. Helping individuals deal with their problems will not be separated from drawing them into the life of the congregation. Heightening sensitivity to God's call will be a part of secular psychological procedures.

Quite different will be the results of selecting other definitions. If health is defined as absence of emotions, attitudes, and patterns of behavior that generate unnecessary problems, and if salvation is understood as afterlife in heaven, then there may be little relation between them. The relation would depend on how the this-worldly conditions for otherworldly salvation were spelled out. If the condition is simply the profession of faith, then the relation would depend on whether such profession, in a given context, generated otherwise avoidable problems or, on the contrary, reduced such problems. If it did neither, then there would be hardly any connection.

The most interesting discussion of relations would come with other selections among the definitions. Suppose we take health to mean the ideal form of life as Christians understand this. Suppose, then, we take salvation to be a this-worldly human condition. The two could then coincide. But they would not be likely to do so if pastoral counselors defined health and theologians defined salvation.

Consider, for example, Schleiermacher's understanding of salvation as the dominance of God-consciousness. This is a specific form of religious experience that pervades one's life. A counselor influenced by Schleiermacher and hence affirming this kind of religious experience as indispensable to the fulfillment of life would nevertheless be likely to devote considerable attention to aspects of emotional life and interpersonal relations not discussed by theologians. Theologians have described the sine qua non of being truly Christian, whereas pastoral counselors have been interested in the fulfillment of the whole personality with special attention to emotions.

Obviously, the relations will not always be so smooth. Even among theologians who have this type of definition of salvation, there are sharp disagreements. The pastoral counselor cannot agree with all of them. But this is a matter of dispute among theologies, not a difference between the health sought by counselors in general and the salvation described by theologians in general. This overall conflict arises only if the counselor is so under the sway of secular psychology that she or he understands health in a way that falls outside the Christian faith. This, too, can happen.

There is, here, an important opportunity for cooperation between theologians and counselors that could enhance both's work. The theological habit of seeing only the sine qua non of Christian existence tends to depict salvation quite abstractly. This is at least as true of those who identify faith with New Being (Tillich), authentic existence (Bultmann), assurance (Ebeling), or responding to God's aim (process theology) as with those who speak with Schleiermacher of a particular religious experience. It is difficult for counselors, whatever their intentions, to make effective use of such definitions in dealing with most of the problems brought to them by their parishioners. Any effort to introduce theology in this way is likely to be artificial.

On the other hand, the counselors' tendency to emphasize emotional health leads to neglect of what is distinctive in Christian existence. God-consciousness, New Being, authenticity, assurance, and conformation to God's aim may not be useful for counseling if introduced abruptly, but they are not irrelevant to the health of the counselee. Thinking through these relations, and especially developing bridges between the most general features of Christian existence and particular situations, is an important task still awaiting cooperative work between theologians and counselors.

I have presented these various pairings of definitions as alternatives. They need not be such. One may find value in more than one definition of health and of salvation. If so, more than one pairing will yield fruitful results. These can supplement one another rather than be in conflict.

CONCLUSION

The assumption underlying this essay is that if we give up the idea that each key term has one correct definition, our discussions will gain richness and realism. This essay has tested this assumption in relation to health as it is thought of in theology. I have proposed three types of definition for health and six for salvation.

I do not find all of them equally fruitful, and I have indicated my concerns about making use of some of them. But I do believe that reflection about the place of pastoral counseling in the church can be advanced by employing several pairs of definitions. In the process it can be seen that some arguments have been misdirected and that new discussions are warranted. May the conversation continue.

4

Projective Identification and the Image of God: Reflections on Object Relations Theory and the Psychology of Religion

CHARLES V. GERKIN

When James Lapsley wrote his remarkably salient book, *Salvation and Health*, in 1972, he joined forces with a number of writers in the now burgeoning field of clinical education for ministry in the effort to inform our understanding of important theological concepts by way of serious dialogue with the social sciences. His old colleague at Princeton, Seward Hiltner, who received much more public acknowledgment of his work than did Lapsley, wrote more and was in some ways a public figure. Meanwhile, in a more quiet and no less deliberate way, Jim Lapsley pressed ahead with his own efforts. The result of those efforts eventuated in the book that alone makes Lapsley a significant person to be honored by his colleagues in pastoral theology. I am gratified to be invited to join with others in this set of essays that finally recognizes just how important Lapsley's contribution has been.

I want to join Lapsley in his and my own efforts to appropriate a contemporary form of psychotherapeutic psychology for theological purposes. For Lapsley in *Salvation and Health*, that appropriation was oriented toward the work of ego psychology and to a lesser extent the work of A. H. Maslow. Maslow's ideas about such things as the hierarchy of human needs and peak experiences offered possible directions for the practical work of the pastor as theologian. Here I will be looking toward a somewhat different direction; namely, those psychologies and psychotherapeutic techniques that have come from the school of contemporary psychology known as object relations theory. My purpose, however, will

52

be much the same as Lapsley's. I am interested in the set of questions and possible suggestive answers that may appear when psychological approaches are used to seek to understand the human-God relationship.

The occasion that led me in the direction I will take was a brief two-day seminar sponsored by the Georgia Association for Pastoral Care for pastoral counselors and others who were intrigued by the work of David E. and Jill Savege Scharff in their book published in 1991 under the title *Object Relations Couple Therapy*.[1] I was asked to make a presentation concerning the possible theological implications of that contemporary movement to meet some of the challenges that arise in assisting marital partners.

I must begin by acknowledging that the ideas I want to explore probably are best categorized as explorations in the psychology of religion rather than as theological explorations in the true sense of that discipline. Theology is a unique and self-defined mode of discourse with its own tradition, its own rules of language, its own ways of viewing the cosmos and human behavior. Theology's world is populated with its own images and themes, its own set of persistent metaphors, its own modes of reasoning. As such, the world of theology cannot be reduced to or even directly translated into the modalities of another way of speaking, another tradition of thinking about the human condition. It cannot simply engage in direct conversation with the language of any other discipline. Yet the languages of other disciplines can be of great assistance to the theologian in what has come to be called a "mutually critical dialogue."[2] David Tracy's colleague, Don Browning, has been most influential in bringing that modification of Tillich's method of correlation into use in pastoral theology.

Object relations theory owes its origins to another language world—that of the psychoanalytic tradition. That world is likewise a unique world with its own images, its own themes of human development and relationships. Those metaphors likewise resist direct translation into the language of theology.

Thus theology and object relations theory remain, as it were, strangers to each other, citizens of two different homelands. Those of us who travel back and forth between those two homelands may carry messages back and forth so that the two traditions may be brought into dialogue with each other—may sometimes even argue with each other and be in fundamental disagreement. Thus the two languages, as Lapsley demonstrated so clearly, may in significant ways learn from each other. But they can never be integrated in the sense of coming to speak the same language. To dwell in both worlds without confusion means, in very important ways, to become bilingual.

Yet somewhere between the language worlds of theology and psychoanalytic thought there is a middle ground about which and to which both theology and psychoanalytic thought can speak. The traditional ways of speaking about that middle ground are to call it the arena of the psychology of religion. The use of the term *religion* here is significant. To be a student of the psychology of religion is not to construct a theological psychology. Nor is it psychological theology. Rather, the term *religion* is used to indicate that what we are concerned with here is the varying and often very particular ways that individuals, families, and cultural groups appropriate religious images, traditions, rituals, objects, and ideas— the so-called stuff of religious life. That concern is in fundamental ways a psychological one. It is a concern that the thought forms and theoretical formulations of psychotherapeutic psychology can speak to and speak about, including the thought forms and theoretical formulations of object relations theory. Theology can also speak about that concern, most particularly from a normative perspective as we make judgments about the value and truth of the varying forms of religious life.

Psychoanalytic Origins:
Freud's Psychology of Religion

Although many theologians and other religious leaders have come to see many of Freud's ideas about the human condition— most notably his fresh emphasis on the power of unconscious motivation and experience—as theologically and pastorally useful, his lifelong stance toward human religious life was fundamentally critical and negative. Perhaps the most succinct statement of his view of religion is found in the following quotation taken from a paper he presented in 1907 titled "Obsessive Actions and Religious Practices": "One might venture to regard obsessional neurosis as a pathological formation of religion, and to describe that neurosis as an individual religiosity and religion as a universal obsessive neurosis."[3] Thus, for Freud, religion was by definition pathological. It arises, as he later wrote in *The Future of an Illusion*, out of the Oedipus complex, out of the relation to the father. Thus religion is always rooted in the illusional rather than in reality and, therefore, is a product of neurosis. Furthermore, it is for Freud always rooted in the relationship of the developing self to the father, whom Freud saw as the seat of authority in the life of the family. In Freud's male-dominated psychology, the struggle of the child to claim its own identity as over against the authority of the father was primary and, therefore, primal in the neurotic formation of a fantasied relationship with an imaginary God.

Most classical Freudians have not challenged this view of the matter. Among nonclassical Freudians, however, Philip Rieff has issued the strongest challenge. He speaks of Freud's "genetic disparagements of the religious spirit" and says that Freud will admit as religious feelings only feelings of submission and dependence; others are dismissed as intellectual delusions or displacements of the primary infantile sentiment.[4] Rieff quite apparently wanted to admit to the realm of religious development both other aspects of emotional life and postinfantile developmental experience.

Negative as is this Freudian view of religious experience, it set a direction for later psychoanalytic explorations of the psychological origins of human religious life. It set the direction as a psychogenetic one; namely, as a search for the developmental origins of human religious experience and for the early developmental experiences that provide the psychological core out of which later religious life develops.

The British School

For our purpose here, perhaps the most positive new direction that followed Freud's psychogenetic road map was that set by the British psychoanalyst Donald W. Winnicott. Like Freud, Winnicott's focus was on the early life of the infant. Unlike Freud, Winnicott turned for his formulations to his direct observations of infants and their mothers. The problem that attracted Winnicott, as was the case with most of the members of the British Object Relations School, was the puzzling question as to how the infant first began to experience a self separate from its world—the self as an object separate from other objects, most notably the mothering figure.

It is thus the mother who provides what Winnicott termed the "good enough" holding environment that so responds to the infant's needs that the child is enabled to make the transition from experiencing itself as fused with its environmental world toward experiencing itself as separate from but related to the world of reality. Said another way, it is that holding environment provided by the mothering object that fosters the formation of the self of the infant. Whether and to what extent that self formation is that of a "true" or "false" self will depend on the quality of care provided by the mother.[5]

One further elaboration of Winnicott's theory of self formation has proved to be of considerable interest to students of the psychology of religion, namely, his theory of the "transitional object." Winnicott posits that, in order for the infant to retain something of the primary narcissistic control of its world with which it began while yet recognizing the separateness of the world of reality that is beyond the infant's control, there develops an arena of thought and experience midway between fantasy and reality. This transitional space is occupied by both illusion and reality. Real objects separate from the self are imbued with fantasied meanings that allow the child to live in both worlds—the world of reality and the world of illusion. This is the world of the infant self in relation to a favorite toy, the famous teddy bear, or Linus blanket.

According to Winnicott's transitional space theory, it is out of this arena of symbolic thought and fantasy/reality experience that, with the further maturation of the child, the world of culture, the arts, and religion develops. Psychologically speaking then, human participation in religion involves both the recognition of a universal and cosmic reality and the expression of certain illusory meanings about that ultimate reality. It is important to recognize that in this formulation, Winnicott departs drastically from Freud's view of illusion. For Freud, illusion always had the meaning of a distortion or contradiction of reality in the service of wish fulfillment. For Winnicott, the illusory creation of meanings is central to human creative experience. Rather than seeing illusion as negative, Winnicott saw illusion as potentially positive, even necessary, if the self is to sustain itself through a life of multifaceted experience.

Other psychologists of religion, most particularly Ana-Maria Rizzuto, William W. Meissner, and Paul Pruyser, building essentially on Winnicott's theory of transitional objects, have further developed the notion of God as, psychologically speaking, a transitional object. Like Freud, these psychologists of religion root the person-to-God relationship in the early experience of the child with its parents. The vicissitudes of the developing relationship with a God representation are inexorably and in complex ways linked to the vicissitudes of the human relationships of the self with its parental objects. In the transitional space of reality and illusion, the relationship to God takes form as the child seeks to work out its own selfhood in relation to whatever reality exists between itself and the parents.

> From the genetic point of view, . . . the psychological phenomenon of a God representation confronts us with problems of maturation, that is, the epigenetic development of the capacity to represent a nonexperiential object sensorially. It also confronts us with questions about the developmental psychic conditions for progressive object relations from symbiosis to maturity: it poses questions about the capacity to sublimate wishes and to transmute parental images and representations into more or less separated God representations. It also poses questions from the point of view of narcissistic equilibrium and object love. . . . The God representation does not escape the normal vicissitudes of other objects, however. Ambivalent feelings mix with longings; wishes to avoid God intermingle with wishes for closeness. The search for love, approval, and guidance alternates with noisy and rebellious rejection, doubt and displays of independence. The pride of faithful service to God contrasts with painful doubts about being unworthy.[6]

Here Rizzuto seeks to acknowledge both the close connection between the formation and maintenance of the God representation and parental object relations, on the one hand, and the increasingly complex set of relationships that develop between the self and other aspects of its world, on the other. As William Meissner points out, however:

> While God shares the transitional space with other cultural representations, the God-representation has a special place in that it is uniquely connected with [the human's] sense of [self], of the meaning and purpose of [human] existence and [human] ultimate destiny. Perhaps more important than anything else is the fact that once this transitional object representation is created, whether it is dormant or active, it remains available for continuing psychic integration.[7]

W. R. D. FAIRBAIRN, MELANIE KLEIN,
AND THE CONCEPTS OF PROJECTIVE
AND INTROJECTIVE IDENTIFICATION

In regard to the workshop to which I referred earlier, I was prompted to review not only the Scharff's significant work with object relations theory in relation to work with families and couples having marital difficulties, but also to look at some of the sources from which they have built the model for their work.[8] I sought to relate that body of literature to the interests of pastoral counselors and others concerned with the connections between object relations theory and religion. Thus began a search for several somewhat different but related relationships among theorists.

I must first acknowledge that what I here propose belongs most appropriately within the field of the psychology of religion rather than in that of theology as that discipline has been handed down through the generations by pastorally oriented persons. What I have chosen to do is to consider whether object relations theory, particularly that of certain of the founding figures in the British School, offers any assistance in our efforts to understand the human relationship to God. It remains to be seen whether these developments in the secular psychotherapeutic psychologies can move us forward in that search. Here, I follow closely the thought of the philosopher Hans-Georg Gadamer. One of Gadamer's important contributions to theological or other religious research is his notion that the true purpose of understanding is, to use his phrase, to "move ahead" in the search for truth.[9]

Although the Scharffs are cognizant of and make substantial use of many of the core concepts first proposed by Donald W. Winnicott, quite apparently a close reading of their work in marriage and family therapy reveals that the primary figures from which they draw are Melanie Klein and W.R.D. Fairbairn, the first generally considered to be the founder of the British School, and the second a physician with particular interest in religious experience.[10]

The following is from the Scharffs' book on couple therapy:

> He [Fairbairn] began by proposing that what organizes the baby in the beginning is the need for a relationship with a primary care-taker, usually its mother (although a father or substitute can do the "mothering"). The baby takes in the *unsatisfying aspects* of its inter-

actions and splits them off from experience, repressing them from consciousness. Two major aspects of painful experience are thus put underground: The *need-exciting* (which he called "libidinal") relationship with the mother, and the *rejecting or frustrating* (which he called "antilibidinal") relationship with the mother. The need-exciting relationship is one in which the baby is left longing for satisfaction, which is beyond reach. In the rejection constellation, the baby feels the mother is rejecting, angry, or frustrating its needs. The baby therefore becomes angry and sad. Finally, there is an area of reasonably satisfying relating between the child and mother, which Fairbairn located in the realm of the "central ego" in relationship to its internal object, the "ideal object." A reasonable range of affects characterizes this area of relating. Fairbairn also described the way that the rejecting object system acted to exert a further "hostile repression" on the need-exciting object system.[11]

Keep in mind these three aspects of experience as we proceed, two of which, according to Fairbairn, tend to be repressed into the unconscious by the nascent infantile self. Only the central ideal object is retained in consciousness. Somewhat in passing, it is interesting to note that Fairbairn speaks of this object as the *ideal* object rather than the "real" or "realistic" object. Thus he suggests that the retention of the mothering object in consciousness necessarily involves a certain degree of idealization. For Fairbairn then, anything negative or need-exciting about that relationship tends to be repressed.

The Scharffs then give great attention to two concepts first proposed by Melanie Klein, namely, those of projective and introjective identification. Stated very simply, these concepts proposed that the unacceptable, repressed aspects of the self—the need-exciting and rejecting or frustrating aspects—are projected into the other (in infancy, the mother) and that the "other person unconsciously takes it in and feels like that projected part through projective identification, and then behaves in such a way as to confirm it or, in more mature states, to modify it."[12]

Later in their book, the Scharffs develop much more fully than space allows here the controversies and differences among various object relations theorists relative to the concepts of projective and introjective identification. They then proceed to make very creative and significant use of these concepts both in relation to the diagnostic aspects of marital therapy and in reflecting upon and carrying out of marital therapeutic intervention. About that central and therapeutically challenging aspect of their work, I will have little to say here. Certainly, they provide a most useful object relations framework for the work of marriage counseling and psychotherapy.

The only precaution I would suggest to pastors and others using this enormously useful therapeutic set of ideas is that it not be used in a manner that risks reductionism to a single theory as adequate for all situations. That would be to suggest that all marriage conflicts could be reduced to the appearance of primary repressed object relations. Surely there are other levels of conflict—economic, value, and cultural conflicts, for example—that play significant roles in many marriage difficulties. Object relations is then a useful, but nevertheless limited, perspective for pastoral or other therapeutic work.

What I do want to do with the notions of projective and introjective identification is to try to relate them in a very tentative and somewhat playful way to what I reported earlier concerning the use psychologists of religion have made of Donald Winnicott's concept of the transitional object. The question I want to pursue has to do with whether or not we can move that work forward just a bit by considering the possibility that in the formation of an individual's representation of God as an ultimate transitional object, the processes of projective identification may also be at work. Furthermore, what, if anything, can be added to our understanding of individual religious experience if we consider the notion of introjective identification in relation to the meaning shape that certain individuals find in their relationship with God? Is it possible that some of the highly complex and idiosyncratic conflicts that some persons experience in their relationship with God have psychological rootage in the process of primary repression of unacceptable need-exciting and rejecting or frustrating aspects of infantile experience?

THREE OBJECT IMAGES

Consider then the possibility that in the formation of the God representation by a given individual there are at work three object images: the image of God as the exciting object, the image of God as the rejecting object, and the image of God as the ideal object.

What then comes into view that may help us to understand the rich variety of images and themes that play and interplay in the formation of the human-to-God and God-to-human relationship?

First, I would ask the reader to think with me about the variety of phenomena we can observe in persons relative to God as the need-exciting object. In my own reflections, I find myself thinking of those persons I have encountered in the course of my pastoral work who seem unconsciously to relate to God as if God were the figure who should and can fulfill all their needs, as if God were the fulfiller of all wishes. Theirs is not a God of judgment or justice as was the God of the prophets of Israel. No, theirs is a God only and overwhelmingly of love and intimate spiritual communion. If they are Christian believers, their image of Jesus tends likewise to be a soft and tender image—an image of the Christ-figure who primarily goes about fulfilling the needs and wishes of the persons he meets along his way.

Although I am not a historian, I would hazard a guess that a significant amount of the literature coming out of medieval centers of monastic search for union with God could be categorized as literature that, often in highly poetic, even eroticized language, seeks to express a human relationship with the need-exciting God. Here again, let me remind the reader that I am not engaged here in reductionism!

Likewise, if one searches the narrative and poetic texts of the Bible with this thought in mind, one can find numerous examples of such imagery in relation to God. One such text is from Psalm 22.

> "Commit your cause to the Lord; let him deliver—
>   let him rescue the one in whom he delights!"
> Yet it was you who took me from the womb;
>   you kept me safe on my mother's breast.
> On you I was cast from my birth,
>   and since my mother bore me you have been my God.
> Do not be far from me,
>   for trouble is near
>   and there is no one to help.
>   Psalm 22:8–11

There are others who, in quite the opposite mode of relating to the need-exciting God, tend to construct a God representation that takes the form of avoidance of a relationship to the need-exciting God. Theirs is a religion of self-reliance. As in the robust hymn often sung by young people during the 1940s and 1950s, they sing:

> Lord we are able. Our spirits are thine.
> Remold them; make us like thee divine."[13]

Second, I would ask my readers to reflect and consider those with whom they have worked in pastoral relationships whose God representation has been that of the God who rejects and frustrates the self. These are the guilt-ridden of the world, the ones who seem always to cower in shame before their image of God. Always unworthy, they seem unconsciously to have a need to grovel before a God they can never please. With these persons it would seem that, if we follow the theory of projective and introjective identification, there lies at the core of their religious development profound experiences of the rejecting mothering object. (Here I do not necessarily mean the mother of the child, but anyone who fulfills that role.) Their God is quite perpetually a God who has introjected the unacceptable feelings of rejection so that they are unable to experience a God representation characterized by forgiving love and acceptance. Rather, they must continue to strive unsuccessfully to please while bearing the burden of profound unconscious condemnation by the rejecting God.

Finally, consider how most of us struggle in our conscious reflections about God and our relationship to that mysterious Other between the desire to idealize, to imagine God in the images of perfection, omnipotence, and omnipresence, on the one hand, and the gnawing questions that haunt us concerning God's absence, the ultimate mystery of the God who is beyond our ability to understand, on the other hand. At times we are very aware of the reality of our own reliance on ourselves and our fellow travelers on the road of life. At other times, we sense that there is indeed an Other upon whom we and all of creation depend.

If Fairbairn is correct in this theorizing about how internal images are formed, and if our extrapolations from his theory are reasonably accurate, it is at this level of the object representation of God that we and those with whom we work are most open to the appropriation of new experience so that our ambivalences about our God representation may find some new resolutions. This is the God representation most accessible to change and creative transformation, for it is the God representation who functions at the level of conscious interaction.

POSSIBLE TRANSFORMATIONS

What of those who, in ways not unlike the couples that the Scharffs describe in their case examples, are caught in interactions with a God representation that is deeply embedded in the unconscious dynamics of hidden projective (and, at least at the symbolic level, introjective) identifications? How are those often destructive and infinitely painful relationships to be offered healing and the possibility of transformation? To respond even cursorily to those questions would require another essay. I can imagine easily a conversation with Jim Lapsley in which he and I would come to some agreements and some sharp differences! Instead, I offer a few tersely stated and very speculative, perhaps even much too tenuous, thoughts about these questions.

First, to open up the possibility of transformation of deeply embedded unconscious need-exciting and rejecting/frustrating God representations with persons will involve inviting the God representation of the help-seeker into the pastoral consulting room in ways not unlike inviting members of a marriage to sit together and examine with care their unconscious modes of interaction. Speaking strictly in psychological terms, that means that other persons need to be encouraged to speak as openly and in a freely associative manner as possible over an extended period of time about their relationship with God.

Second, allowing whatever God representation exists in the person to be fully experienced and explored will inevitably involve the exploration of projective and introjective identifications within the transference relationship with the helper. A "reading" of the projective identifications involved in any given individual's relationship with her or his God representation will necessitate a "reading" of transference and countertransference phenomena. Just what forms that projection of the God representation onto the helper and/or the person seeking help will be both numerous and quite unpredictable. The same care must therefore be exercised by the helping person in this level of conversation about the human-God relationship as is necessary in working with persons concerning their human-to-human relationships.

Third, what I have just said means that the pastor/helper's own conscious and unconscious interactions with his or her God representation will play a significant role in both the quality and the direction of the helping process that takes place. Because I am here assuming what all psychoanalytically-oriented helpers take for granted, much of the most significant interchange will take place at an unconscious level. Thus the transformation of the self-God relationship at the deepest levels of human interaction is in certain ways beyond the conscious control of either helper or help-seeker.

Fourth, if such a relationship between helper and help-seeker can be established with openness and consistency, both helper and help-seeker may find their God representations being made subject to change. By reasonable logic this will indeed be the case, though seldom is that reality given the degree of self-reflection it deserves. However, if we think carefully about the matter, it will become apparent that automatically, in ways beyond our conscious intent, such self-reflections do take place. Certainly, they take place when two or more helpers who fundamentally trust each other get together to talk about their work.

Fifth, although I began this essay by locating it within the psychology of religion, I want now to speak in a certain sense theologically. The norms that should give control to the helper-to-help-seeker search for a transformed God representation should be norms that transcend the boundaries of the dyadic relationship. They need to come from a mutually recognized community of faith and tradition that preserves a certain vision of what the human-God relationship is and should be. For those of us within the Judeo-Christian tradition, that vision is in a certain sense held in common because it originates with the experience of the community of ancient Israel of their God. For Christians that vision has been fulfilled with the coming of the Christ.

In this essay I have attempted to explore what is for me some very new and unexplored territory. The realm we have entered together is not unlike the realm James Lapsley entered when he made his contribution to the relationship of the self to God. Both Lapsley and I have sought to relate a psychological/theological perspective to the same set of problems. Lapsley found his psychological sources within ego psychology with a hint of humanistic self-actualization psychology. Writing in a different time, I have chosen another set of psychological theories. But the search is the same, and it is one that will continue for some time. As Jim Lapsley might say, I would not want anything I have said to be taken as firm and final truth on these matters. If I have stimulated consideration of what to me are very difficult and challenging mysteries, I will be quite satisfied, as I hope Jim Lapsley was satisfied when he opened for pastoral theology greater dialogue with the psychologists concerning religious experience.

NOTES

1. David E. Scharff and Jill Savege Scharff, *Object Relations Couple Therapy* (Northvale, N.J.: Jason Aronson, 1991).

2. David Tracy, "The Foundations of Practical Theology," in *Practical Theology*, ed. Don S. Browning (San Francisco: Harper & Row, 1983), 61–82.

3. Sigmund Freud, "Obsessive Actions and Religious Practices," in vol. 9 of *Standard Edition of the Complete Psychological Works of Sigmund Freud*, ed. James Strachey (London: Hogarth Press, 1986), 115–28.

4. Philip Rieff, *Freud: The Mind of the Moralist* (Chicago: University of Chicago Press, 1979).

5. Donald W. Winnicott, *Maturational Processes and the Facilitating Environment: Studies in the Theory of Emotional Development* (Independence, Mo.: International University Press, 1965); and idem, *Playing and Reality* (New York: Routledge Chapman & Hall, 1982).

6. Ana-Maria Rizzuto, *The Birth of the Living God: A Psychoanalytic Study* (Chicago: University of Chicago Press, 1981).

7. William W. Meissner, *Psychoanalysis and Religious Experience* (New Haven: Yale University Press, 1986).

8. David E. Scharff and Jill Savege Scharff, *Object Relations Family Therapy* (Northvale, N.J.: Jason Aronson, 1987); and Scharff and Scharff, *Object Relations Couple Therapy*.

9. Hans-Georg Gadamer, *Truth and Method* (New York: Crossroad, 1982); and idem, *Philosophical Hermeneutics* (Berkeley: University of California Press, 1976).

10. Harry Guntrip, *Psychoanalytic Theory, Therapy and the Self* (New York: Basic Books, 1973).

11. Scharff and Scharff, *Object Relations Couple Therapy*.

12. Ibid., 8.

13. Harry S. Mason, "Are Ye Able?" in *The Methodist Hymnal* (Nashville: Board of Publication of the Methodist Church, 1966).

5
K'ung Fu-tze, Meet Jim Lapsley

JAMES G. EMERSON, JR.

The futurologist Alvin Toffler wrote a book titled *The Third Wave*. In the West, the first wave of pastoral theology might well be marked by the line from Schleiermacher to Boisen. The second wave, which takes in the history from Boisen to Hiltner, Johnson, Clinebell, Weiss, and their scholar/practitioner descendants, includes major women writers in the field and men such as Jim Lapsley. The "third wave" to which we now move centers on the globalization of theology, the growth of women's studies, and the Protestant concern for spiritual formation.

Today in theological education, globalization has become the context in which all other matters are evaluated and studied. This is especially true with regard to the question "What does it mean to be human?"

Even though I am not Asian, I welcome the invitation to reflect on the Asian contribution to our Western concerns. I write with appreciation for the correctives to my own thought that I find in the Asian context. Further, though I do not quote them specifically, I express the appreciation of many of us to David Augsburger in the United States, Sudhifa Kakar in India, and the late Erik Erikson, whose works have been in the global context almost from the start.

As one travels throughout Asia at the present, the dominance as well as the impact of Western counseling practice becomes evident. Taiwan has its clinical pastoral education training centers. India has its counseling centers in Vellore, Bangalore, and Delhi. One Indonesian theological seminary has a library and counseling program that would stand with any in the West. Although the leadership of these centers is thoroughly Eastern, the basic training of those leaders has taken place in the United States, Britain, or Germany.

Happily, the *Asian Theological Journal* and many parts of the lesser known but equally excellent journals from different parts of Asia have begun to make their own contribution. Articles that reflect on family counseling in an Asian context, that speak to personality development in a Hindu context, and that explore the "guru mentality" demonstrate the coming Asian contribution to pastoral care and pastoral theology. Lapsley's own writings indicate a clear and proper awareness of his being "in the West." His latest book on the subject of aging shows awareness of different cultural worlds within which pastoral care takes place.[1]

Lapsley's specific interest in anthropology, from a theological standpoint, lifts up the question "Who is the human being?" As we look back, his studies focus on Western writers—especially H. Richard and Reinhold Niebuhr, and Heinz Kohut. Lapsley's thinking, however, thrusts forward to the issue of "who is the human being?" at every age of life and in different cultural worlds. This look in two directions itself suggests the nature of moving from a past into a new era—the coming "third wave"—of pastoral theology. Lapsley raises the issues of anthropology in *Salvation and Health*.[2] His later works lead us into a cultural look at a theology of anthropology. The implications for the field of pastoral theology stand out. Today, "our" field will either come to terms with those implications or risk irrelevance in the decades ahead.

Perhaps the lifting up of the anthropological issue itself is a major contribution of Lapsley. Perhaps the reality of Asian perspectives different from our Western perspectives on this anthropology is the key contribution to a global pastoral theology.

WHO ARE WE AS HUMAN BEINGS?

At the end of World War II, preacher after preacher told the story of a certain veteran who suffered from amnesia. This man appeared at a veterans' function and said to the assembly, "Does anyone know who I am?" In those same years, Arthur Miller published his stage success *Death of a Salesman*. That play ends with one of the brothers standing at the grave of Willie Lohmann say-

ing, "He never knew who he was." Both stories became parables
of a postwar generation that did not know who it was or where it
needed to go.

From the days of the Genesis story until now, the questions
regarding "who we are" and "where we are going" have been
linked. Adam and Eve let themselves be seduced by the serpent
who enticed them with the promise to be something other than
they were—like God. Cain killed Abel and said, "Am I my
brother's keeper?" Both stories show that the questions of who we
are, what we do with who we are, and where we fit into the
scheme of things go back to the beginning of human experience.

Lapsley lifts up the issue in relation to a spirit-self model.[3] In his
writings, he argues that effective pastoral care demands coherent
thinking about what it means to be human. Not only does he ask
what it means to be human, but he also asks what it means to be
human at different stages in life. He recognizes that much of developmental psychology has spoken to humanness with models from
youth or young adult years. In his latest book, he now pushes us to
look at the issue in the model of aging adults.[4]

Over the centuries, Asian thought has recognized and debated
the crucial nature of "who are we and what are we to do?" Out of
the works of Buddha, for example, we find denial of the concept of
an inner spirit that in any sense is different from the body. There is
no personal self and there is no personal God.[5] The Buddhist approach would see Lapsley's "spirit-self" as flawed from the outset.

On the other hand, K'ung Fu-tze, known to the Western world
as Confucius, posits the concept of "jen," a genuine self, a mature
self, a self that grows through stages. Therefore, in the difference
between the Buddhist and the Confucian views from Asia, we have
a Western parallel in the debate between the behaviorists and those
who see the self as real—to say nothing of those who see the self as
God-created. Yet in Asia, whether in a Buddhist or Confucian
framework, the questions of who we are as humans are not seen in
the context of Freudian drives or ego functions. Instead, questions
of human nature are seen in the context of relationships—to the
cosmos, to the tribe or clan, to the community, to other individuals.

As his own writing has moved on from the matter of salvation
in his early years to that of aging, Jim Lapsley has himself shown
something of a progression. Although *Salvation and Health* rec-

ognizes the interpersonal nature of personality,[6] his latest book seems to involve more fully than his early ones the role of community.

Although most Westerners seem to lean toward Buddha when they look East because of Buddhist strengths in the area of meditation, I join with those who feel that the more fruitful dialogue is with K'ung Fu-tze. Although meditation and spiritual formation have a central place in my own thinking and life, for the questions of this essay, I prefer to concentrate on K'ung Fu-tze. His views of who we are as humans and what we should do with who we are seem to me more suggestive for our discussion purposes of this dialogue and this essay: "K'ung Fu-tze, meet Jim Lapsley; Jim Lapsley, greet K'ung Fu-tze!"

A Dialogue

Lapsley: Mr. Moderator, I do appreciate your bringing us together. I have made it quite clear in my publications that I write from a Western perspective. Yet, as you have already indicated, humans are human whatever the culture. We can learn from each other. I am most pleased to meet Mr. K'ung Fu-tze.

K'ung Fu-tze: The honor is mine. We have much to learn from each other.

Moderator: Gentlemen, the issue of who we are and whether or not we see ourselves from a Western or an Asian frame of reference is not merely an ideal one. The issue has practical implications not only for our view of human nature but also for how we understand society, how we organize a church, how we put together a service of worship, and how we evaluate a verbatim report.

K'ung Fu-tze: Indeed, for example, my format for approaching both practice and organization even pulses through today's China. Why recently, I heard a Chinese seminary student in Beijing explain her reasons for entering the ministry with reference to my four ethical virtues.

Lapsley: Interesting. As a Westerner and a Presbyterian, I would have expected her to speak of a sense of calling, a sense of vocation. Now tell me, honored Sir, how do you view human nature? Who are we?

K'ung Fu-tze: Not only I but others who think as I do, such as Mencius, are optimistic. We see human nature as basically good.

On that goodness we can build an ethic—a rationale for both organization and behavior within the organization.

LAPSLEY: In Western experience, we found something similar in Carl Rogers and others who took an optimistic approach to human nature. For him, this positive view led to a concept of what one did or did not do in a one-on-one interview to allow for personal health. Others developed it in relation to group therapy. However, we also had those who moved to the questions of morality. I think of Don Browning.

MODERATOR: True enough, but the Browning approach, although a step toward the Confucian line, still has a frame of reference that is quite Western. The Western approach tends to move from the individual. The Asian approach looks at the community and then moves to the individual. The Asian, influenced by the community context, seeks to live up to the potential that he or she has. In the concept of reincarnation, especially in Buddhist thought, the individual seeks to fulfill his or her karma in this life so that in the next, he or she may live at a higher level.

K'UNG FU-TZE: You are getting there, Mr. Moderator, but permit me humbly to add a thought. I would see the task of the individual as learning how to live up to the goodness that is within one. Whatever one's station may be—a child, an adult, a teacher, a ruler, a person of business—that means living up to the potential as seen by the community.

MODERATOR: What then is the consequence of failing to live up to this "goodness"? Is it a sense of guilt?

K'UNG FU-TZE: Failure to live up to potential leads to shame. I look at that failure as more a matter of shame than guilt. The sense of community, the sense of shame, and the basic goodness of human nature—these are key in my thought and understanding of what you call "human anthropology."

LAPSLEY: Thank you, Mr. K'ung Fu-tze. You have given us a good beginning. I appreciate the fact that in your sense of community, you have not lost the sense of the individual—of the self. I would also hold that we must speak of responsibility, guilt, and evil. Your lifting up of the matter of shame in the context of community I find insightful and a helpful expanding of my own views—especially with regard to the aging. We must talk again.

I am not sure whether K'ung Fu-tze or Jim Lapsley (or even Don Browning) would be the more horrified by my characterization of them. Fanciful as the dialogue may be, I trust that the short discussion puts before us not just the thought but the "feel" of an Asian perspective on the anthropological insights that come from Jim Lapsley.

ASIAN PERSPECTIVES ON ANTHROPOLOGY

Let us now look specifically at three areas: community and identity; shame; and the actualization of goodness.

The Issue of Community and Identity

Popularly, people speak of the West as oriented to the individual and the East as focused on the community. My colleagues in India and Taiwan feel the distinction is overdone, and I agree. Nevertheless, the stereotype has sufficient validity that I keep it for the purpose of this look at Lapsley's anthropology. K'ung Fu-tze has great concern for what will allow the state, the community, and the society to function. The mind-set of many Americans centers on "Who am I?" "Where do I fit?" "What are my rights?" Therefore, the distinction holds.

Lapsley, in his discussions of the self, raises the identity issue. He recognizes the difference between the "I-self" and the "we-self."[7] Biologically speaking, the aging process has its effect on the way the "I" of an individual can be expressed. An aging person cannot run as fast as he or she once did. He or she moves from total physical dependence at birth, through strong independence, to sometimes total physical dependence in the frailty of old age. In the writings of Victor Frankel and others, Western identity may come through one's purpose (logotherapy) or one's calling (Calvin).

The Asian approach sees the individual identity as coming from the group. Chang Jung speaks in communist China of decisions being made on the basis of what was good for the group and the rightness of that group frame of reference.[8] However, that approach did not start with communism. Today we see it in Korea, China, and Japan. In Taiwan, with the tremendous influence of both Japanese and United States business interests, we see a mix. (In relating to a modern young citizen of Taiwan, an outsider must be sensitive to the fact that at one moment, the young adult may seem as independent as any Westerner and at the next moment will seem "very Chinese.")

Lapsley has come at this issue with a most interesting concept of relational vectors. He writes:

> Vector is a term in mathematics used to denote direction and magnitude, usually represented by a straight line. In this discussion, the term will be used metaphorically to indicate different objects (or subjects) of relationships (direction), and kinds and degrees of attachment (magnitude). This metaphorical use introduces the notion of difference in kind not found in the mathematical term, but it still seems best for my purpose.[9]

Although I have some concern about the use of the word *vector* simply because of its "straight line" connotation, Lapsley's definition of the word emphasizes relationship. Relationships suggest types of community. Awareness of different magnitudes of relation and different "subjects" of relationships makes a positive contribution. That awareness gives a basis for carrying out the East-West dialogue on the relation of community and identity. The vector metaphor itself gives a basis for acknowledging the different mixes of individualism and community centeredness in such a place as Taiwan. The concept recognizes that no one is "purely" Eastern or "purely" Western in a world that has become the proverbial global village. Within the vector metaphor, Lapsley identifies spousal relationships, the relation to oneself, child/parent relations, friends, the human community, nature and culture, and God.

Much of this discussion by Lapsley comes not under the heading of "self" but under the heading of "spirit." That, to Asian eyes, looks like a note of hesitance in lifting up the community dimension of the self—and maybe it is. Yet Lapsley's writing takes the incarnation seriously. The anthropology he presents is not just a biological anthropology. The whole person must be seen as a "spirit/self," not just a self alone—whether a neurological or biological self. Lapsley's use of "spirit" ties nicely with the Confucian sense of a relation to the cosmos, the "mandate of heaven."

In the dialogue with Jim Lapsley, K'ung Fu-tze would push for courage in thinking more about the role of community in understanding "who we are." K'ung Fu-tze would not speak of the relation to God, for example, as Lapsley does, but of the creation. In fact, especially in India today, there is increasing concern that Western thought has not taken the theology of creation seriously enough in its understanding of the diverse nature of culture.[10] The

Asian view of the "mandate of heaven" grows out of a deep Asian consciousness of our community relation with all of creation, not with just our own personal lives.

From a biblical standpoint, the role of the tribe and the place of the "people"—including the "people of God," or the community of faith—become part of understanding "who we are." The role defines what pastoral care means in ministering to "who we are" and "what we must do." K'ung Fu-tze would feel at home in that approach.

In regard to modern pastoral practice, for example, this focus on community would raise questions such as: What does the reality of a "we self" have to say to a retirement community? To a church in which retired people worship? To how we live and how we die? What does the concept of the "we self" say to the process of prayer? To the way we understand the communion of saints? To the place of genealogies? To ancestor worship?

(With regard to ancestor worship, for example, the Chinese Christian may well have moved away from the practice as such. Yet the Chinese Christian continues to hold a memorial service on the first, second, and third anniversaries of the family members who have died. That practice cannot be dismissed as just private "grief work." The practice brings a sense of community with the deceased that suggests something to the practice of pastoral care in the West. In our Protestant individualistic understanding of the nature of self, do we need a balance that recovers the Jewish Kaddish or the Asian annual remembrance?)

The Issue of Shame

In Western writing, the concept of shame has gained much attention over the last ten years. Donald Nathanson of Johns Hopkins University sees shame as a drive; others, like Erik Erikson, see shame as part of the developmental process.[11] Both approaches see shame as a part of awareness of the self—a part of developing a sense, not of right/wrong, but of potential fulfilled or not fulfilled.

The power of this type of shame came to me most forcefully in a visit with my aging father. At the age of eighty-four, he clearly was failing. In going through his library, I found his college yearbook. In an enjoyable afternoon of reading it to him—in effect, of dealing with what Lapsley, following Kohut, calls the "cohesive-

ness of self"—we came upon a special page.[12] The editors had
devoted that page to my father and his success as the first Iowan to
win the National Collegiate Oratorical Contest. The review went
on to identify my father as the William Jennings Bryan of the
future.

When I finished reading the page, I looked at him with pride.
He looked at me and burst into convulsive sobs! "I never made it,"
he said, "I never lived up to what I expected to do."

It made no difference that he had spent ten years in tubercular
sanitoriums as a result of disease contracted in the trenches of
World War I and had gone on to be among the most sought-after
professors of his day at Stanford. The fact that the Stanford community and family community considered him a success had little
effect. He felt he had not fulfilled his potential—he felt shame.

Lapsley distinguishes between "the tragic man" and "the guilty
man."[13] Surely, my father seemed tragic in that moment. Just as
surely, the form of pastoral care required at that time needed a
different style and approach from that demanded in one who had a
deep sense of guilt. Failure to live up to potential and guilt for
having lived the wrong way are two different things.

Not just Lapsley, but most Western writers discuss the issue of
shame, the "tragic man" and the "tragic woman," as individuals
who have not fulfilled what was within them. Where that short-
coming is the origin of shame, then that truth speaks to the form
of pastoral care appropriate to that sense of shame. Lapsley, in line
with Kohut, would, I believe, call for a strong sense of empathy on
the part of the caregiver.[14]

Yet, in many ways this Western view of shame is narrow.
Granted, not all Westerners see shame in the narrow confine of just
individual development. Granted that this individualistic sense of
shame also appears in some instances of Asian experience. The
typical Asian sense of shame has, I believe, a different base and
requires a different sense of pastoral care.

Whereas in the West, shame comes when one feels he or she has
not lived up to his or her own expectations of the self; in Asia,
shame comes when an individual or the community feels that the
community expectations have not been met. The orientation of the
shame in the Asian culture lies not so much in private accomplishment as in community honor. Has or has not a person brought
honor to the community by what one has or has not done?

Therefore, when a scandal rocks a business in Japan, the head of the company resigns even if he himself has been betrayed by the scandal. He is head of the community in which the scandal surfaced. In such a context, the chief executive officer must restore the honor of all by himself taking on the failure and the act of atonement. Fortunately, hari kari (a ritual suicide) is not practiced today in the way that it was forty years ago; yet a resignation is a symbolic suicide.

This is not the time to go into the meaning of this analogy for the doctrine of the atonement. It is the place to suggest that the community approach to "who we are" and "what we are to do" speaks to the whole matter of how we understand anthropology, human nature, salvation, and the work of pastoral care.

Particularly in his book on aging, Lapsley has raised the issue of living up to potential and the dynamic that surrounds it. In his discussion of Kohut and Niebuhr, he also sees the difference between a narrow view of self and a broad view. From that, one can easily move from a narrow (individualistic) view of shame to a broad (community) view. From the perspective of K'ung Fu-tze, however, the question to all of us in the West still comes, Have you fully recognized the community dimension of the self in your theology of anthropology?

In the pastoral care section of his latest book, Lapsley himself lifts up the role of the community in the care needs of people as they age. I call that the "community as caregiver." Here, one finds genuine links with the Asian perspective, for here the matters of personal worth and honor of the community come together. Here one finds a fruitful base for the future dialogue between K'ung Fu-tze and James Lapsley.

The Asian approach to shame and the mature person (the person of jen) does this: it gives a community frame of reference in which to understand shame and honor. In doing so, the Asian approach does two things: (1) it calls those of a Western mind-set to a way of thinking that is fundamental for understanding the Bible; and (2) it calls upon the Westerner to see more in the sense of shame in human nature than just the individualistic dimension.

In addition to what has been said about shame versus guilt in the understanding of "who we are," let us consider also personal worth.

We stated that shame comes from feeling that we have not lived up to potential. The "worthy" person is the person who has done all that he or she could do with what he or she had. The worth of an individual rests on that accomplishment.

As a person ages, "what that person has" may decline from a physical standpoint. How often do we hear, "I just do not have the energy anymore"? In the East, such a decline does not mean that the matter of worth decreases. On the contrary, because of experience, that worth increases.

A case in point is a tomb outside of Turfan, China. Four frescoes appear on the wall of the underground tomb. These frescoes represent four men in four stages of life. The last stage shows a man reflecting on what life has been. Out of this Confucian reflection, there comes wisdom. This last stage cannot be as active as the first. Yet this last stage has as great a worth as the first; it has the worth of wisdom.

As the Asian raises the matter of community, so the Confucian raises the point that the worth of the individual grows with age. This view comes from and affects the Asian perception of who we are because it takes with radical seriousness "who we are in relation" to the community. The Asian perspective calls for a dynamic of valuing—to which we now turn.

Actualization of the Good

A clear point of difference between the Confucian (Eastern) point of view and that of Lapsley (and the West) comes at the point of evil/sin. That same conflict appears again in the tension between the Confucian culture of the mainland Chinese and the emphasis on Western Marxism. So varied are the ramifications of this difference that we cannot explore them in this essay. With the background of the Niebuhrs and Kohut, much could be said about evil in Lapsley's sense of anthropology. However, for our purposes, let us move to the point where pastoral care breaks through the bondage to past sin and looks to the point of healing, of goodness.

In human experience, when a person gains insight into the reality of evil, the individual still needs that which actualizes the goodness in life. We see the difference in the distinction between a revival meeting and a service of worship. The former calls for a recognition of sin and moving in a new direction. The latter assumes the recognition and seeks "growth in grace."

At this point, Lapsley makes a genuine contribution with his sense of the anthropology of the spirit. Writes Lapsley:

> The interaction between spirit and self is at the core of the person. Neither can be said to characterize completely any human action, attitude, thought, or emotional state. Rather both are involved in some degree, and their interaction gives each person his or her uniqueness.[15]

He goes on to suggest how this spirit-self model will illumine the lives of older people even though he thinks it to be applicable to all.

Indeed, that anthropological model is "applicable to all." The task in the caregiving process is to bring out the sense of "self-spirit" so that the individual knows who he or she is and can own that self-spirit.

That which allows this goodness to come alive in the person I have elsewhere called "symbol work."[16] Symbol work is what one does to "own" who he or she is. In this case, the symbol work is what a person does to own the goodness that has come alive in him or her. The task of the pastoral caregiver lies in helping find the symbols that bring the goodness alive. The caregiver may do that in counseling, in worship, in many different arenas. K'ung Fu-tze saw this in his concern for ritual. Lapsley sees this in his concern for the very process of the pastoral care. For both Lapsley and K'ung Fu-tze, the need is to have that "right action" which actualizes the goodness.

Therefore, in ancient China, K'ung Fu-tze worried about ritual—the right way of doing things in the court and in the home. As a result, Chang Jung, in her autobiographical book on growing up in modern China, documents again and again actions expected of her father, her party, and even herself.[17] Likewise, in his latest book, Lapsley gives several chapters of theory and then moves into a review of that theory in the light of practice—of actions.[18]

This emphasis on right action is action within the community. The concept comes as no surprise to those aware of biblical Hebrew.[19] Therefore, to speak of a God of righteousness means to speak of a God in right and appropriate relations with humankind. The righteousness on God's part is understood in God's acts; for the Christian, God acts in Jesus Christ.

THEOLOGICAL OBSERVATIONS

This essay concludes with observations on the role of yin and yang and the relationship of conversion and sanctification.

The Role of Yin-Yang

In the last decade, especially with the Olympics in Korea, all the world has become familiar with the symbol of the black and white teardrops intertwined in a large circle. These represent the yin-yang of Asian thought.

The yin-yang concept reflects the male-female, the positive-negative (as in electric charges), the black-white, which are a normal part of all created life. "Black" does not represent evil any more than "white" represents goodness. Both are necessary for the full life. Both are found in each individual and in each community. Both form part of the basic goodness with which "who we are" came into being.

However, this basic goodness has been destroyed both in East and in West. Whether one goes back to the Holocaust, looks at ethnic cleansing in Bosnia, or Hindu-Muslim riots in India, the goodness stands shattered or at least betrayed. That fact stands whatever the rationale of theology of that destruction/betrayal.

The reality of evil, says the Asian perspective, requires the right rituals to help one come out from bondage to it. K'ung Fu-tze established rituals to deal with the chaos in society. These rituals had to do not only with religious norms, but forms of conduct in the home, in the workplace, in the government. The emphasis on the community of the home lay in that, there, one had the school that prepared one for life elsewhere.

In his *Politics*, Aristotle provided the same basic insight for the West as K'ung Fu-tze did for the East. In the family, Aristotle saw both the model and the training ground for administrative life.

The Asian, with this background and concern for ritual, upholds then the need for those symbols of life that make real who we are and who we are in relation to others. Today's generation of Asians may well reject kowtowing—the act of going on one's knees and touching the head to the floor of the person honored. Yet the need for symbols that make alive who we are and who we are in relation remains.

Lapsley, in the case studies of his new book on work with the elderly, entitled the book *Renewal in Late Life through Pastoral Counseling*. What is the role of the counselor? The very use of the word *renewal* makes clear that just accepting one's fate is not the role. Rather, the task is to help the individual and the group find those symbols that make alive who we are.

Lapsley speaks, for example, to the excessive neatness found in Sun City, Arizona. He writes:

> This characteristic [of neatness] is of some importance in this study. For one thing, it shows the investment that the communities have in neatness as such. But it also shows that, in keeping with continuity theory, neatness characterized these older persons long before they came to the Sun Cities.[20]

The neatness expresses who the people are, brings alive their sense of worth, makes clear something about themselves at this stage of life. Symbols have that specific function—the function of making visible outwardly what is true but invisible, inwardly.

In the Western culture, when one retires, a person often loses those symbols that give a sense of identity—of who one is. The walk or ride to a place of work, the name on a door or the wearing of coveralls, the right to say "I am a . . ." Never will I forget the moment when I introduced a pediatrician to a young mother, new to the community, with the words, "This is Dr. Verpleugh, a retired doctor in our community." Came the quick reply, "I am a doctor; I am not retired; I just no longer have an office."

The word *retired* carried the message that he had lost his professional standing and his place of worth. His retort sought to reclaim—"renew" in Lapsley's words—his place of worth as a man of standing. Therefore, the pastoral counselor, whether in worship and preaching or in counseling and the giving of care, is facilitating the discovery of those symbols that allow an elderly person to come alive as to who he or she is.

Theological anthropology, as it relates to the work of pastoral care, then, sets the agenda for the practice of care. In the case of shame, that agenda is one of finding the symbols that restore the sense of worth and thus overcome the shame.

Conversion and Sanctification

The concepts of conversion and sanctification need to be kept in balance and in tension. Where in society or the life of the individual, evil abounds, we need awareness (confession) and change (conversion). We need to set up structures that protect against codependency. In Kohut's view of the difference between pathological and healthy narcissism, we need the form of care that allows for change.

However, Lapsley's discussion of the "cohesiveness of the self" suggests also that the church must provide that which nurtures the self that has already changed. This view historically has carried the name "sanctification."

Some approaches to pastoral care emphasize the conversion model and others the sanctification model. The fact is that both are needed.

Conclusion

I cannot say that I am an expert either of Asian or Lapslian anthropology. In fact, who can speak confidently about another person's or culture's view? Yet, in this mythical conversation between Lapsley and K'ung Fu-tze, we sense a creative view of anthropology—of "who we are."

In the rapid changes around the world, one senses that this dialogue may be the key dialogue of the next decade. The dialogue makes the decade and the pastoral theology of A.D. 2000 both relevant and exciting.

Notes

1. James N. Lapsley, *Renewal in Late Life through Pastoral Counseling* (New York: Paulist Press, 1992).

2. James N. Lapsley, *Salvation and Health: The Interlocking Processes of Life* (Philadelphia: Westminster Press, 1972).

3. James N. Lapsley, "Spirit and Self," *Pastoral Psychology* 38, no. 3 (Spring 1990): 135–46.

4. Lapsley, *Renewal in Late Life*.

5. Gerald Roscoe, *The Good Life: A Guide to Buddhism for the Westerner* (Bangkok, Thailand: Asia Books Co., 1990), 34–35.

6. Lapsley, *Salvation and Health*, 70.

7. James N. Lapsley, "The 'Self,' Its Vicissitudes and Possibilities: An Essay in Theological Anthropology," *Pastoral Psychology* 35, no. 1 (Fall 1986): 36.

8. Chang Jung, *Wild Swans* (New York: Simon & Schuster, 1991).

9. Lapsley, "The Self," 45.

10. Stanley Samantha, *One Christ, Many Religions* (New York: Orbis Press, 1991).

11. Donald Nathanson, *Shame and Pride: Affect, Sex, and the Birth of the Self* (New York: W. W. Norton, 1992); Erik Erikson, *Childhood and Society* (New York: W. W. Norton, 1950).

12. Lapsley, *Renewal in Late Life*, 44.

13. Lapsley, "The Self," 32.

14. Lapsley, *Renewal in Late Life*, 29.

15. Ibid., 52.

16. James G. Emerson, Jr., *Suffering: Its Meaning and Ministry* (Nashville: Abingdon Press, 1987).

17. Chang Jung, *Wild Swans*, 8.

18. Lapsley, *Renewal in Late Life*, last two chapters.

19. *Gesenius' Hebrew and Chaldee Lexicon to the Old Testament Scriptures* (Grand Rapids: Wm. B. Eerdmans, 1949), 702 (the meaning of "sadaq" in regard to persons).

20. Lapsley, *Renewal in Late Life*, 88.

6
The Soul as the
"Coreness" of the Self

DONALD CAPPS

James N. Lapsley has devoted much of his long and distinguished career to what is today called "theological anthropology" (formerly called, in the days before gender-inclusive language, the "doctrine of man"), an endeavor that seeks to describe, analyze, and explain the human situation for the purpose of discerning how Christianity may work toward its amelioration. Because he engages in theological anthropology from the perspective of pastoral theology, a field that is noted for its openness to dialogue with the so-called secular world, Lapsley has made considerable use of the human sciences, especially psychoanalytic psychology, to inform his understanding of the human situation. His theological orientation is fundamentally in the Reformed tradition, for he was reared Presbyterian and has been a lifelong clergyman of the Presbyterian Church (U.S.A.). As a graduate student at the University of Chicago in the late 1950s, he also developed an appreciation for process thought (the dominant philosophical orientation of Chicago's Divinity School at that time, though certainly not exclusive to Chicago, as the work of Union Seminary's Daniel Day Williams readily attests). His theological anthropology may thus be viewed as one in which process thought, Reformed theology, and psychoanalytic psychology are creatively joined.

One may initiate a theological exploration into the human situation at different levels of analysis, but it has been Lapsley's practice to begin with the person and to move outward from there. The person, we might say, is the smallest unit of analysis; and it is, therefore, an appropriate place to begin a description, analysis, and explanation of the human condition. As the exploration proceeds, the person's social location is introduced as well, with particular attention given to the complex and multifarious ways in which person and social world interrelate. Yet the person is the focal unit of analysis. This enables the pastoral theologian to focus on intra-psychic processes, on the things that are going on "inside" the person. This "insidedness" of the person is often referred to as "the self."

Throughout his career, Lapsley has been concerned with exploring the relationship between person, self, and social world. In this essay, I have chosen to focus on the feature of his work that concerns the "inner workings" of the person (his or her selfness), for I believe that it is here that Lapsley has made his most enduring contribution to pastoral theology. Although his work on this issue reaches back to the early 1960s, I will concentrate on his most recent formulations, both because these are the most accessible to today's reader and because they reflect his own most recent, and mature, reflections on the issue.

A MODEL OF THE HUMAN BEING

In *Renewal in Late Life through Pastoral Counseling*, Lapsley devotes a chapter to the formulation of a "model of the human being" based primarily on theological, psychological, and experiential sources. He declares that this model "may be called a self-spirit model, as it centers on the interaction of these important dimensions of human life, when they are properly understood."[1] He begins by discussing the key terms of the model separately, giving attention to the history of these terms and their contemporary usage and meaning in the model, and he then describes their interaction.

The first key term of the model is the *spirit*. Historical review, focused primarily on the Bible and Greek philosophy, leads him to define the human spirit as "the human form of life itself. *It provides intensity of motion and direction toward other beings and toward a vision of the future*. Other beings include especially other human beings and God. The future is centered on a central purpose."[2]

The second key term is *self*. Historical review suggests that the current understanding of self as "the felt awareness of one's own

personhood" has its beginnings in the Middle Ages, when the word
self was used as a reflexive intensifier to distinguish one person from
another, as in the phrase "he, himself." Implicit in this view of the
self is that it has "sameness," or continuity over time, and "ownness," or distinctiveness from other persons. More recently, self has
also come to refer to the core of one's person, as distinguished from
the periphery, so that when we say, "I was not myself," we are
referring to some behavior that we do not want to "own." Thus we
can distinguish between the true self and those aspects of the person
that may lie outside the self.[3] Lapsley defines self as "the felt sense of
ownness and sameness that a person perceives, together with their
connections below the surface of awareness, and sometimes to disconnected fragments below the surface."[4] He notes that this definition emphasizes the "subjective self," as opposed to the "objective
self" as perceived by someone else. He recognizes, however, that
this distinction is not clear-cut, because the observer is perceiving
what is communicated by the person about that person's self. Also
emphasized in the definition is the fact that "there are psycho-physi-
cal structures which underlie awareness," and that "these structures
may also be said to be the self." Hence, the definition includes not
only the "felt sense of ownness and sameness that a person perceives" but also "their connections below the surface of awareness"
and "disconnected fragments below the surface."

Having defined spirit and self, Lapsley goes on to discuss the
interaction between spirit and self, noting that it is this interaction
that is "at the core of the person." In any human action, attitude,
thought, or emotional state, both are involved in some degree, and
their interaction gives each person his or her uniqueness. The spirit
is dominant in actions, attitudes, thoughts, or emotional states
where there is relational outreach and aspiration toward the future.
The self is dominant where there is assertion of one's felt sense of
ownness and sameness. But in all instances both are involved to
some degree and are interactive.[5]

In the course of his discussion of the spirit, the self, and their
interaction, Lapsley makes two significant observations. One concerns the idea that the self refers to the *core* of one's person. He
notes that "this 'core' meaning of the self has many of the same
characteristics once carried by the term 'soul.' Hence, 'self' is often
used in modern translations of the Bible to express the term *psyche*,
formerly translated by 'soul.' "[6] The other concerns this assurance:

In focusing on the interaction of spirit and self I do not intend to neglect the body as the vehicle of interaction. Without proposing a "solution" to the mind-body problem, I affirm the embodiment of both spirit and self with respect to human beings. Without the body the human spirit and self do not exist as human. From a theological perspective, the spirit, indeed, we are taught, will return to God upon the death of the body and the self. Nevertheless, as human spirit it requires embodiment. The self permeates the body and is not localized in the brain or the nervous system, even though these organs are more central to its functioning than others.[7]

The first observation—that the idea of the self having a core is reminiscent of traditional notions of the soul—prompts us to ask whether Lapsley has too easily conflated the "ownness" and "coreness" of the self, and whether his definition of the self could be improved by recovering traditional notions of the soul? Specifically, such notions may help to account for the fact that the self is split between that which a person perceives and that which is "below the surface," and to explain the existence of "disconnected fragments below the surface." Regarding his emphasis on the embodiment of both spirit and self, notions of the soul are also relevant, for they may help to explain how this embodiment works, in both instances. Thus the thesis I want to offer here is that a model of the human being requires a third term—soul—which both accounts for the coreness of the self and helps to explain the embodiment of self and spirit. In pursuing this thesis, I also hope to explain why interaction between spirit and self is often self-destructive. The reason for this, I would argue, is that the aspirations of the spirit and the core of the self (or soul) are fundamentally at odds with one another. Such is the human condition and the reason that humans are the unhappiest creatures in all of God's creation.

To support my thesis, I will follow the same procedure that Lapsley himself employed with "spirit" and "self," giving attention both to the history of the term soul and to its contemporary usage and meaning. Because the term soul has fallen out of favor in contemporary usage (as Lapsley notes, modern translations of the Bible and modern theologians, led by the Niebuhrs, have dropped the word soul in favor of the word self), I will make use of the writings of James Hillman, a post-Jungian who argues for the recovery of soul-language in modern psychology. However, lest I be viewed as having abandoned psychoanalysis in favor of analytical psychology, I would note that Freud himself not only used the term *soul*, but gave it a central place in his anthropology.

In *Freud and Man's Soul*, Bruno Bettelheim complains that English translations of Freud are severely defective, and that the most serious error has been "the elimination of his reference to the soul (die Seele)."[8] Bettelheim goes on to note that, although Freud evoked the image of the soul quite frequently, especially in crucial passages where he was attempting to provide a broad view of his system, his reflections on "the structure of the soul" and "the organization of the soul" are almost always translated "mental apparatus" or "mental organization." Furthermore, Freud used the word *soul* to refer to the therapeutic process itself, emphasizing that the soul is the very object of psychoanalytic treatment. It is the soul that is sick, the soul that requires treatment. On the other hand, the soul effects its own treatment, and the analyst is only a midwife in a process that the soul itself originates and carries through. Thus, in the opening passage of an article entitled "Psychical Treatment (Treatment of the Soul)," Freud writes:

> Psyche is a Greek word and its German translation is "soul." Psychical treatment hence means "treatment of the soul." One could thus think that what is meant is: treatment of the morbid phenomena in the life of the soul. But this is not the meaning of this term. Psychical treatment wishes to signify, rather, treatment originating in the soul, treatment—of psychic or bodily disorders—by measures which influence above all and immediately the soul of man.[9]

Freud's point here is that "treatment" does not mean what is done to the soul from without, but the treatment the soul offers itself.

This idea of the soul as the locus and source of healing is completely lost when the *Standard Edition* translates the word "soul" (Seele) as "mental" and when "psychical treatment" is said to "take its start in the mind." This translation misses Freud's point that treatment has to do with one's very existence and that the pathology being addressed is located in the innermost core of one's being. Thus, here, Bettelheim draws our attention to the fact that poor translations have been responsible for the loss of soul language in psychoanalytic thought and practice. Because the impulse behind such translations was to make Freud's writings sound more scientific, the culprit in this case is science, which, in its desire to demystify and objectify, found it necessary to reduce the language of the soul to what were considered by Freud's translators to be its scientific equivalents.

SPIRIT AND SOUL

In *Re-Visioning Psychology*, James Hillman discusses the tendency of humanistic psychology (especially Abraham Maslow) to deny the soul and its afflictions. Following this discussion, he offers a brief excursus on the differences between spirit and soul. In his view, soul and spirit need to be differentiated because in Christianity, soul has become identified with spirit, to the soul's own detriment: "Already in the early vocabulary used by Paul, pneuma or spirit had begun to replace psyche or soul. The New Testament scarcely mentions soul phenomena such as dreams, but stresses spirit phenomena such as miracles, speaking in tongues, prophecy, and visions."[10]

The images ascribed to spirit blaze with light: "Spirit is fast, and it quickens what it touches. Its direction is vertical, and ascending." Although there are many spirits, and many kinds of spirit, the notion of spirit has come to be associated with "the sublimations of higher and abstract disciplines, the intellectual mind, refinements, and purifications." Thus the philosophers have tended to view spirit as their province, and have kept soul out of their works or assigned it a lower place:

> Descartes confined soul to the pineal gland, a little enclave between the opposing powers of internal mind and external space. More recently, Santayana has put soul down in the realm of matter and considered it an antimetaphysical principle. Collingwood equated soul with feeling and considered that psychology had no business invading the realm of thought and ideas. The spiritual point of view always posits itself as superior, and operates particularly well in a fantasy of transcendence among ultimates and absolutes.[11]

In contrast to images of spirit, soul images are connected with the night world, the realm of the dead, and the moon: "We still catch our soul's most essential nature in death experiences, in dreams of the night, and in the images of 'lunacy.' "[12] Unlike spirit, which extracts meanings (insights) and puts them into action, soul sticks to the realm of experience and to reflections within experience:

> It moves indirectly in circular reasonings, where retreats are as important as advances, preferring labyrinths and corners, giving a metaphorical sense to life through such words as *close, near, slow,* and *deep.* Soul involves us in the pack and welter of phenomena and the flow of impressions. It is the "patient" part of us. Soul is vulnerable and suffers; it is passive and remembers.[13]

Whereas spirit says look up, gain distance, attend to the beyond and above, and travels by means of a *via negativa*—"not this, not that"—for "strait is the gate and only first or last things will do," soul replies, "But this too may have a place—who knows?" So, "the cooking vessel of the soul takes in everything, everything can become soul; and by taking into its imagination any and all events, psychic space grows."[14]

Hillman elaborates these differences between spirit and soul in his article "Peaks and Vales."[15] Here again he attributes the loss of soul to Christianity, which, beginning with Paul, substituted spirit for soul. He notes that at the Council in Constantinople in 869, "the soul lost its dominion. At this council, the idea of human nature as devolving from a tripartite cosmos of spirit, soul and body was reduced to a dualism of spirit (or mind) and body (or matter)." Yet this council only made official "a long process beginning with Paul, the Saint, of substituting and disguising, and forever after confusing, soul with spirit."[16]

A key figure in this development was Tertullian, who contended that the soul may be identified with a kind of "natural" Christianity, or Christianity in its most unreflective and least elevated form. Christians who aspire to a higher level of faith and commitment to God will cultivate the spiritual life and not be satisfied with soul-religion. When the Council of Nicaea in 787 deprived images of their inherent authenticity, soul was associated with images and image worship—with an unreflective, natural Christianity that spiritual Christians might tolerate in others, and even themselves have recourse to in moments of fear and dread, but recognize as base and immature.

In this essay, Hillman continues his critique of Maslow's notion of the "peak experience." He commends Maslow for reintroducing pneuma into psychology, but points out that Maslow, in doing so, also reintroduced the old confusion of pneuma with psyche (or soul). Peak experiences concern the spirit and its elevation, and "the peak experience is a way of describing pneumatic experience." The one who seeks the peak experience "is in search of spirit." But the peak experience has nothing to do with the psyche, or soul; for soul is identified, metaphorically, with the vales of life, and, in the usual religious language of our culture, the vale is a depressed emotional place—the vale of tears, the lonesome valley, and the valley of the shadow of death. As Hillman points out, the first definition of "valley" in the *Oxford English Dictionary* is "a long depression or hollow." Other meanings of the words *vale* and *valley* refer to "such sad things as the decline of years and old age, the world regarded as a place of troubles, sorrow, and weeping, and the world regarded as the scene of the moral, the earthly, the lowly." As Keats suggests in a letter, "Call the world, if you please, the vale of soul-making."[17]

Hillman notes that in mythology the valleys are the places where the nymphs hold sway, and nymphs are personifications of the wisps of clouds of mist clinging to valleys, mountains, and water sources. Thus "nymphs veil our vision, keep us shortsighted, myopic, caught—no long range distancing, no projections or prophecies as from a peak."[18] The desire for spiritual transcendence is strong in us, especially when, in the vigor of youth, we leave behind the low and mundane valleys of our childhood and aspire to transcend the limitations of our lives and to breathe the spirit of limitlessness.

Hillman cautions that the valley world of the soul is steeped in history, whereas in the peak experience of the spirit, history is that which can be overcome, the debris over which we cling in our ascent and must, therefore, be denied:

> Thus, from the spirit point of view, it can make no difference if our teacher be a Zaddik from a Polish shtetl, an Indian from under a Mexican cactus, or a Japanese master in the garden of stones; these differences are but conditionings of history, personalistic hangups. The spirit is impersonal, rooted not in local soul, but timeless.[19]

Spirit ascends the mountain, thinking that it can leave soul behind, and believing that it will not pay a price for having done so. But,

> from the viewpoint of soul and life in the vale, going up the mountain feels like a desertion. . . . Its viewpoint appears in the long

hollow depression of the valley, the inner and closed objection that accompanies the exaltation of ascension. The soul feels left behind, and we see this soul reacting with resentments. Spiritual teachings warn the initiate so often about introspective broodings, about jealousy, spite, and pettiness, about attachments to sensations and memories. These cautions present an accurate phenomenology of how the soul feels when the spirit bids farewell.[20]

So the soul develops its pathologies. There are the depressions and objections that come with spirit's rejections, and the resentments created by spirit's attempt to run roughshod over the soul's local history, resentments that emerge in what psychotherapy terms our "complexes." In mythological terms, the Appollonian spirit, with its desire to make us feel free and open, and responsive to our higher self, has to come to terms with old Saturn, who is imprisoned in paranoid systems of judgment, defensive maneuvers, and melancholic conclusions.[21] If, as the name implies, the spiritual disciplines are disciplines of the transcendent spirit, then it is the task of psychotherapy, as *its* name implies (psyche-therapy), to concern itself with the residues of the spiritual ascent: with soul's depressions, resentments, paranoias, and melancholias.

However, if this contrast between spirit and soul appears to imply that soul is nothing but pathology, this would be the wrong conclusion to draw. As Hillman points out, soul is "a wondrous quality in daily life," an appreciation for things and experiences that spirit considers mere local trivia. Also, whereas spirit assumes a position of humility as it confronts the inevitable limits of self and life, soul goes in for the humorous:

> Humility and humor are two ways of coming down to *humus*, to the human condition. Humility would have us bow down to the world and pay our due to its reality. Render unto Caesar. Humor brings us down with a pratfall. Heavy meaningful reality becomes suspect, seen through, the world laughable—paranoia dissolved.[22]

To illustrate the soul's preference for the humorous, Hillman cites a letter written by the fourteenth Dalai Lama of Tibet. This venerable master of the spirit uses the peaks and valleys metaphor to distinguish spirit and soul, and describes soul as "communal," as loving to hum in unison. But, says the Dalai Lama, soul is not enough, for "the creative soul craves spirit," and "the most beautiful monks one day bid farewell to their comrades to make their solitary journey toward the peaks, there to mate with the cosmos."[23] Meanwhile, the less "creative" souls are content to pass the day sustained by the common ordinary amusements of daily life. Western visitors to Tibet have noted that these folks may spend the better part of the day recounting an amusing event, such as an accidental pratfall by one of their number who failed to notice a stone that lay—or was placed—in the path where he was walking. This is soul, and it manifests itself not in songs of ascent, but in low laughter rising from the gut.

THE SOUL AND HUMAN ANATOMY

Employing Hillman's distinction between spirit and soul, and his use of spatial imagery—peaks and vales—to express it, I now want to consider how this spirit/soul split is embodied. I suggest that Hillman's spatial imagery for spirit and soul—peaks and vales—externalizes a conflict that we actually experience in our bodies. Moreover, I would argue that we resort to such external imagery because internal imagery no longer seems to work once we inflate the pathologies of the soul by considering them signs of spiritual suffering. I propose that to recover the soul, to make it mean something once again, we need to "remedicalize" it; not, however, by translating "soul" into the psychiatric language of "mental process," but by relocating soul in the body and its processes, thus transposing Hillman's spatial imagery into the inner landscape of the human body—in a word, to "anatomize" it.

Thus I propose to reassert the ancient tradition that the soul is "located," as it were, in the digestive system—the lower body—and, more precisely, in the central organ of the digestive system, the liver; and to claim that the spirit has *its* "location" in the higher blood-vascular system, and, more specifically, in the central organ of the system, the heart.[24] I am suggesting, in other words, that Hillman's differentiation between spirit/peak and soul/vale has been replicated in Western (and thus Christian) reflections on the vital organs.

Throughout human history, our premodern predecessors have been vexed and perplexed by the question of the soul's location in our bodies: If you and I have a soul, where is it located? Although it is characteristic of moderns to consider this a meaningless question, usually by asserting that the soul is not an entity but a way of

talking about what transpires between you and me,[25] perhaps it
behooves us, in what is now being called a postmodern age, not to
dismiss the question quite so easily. In any case, I believe that this is
actually a vital question for us to ask if we agree that, while the
reduction of the soul to mental states is bad enough, the inflation
of the spirit at the expense of the soul is even worse. If, as I would
argue, the soul is the coreness of the self, assertion of the spirit's
aspirations without considering their costs to the soul is terribly
self-destructive. This, as I understand it, is what Alcoholics Anony-
mous has been saying for decades.

According to Morris Jastrow, Jr., and Richard Selzer, the
ancients believed the soul is located in the liver.[26] The liver was
regarded as the center of vitality, the source of all mental and
emotional activity, "nay, the seat of the soul itself."[27] The liver
was also considered the organ through which the gods spoke, a
belief that supported divination practices, for priests would slit
open the belly of a sheep or goat and read the markings on the
animal's liver. Selzer points out, however, that with "the separation of medicine from the apron strings of religion and the rise of
anatomy as a study in itself, the liver was toppled from its central
role and the heart was elevated."[28] Evidently, anatomical research
demonstrated that it was not the size or marking of an organ but its
essential function that counted; and, on this measure, the heart
came to be viewed as the true center of human vitality. After all,
the heart is the organ that pumps blood—the lifegiving fluid—
throughout the body.

Christianity, in Selzer's view, became a religion of the heart,
and, moreover, it transformed earlier barbaric heart rituals into a
more spiritualized form. If the ancient warrior cut out the heart of
his enemy and ate it with gusto, believing that to devour the slain
enemy's heart was to take upon oneself the strength, valor, and
skill of the vanquished, the early Christians engaged in the more
civilized, and spiritualized, practice of *adoring* the heart of a saint:
"It was not the livers or brains or entrails of saints that were lifted
from the body in sublimest autopsy, it was the heart, thus snipped
and cradled into worshipful palms, then soaked in wine and herbs
and set into silver reliquaries for the veneration."[29] This veneration
of the heart was also supported by the Greek philosophical tradition, for, as Selzer notes, it was Plato who

placed the higher emotions, such as courage, squarely above the diaphragm, and situated the baser appetites below, especially in the liver, where they squat like furry beasts even today, as is indicated in their term "lily-livered," or "choleric," or worse, "bilious."[30]

Although Selzer's history of the triumph of the heart at the expense of the liver as the seat of human vitality is rather sketchy, it supports nonetheless Hillman's distinction between spirit and soul. If Christianity became the religion of spirit (pneuma), it did so in part by giving special prominence to the heart, displacing the liver as the locus of the divine. Also, as noted above, Selzer's account of the triumph of the heart over the liver supports Hillman's spatial imagery. Heart becomes associated with peaks, whereas liver has its place in the vales below. As Hillman himself points out:

> Sometimes going up the mountain one seeks escape from the underworld, and so the Gods appear from below bringing all sorts of physiological disorders. They will be heard, if only through intestinal rumblings and their fire burning in the bladder.[31]

Selzer's account of the triumph of the heart may also explain why Christians did not have much use for soul-language. If, as Hillman argues, Christianity quickly became a religion of spirit, we may assume that, for Christians, the soul continued to be identified with the liver, and for this reason alone it would need to be devalued.[32]

MELANCHOLY: THE CHRISTIAN FORM OF SOUL-SICKNESS

Melancholy, the most vexing spiritual-psychological disorder throughout the course of Christian history, has seldom been associated with the heart and the blood-vascular system, but has almost always been linked to the liver and the digestive system. In *Melancholia and Depression: From Hippocratic Times to Modern Times*, Stanley Jackson sheds additional light on the plight of the soul by surveying the history of explanations for melancholia and depression. He points out that the term *melancholia*

> had its origins in terms that meant black bile and itself was used to mean the black bile as well as to name a disease. The black bile was a concept embedded in the context of humoral theory, which for

approximately two thousand years was a central explanatory scheme for dealing with diseases. The black bile was considered to be the essential element in the pathogenesis of melancholia.[33]

Writing in the fifth century B.C.E., Hippocrates was the first to include black bile among the four humours (the others being blood, yellow bile, and phlegm); and through the fifth century, black bile was held to be responsible for a great variety of diseases ranging from the headache, vertigo, paralysis, spasms, epilepsy, mental disturbances, and diseases of the kidney, liver, and spleen.[34] Although black bile, unlike the other three humours, is difficult to reconcile with any known substances today, Jackson cited Henry E. Sigerist's point:

> In this as in other cases the Greeks based their theories on observations. We know that the stool of patients suffering from bleeding gastric ulcers is black, as sometimes are the substances vomited by patients with carcinoma of the stomach. A form of malaria is still known as "black water fever" because the urine as a result of acute intravascular hemolysis suddenly becomes very dark, if not black at least mahogany-colored. Similar observations may have led to the assumption that ordinary yellow bile through corruption could become black and that this black bile caused diseases, notably the "black bile disease" named melancholy.[35]

Plato—a younger contemporary of Hippocrates, one who knew his views—employed a version of the humoral theory in *Timaeus*. According to Jackson, Plato conceived of a form of black bile as among the causes of many diseases, its formation being the outcome of flesh decomposing and finding its way back into the blood. Plato noted that this decomposed matter grew black from "long burning" and became bitter, and that sometimes when the "bitter element was refined away . . . the black part assumed an acidity which takes the place of bitterness." He also indicated that the pathogenic forms of the humours have the potential to wander about the body, and, finding no exit or escape, they become "pent up within and mingle their own vapors with the motions of the soul" and thus create an "infinite variety" of emotional distress and mental disorders.[36]

Besides the black bile theory, another important feature of humoral theory and its explanation for the disease of melancholia is the spleen, for this organ was thought to have an especially important connection with the black bile. Whereas Erasistratus declared that the spleen was an organ of little consequence, Galen believed otherwise. In his view, it served to filter out "the thick, earthy, atra bilious humours that formed in the liver."[37] Because "black bile" was not among the three basic humours, but a "corruption" of one of the humours ("yellow bile"), it was inevitable that it would come to be viewed as the cause of many diseases, both physical and emotional. Yet, because it was associated with bitterness and acidity, it was believed to have especially to do with the emotional disease of melancholia, which was reflected in attitudes of bitterness, dejection, resentment, and, in more recent times, with depression. Thus, among the Greeks, melancholia came to be viewed as the pathology of the soul.

In early Christianity, beginning with the writings of Evagrius of Pontus, a fourth-century Egyptian monk, melancholia came to be viewed as one of the deadly sins, and penance was considered the appropriate "medicine" for its healing. Melancholia was also assimilated into Christian views of demonic spirits; Evagrius himself suggested that melancholy was an evil spirit, the effect of the "noonday demon" who attacked ascetics with particular vengeance.[38] On the other hand, later scholastic writers

> considered some instances of acedia (or melancholy) to be derived from an imbalance of the humours, thus making it a disease or the outcome of a disease. . . . The presence of such a natural cause tended to lessen the sinfulness of the vice in the eyes of these authors; it resulted more from disease than moral failing.[39]

Instead of advocating penance for melancholy owing to an imbalance of the humours, they suggested that the afflicted might be helped by listening to soothing music. (This solution is reminiscent of the biblical story of King Saul and his young harpist, David.)

The long-term effect of the Christian ascetic movement, however, was to "spiritualize" melancholy, separating it from the humoral theory in which it had been situated originally. By the late Middle Ages, two competing theories were well established: the original Greek idea that melancholy is attributable to a bilious condition based in the digestive system, and the Christian ascetic view that it has more to do with the passions and is, therefore, associated more directly with the human heart. Robert Burton's monumental

The Anatomy of Melancholy, which first appeared in 1621 and went through several expansions during Burton's lifetime, accepts the humoral views propounded by Hippocrates and Galen, but gives far less attention to the somatic than to the emotional causes, such as sorrow, fear, envy, and malice, as well as to such social and environmental influences as poverty and air pollution.[40] This evolution is precisely what Hillman's excursus on the spirit and soul would have predicted: Melancholy is slowly but irrevocably dissociated from the digestive system, which in turn results in a dissociation of the emotional features of melancholy from their somatic roots, especially in the lower body. Melancholy becomes a "spiritual condition." The digestive system is no longer the seat of emotions like sorrow, fear, envy, and malice; and, as a result, the soul becomes a vacuous concept, for it no longer has anything to do with human emotions and passions. The final indignity to the soul comes when even those who continued to subscribe to the humoral theory treated melancholy as a medical matter only and no longer viewed its physical causes as having anything to do with the soul.

When the melancholic condition is thus spiritualized, the result is a failure to take any real account of the price that accompanies any spiritual ascent—the bitterness of a soul that has been left behind to nurture its resentments, paranoia, and other pathological defenses. When the soul was believed to have its locus in the liver, the fact that the soul could exact a price for efforts to live as disembodied spirits—as hearts lifted from the body in sublimest autopsy—could not be ignored.[41] Now the soul is an empty and vacuous notion, and digestive disorders are merely of medical interest. They are not, as in original theories of melancholy, symptoms of a sick or pathologizing soul. The spirit need no longer answer to the soul, for the soul itself has been rendered innocuous. It either ceases to exist at all, or, if it does continue to exist, it has no power to hurt or to take its revenge on the spirit, which has abandoned it.

THE SOUL AS SELF-REGENERATIVE

What we also lose when the soul is detached from the body is the sense that it is potentially beneficent. Through its association with the liver, the soul could be understood to be the regenerative agent within the human self. Through direct observation, the ancient Greeks recognized that the liver is self-regenerative, the only organ of the body that has this capacity to regenerate itself. Selzer describes its self-regenerative powers, citing the case of Prometheus:

> Remember Prometheus? That poor devil who was chained to a rock, and had his liver pecked out each day by a vulture? Well, he was a classical example of the regeneration of tissue, for every night his liver grew back to the ready for the dreaded diurnal feast. And so will yours grow back, regenerate, reappear, regain all of its old efficiency and know-how. All it requires is quitting the booze, now and then. The ever-grateful, forgiving liver will respond joyously with a multitude of mitoses and cell divisions that will replace the sick tissues with spanking new nodules and lobules of functioning cells. This rejuvenation is carried on with the speed and alacrity of a starfish growing a new ray from the stump of the old. . . . How unlike the lofty brain which has no power of regeneration at all. Once a brain cell dies, you are forever one shy.[42]

When we associate the self-regenerative nature of the liver with the soul, as the ancients did, we can readily appreciate the soul's beneficent nature. The self-regenerative nature of the liver calls attention not to the soul's bitterness, but to its capacity to forgive, especially its forgiveness of the spirit's grandiosity, its visions of limitlessness, its callous denial of the debris over which it climbs in its dreams of transcendence. Thus we may say that "soul-loss" need not be permanent or final, for the soul is self-regenerative and sees to its own recovery. Unlike spirit, which seems to need an external "director,"[43] soul, as Freud argued, is able to treat itself.

A dramatic example of the liver's capacity for self-regeneration is the recent liver transplant from a baboon to a human. At the news conference following the recipient's death seventy-one days after the transplant operation, the medical team acknowledged that their "almost pathological fear of [organ] rejection" may have contributed to the patient's death, because their fear of organ rejection, which "had been seen in a virulent form in every other case ever done," led the team to order far more diagnostic testing than customary, and one such test precipitated a serious reaction that may have contributed to the patient's death. As it turned out, the medical team need not have worried, for the liver adapted itself to the recipient's body: "Within a month of the transplant operation, the baboon liver had tripled in size on its own to meet the metabolic

needs of the recipient." According to the pathologist who performed the autopsy, "It adjusted nicely for a man of his size and
weight." Noting that "the liver is an unusual organ because it has
the capacity to regenerate," he marveled, "No one knows why the
liver grew and why it stopped when it did."[44]

If we moderns can no longer believe that the soul is actually
located in the liver, then surely the fact that the liver is self-
regenerative is enough to support belief that the liver is an apt
metaphor for the soul. For what the liver tells us—what its markings, in a sense, show us—is that we can try to kill the soul, yet it
always has a way of coming back, of renewing itself. For the one
who—whether the host self or external enemies—has tried to kill
it, this is an ambiguous prospect, for the soul may forgive, but it
may also avenge itself. As the pathologist suggests, "the liver is an
unusual organ because it has the capacity to regenerate." And so,
we affirm, does the soul.

The Digestive System and Soul-Recovery

Shortly after its publication in 1958, Erik H. Erikson's *Young
Man Luther* provoked a great deal of controversy in theological
circles, and not a little ridicule, mainly for its claim that Luther's
"theological breakthrough" occurred when he was sitting in the
"sweat chamber" (or toilet). For Erikson, it was of considerable
significance that Luther's experience of divine grace happened
when he was sitting on the toilet. He takes the psychiatrist Paul J.
Reiter to task for stating that the location really doesn't matter. On
the contrary:

> This whole geographic issue . . . deserves special mention exactly
> because it *does* point up certain psychiatric relevances. First of all,
> the location mentioned serves a particular physical need which
> hides its emotional relevance as long as it happens to function
> smoothly.[45]

As Erikson notes, Luther suffered from lifelong constipation and
urine retention. Thus, "In this creative moment the tension of
nights and days of meditation found release throughout his being
—and nobody who has read Luther's private remarks can doubt
that his total being always included his bowels."[46] Thus, for Erikson, there is something profoundly physiological in Luther's new

understanding of God as one who is "no longer lurking in the periphery of space and time," but is rather "moving from inside" of us, and is thus, in a very real sense, "what works in us."[47]

This analysis of Luther's breakthrough, of his experience of the grace of God, suggests that the digestive system is implicated in the recovery of one's soul. Yet Erikson's analysis was ridiculed by the theological community, because it could not imagine that God and the digestive system have anything remotely to do with one another. This is not surprising, of course, for it is consistent with the history of Christian asceticism we have just reviewed; namely, of soul-denial motivated by a commitment to some higher spirituality.

Nor could the theological community recognize, as Luther (and Erikson) surely did, the obvious humor in this odd collusion of divine grace and the digestive system. As Erikson shows throughout *Young Man Luther*, Luther's own ribald humor often centered upon the vicissitudes of the digestive process, even as this same process figured in Luther's melancholic moods as well. As Erikson points out, "In melancholy moods, [Luther] expressed his depressive self-repudiation also in anal terms: 'I am like ripe shit,' he said once at the dinner table during a fit of depression (and the boys eagerly wrote it down), 'and the world is a gigantic ass-hole. We probably will let go of each other soon.' "[48] This is soul-talk. This is not the spiritual Luther of whom Erikson could say, "I will state, as a clinician's judgment, that nobody could speak and sing as Luther later did if his mother's voice had not sung to him of some heaven."[49] Rather, this is the soulful, gut-rumbling Luther, who assuaged his melancholia by means of self-deprecating humor.

It is worth noting that the reaction of the theological community to *Young Man Luther* was similar to its reaction in Luther's time. As Burton points out in *The Anatomy of Melancholy*, it was Luther's follower, Philip Melancthon, who added "spirit" to the four humours and who held "the fountain of these spirits to be the heart," as "spirit," the "instrument of the soul . . . is expressed from the blood."[50] In effect, Melancthon "spiritualized" Luther's understanding of divine grace, lifting God from vale to peak, from liver to heart, and, in so doing, rendering Luther's theology soulless. Ever since, Lutheranism has honored a sanitized Luther and has viewed his preoccupation with his digestive system as merely a function of his sociocultural background, and therefore as integral neither to his own religious experience nor to anyone else's.

THE DIVIDED SELF

In addressing the issue of the embodiment of the spirit and the self, Lapsley noted that "the self permeates the body and is not localized in the brain or the nervous system, even though these organs are more central to its functioning than others."[51] I believe that the brain or the nervous system is central to the functioning of the self in its "sameness" and "ownness," as these have especially to do with the self's perception of its continuity over time (sameness) and distinctiveness from other persons (ownness). Persons who have suffered brain injury or who have a neurological disease are especially vulnerable to the loss of this felt sense of sameness and ownness.

The foregoing discussion of the soul suggests that there is another aspect of the self—its coreness—for which the digestive system is most central. Precisely because the digestive system is associated with feelings (e.g., pain and pleasure) and not with such higher-order processes as memory, which is required for a sense of sameness, and self-other differentiation, which is required for a sense of ownness, it represents that aspect of the self that is vulnerable to being split off, of becoming the "disconnected fragments below the surface." In psychoanalytic language, this is the region of the self that is unconscious, outside the self-reflective process with which the neurological system is associated. It is, therefore, easily ignored or denied precisely because it falls outside our conscious awareness. Yet we ignore and deny it at our peril. When it pathologizes, it does so especially by attacking some element of the digestive system. Addictions that disrupt or even destroy the digestive system (e.g., alcoholism and eating disorders) are to the coreness of the self what neurological diseases are to its sameness and ownness. Thus, by insisting that the notion of the soul be retained in its own right and not merely replaced by self language, we provide an explanation for why the self is at odds with itself, having parts that are disconnected with one another. Although sameness and ownness seem to function well together and are mutually reinforcing, coreness is often at odds with them, and they with it.

Our analysis also explains why the self is often at odds with the spirit. As Hillman's analysis shows, it is the coreness of the self that threatens, and is threatened by, the spirit. This conflict between self and spirit is embodied in the conflict between the blood-vascular system, which expresses the aspirations of the heart, and the digestive system, which gives voice to the hurts and humors of the soul. If our model of the human being fails to take account of the soul-spirit conflict, we will depict the *self*-spirit interaction much as Lapsley does, as an interaction in which one or the other is dominant, and we will not give adequate attention to the ways in which self and spirit are in conflict with one another, usually to the detriment of the self. Although the aspirations of the spirit and the sameness and ownness of the self are often congruent with one another, and able to function in unison, the spirit's aspirations are typically in direct conflict with the coreness of the self. I would suggest that the aspirations of the spirit and the coreness of the self have an inverse relationship to one another, and, therefore, that the soul bears a heavy responsibility when our spirits (or hearts) are broken; and the spirit bears an equally heavy responsibility when our souls are sick.

On the other hand, I believe that if we are aware of this primordial conflict between spirit and soul, there are ways to minimize it. Soul's tendency to deflate the spirit through humor is one such method, for it reminds us of the limitations of the self and calls into question the grandiose aspirations of the spirit. Conversely, the spirit challenges the soul's tendency to pathologize itself by rekindling renounced or abandoned desires. With effort, spirit and soul can work together, for, as long as the body lives, they cannot but coexist because there is for neither any exit or escape.

What are the implications of this expansion of Lapsley's model of human being or pastoral care? In discussing his model, he suggests one way in which a caregiver may assist the self. This is when the caregiver, as observer of the self, "assists the person to a fuller and more accurate perception of his or her self."[52] This is a very important insight, for it gives warrant for the role of the pastoral counselor. But Freud's observation that the soul sees to its own treatment is equally important, for it suggests that there are limits to the role of the pastoral counselor precisely where the soul is concerned. Indeed, as the example of the medical team that performed the first baboon liver transplant reveals, there is the danger that we, as caring pastors, will overreact to the soul's pathologizings and fail to respect the soul's own regenerative powers. Thus, as we begin to recover the language of the soul, we will need to recover the ancient designation of our vocation as "the cure of souls." We do so, not, however, in order to describe what we do, but to delineate the *limits* of what we do, differentiating between what we can do for another and what we must allow the soul to do for itself.

NOTES

1. James N. Lapsley, *Renewal in Late Life through Pastoral Counseling* (New York: Paulist Press, 1992), 29. See also idem, "The 'Self,' Its Vicissitudes and Possibilities: An Essay in Theological Anthropology," *Pastoral Psychology* 35, no. 1 (Fall 1986): 23–45; and "Spirit and Self," *Pastoral Psychology* 38, no. 3 (Spring 1990): 135–46.

2. Lapsley, *Renewal in Late Life*, 32.

3. Ibid.

4. Ibid., 33.

5. Ibid., 34.

6. Ibid., 32.

7. Ibid., 34.

8. Bruno Bettelheim, *Freud and Man's Soul* (New York: Vintage Books, 1984), 70.

9. Quoted in ibid., 73–74.

10. James Hillman, *Re-Visioning Psychology* (New York: Harper & Row, 1975), 68.

11. Ibid.

12. Ibid.

13. Ibid., 69.

14. Ibid.

15. James Hillman, "Peaks and Vales: The Soul/Spirit Distinction as Basis for the Difference between Psychology and Spiritual Discipline," in *Puer Papers*, ed. James Hillman et al. (Irving, Tex.: Spring Publications, 1979), 54–74.

16. Ibid., 54.

17. Ibid., 58.

18. Ibid.

19. Ibid., 62.

20. Ibid.

21. Ibid., 72.

22. Ibid., 64.

23. Ibid., 59.

24. See Henry Gray, *Anatomy: Descriptive and Surgical*, ed. T. Pickering Pick and Robert Howden (Philadelphia: Running Press, 1974).

25. See Steven Kepnes, "Buber's Ark: The Dialogic Self," in *The Endangered Self*, ed. Richard K. Fenn and Donald Capps (Princeton, N.J.:

Princeton Theological Seminary Center for Religion, Self, and Society Monograph No. 2, 1992), 101–13.

26. Morris Jastrow, Jr., "The Liver as the Seat of the Soul," in *Studies in the History of Religions*, ed. David Gordon Lyon and George Foot Moore (New York: Macmillan Co., 1912), 143–68; and Richard Selzer, *Mortal Lessons: Notes on the Art of Surgery* (New York: A Touchstone Book, 1974), 62–77.

27. Selzer, *Mortal Lessons*, 64.

28. Ibid., 65.

29. Ibid., 63.

30. Ibid., 65–66.

31. Hillman, "Peaks and Vales," 71.

32. Jastrow notes that ancient India privileged the heart: "In Sanskrit literature the heart is the seat of thought, and since thought is the most significant and most direct manifestation of the soul, the heart is identified with the soul, and as such, becomes also the source of all emotions and the general symbol of vitality" ("The Liver as the Seat of the Soul," 144). In contrast, the ancient Hebrews held that the liver is the seat of the soul, and Jastrow cites various verses to support this (Lam. 2:11; Job 16:13; Prov. 7:23; Ps. 7:6; Ps. 30:13). Also, the Talmud refers to medical remedies that employ the liver of a dog or the gall of a fish: "Both remedies are clearly based on the supposition that the liver as the seat of life or of the soul is capable of restoring the intellect and sight, which are manifestations of soul life" (p. 150).

33. Stanley Jackson, *Melancholia and Depression: From Hippocratic Times to Modern Times* (New Haven: Yale University Press, 1986), 7.

34. Ibid., 8.

35. Ibid.

36. Ibid., 8–9.

37. Ibid., 9–10.

38. Ibid., 67–68.

39. Ibid., 71.

40. Robert Burton, *The Anatomy of Melancholy*, ed. Joan K. Peters (New York: Frederick Ungar, 1979), 35–68.

41. William Safire suggests that President Bush suffered from melancholia after the euphoria of Desert Storm died down: "The self-assured Bush served the nation well through the Persian Gulf crisis; nobody can ever take his hundred hours of greatness away from him. . . . Then Bush the winner was replaced by Bush the loser. For the first half of 1992, he seemed dispirited; many thought he was ill. . . . [H]e seemed to slide into melancholia" ("Bush's Gamble," *The New York Times Magazine*, 18 Oct. 1992, 32). Safire attributes Bush's melancholia to the erosion of his approval rating and the economy's failure to respond to the Federal Reserve

Board's dramatic interest rate cut in December. I would not question this, but I would also suggest that this melancholia was a *direct* consequence of Desert Storm, even as it seems to have been for the American public in general. I would also note that the low point for Bush was his public vomiting episode in Japan in December 1991, a certain indication that, unbeknownst to him, his soul was troubling him.

42. Selzer, *Mortal Lessons*, 76–77.

43. See Michel Foucault, "Technologies of the Self," in *Technologies of the Self: A Seminar with Michel Foucault*, ed. Luther H. Martin, Huck Gutman, and Patrick H. Hutton (Amherst: University of Massachusetts Press, 1988), 16–49.

44. Quoted in *New York Times*, 9 Sept. 1992, sec. A, 13.

45. Erik H. Erikson, *Young Man Luther: A Study in Psychoanalysis and History* (New York: W. W. Norton, 1958), 204.

46. Ibid., 205.

47. Ibid., 213–14.

48. Ibid., 206. I believe Luther would have been most sympathetic with the following Jewish prayer, which is said after using the toilet: "Blessed art thou, Lord our God, King of the universe, who hast formed man in wisdom, and created in him a system of ducts and tubes. It is well known before thy glorious throne that if but one of these can be opened, or if one of those be closed, it would be impossible to exist in thy presence. Blessed art thou, O Lord, who healest all creatures and doest wonders."

49. Erikson, *Young Man Luther*, 72.

50. Burton, *The Anatomy of Melancholy*, 38–39.

51. Lapsley, *Renewal in Late Life*, 34.

52. Ibid., 33.

7
Whose Participation and Whose Humanity? Medicine's Challenge to Theological Anthropology

Brian H. Childs

With the publication of *Salvation and Health* in 1972, James N. Lapsley made one of his keen observations/diagnoses about the state of the crisis in the church. The church had lost much of its creditability because it was using an outdated and worn-out notion of what it is to be human and what human destiny is about. Specifically, Lapsley lamented that at the time of the publication of the book, the church was still assuming a theological anthropology that was two hundred years old. Although acknowledging the impact of the likes of Tillich and Barth in the first half of the twentieth century, Lapsley found normative understandings of what it is to be human lacking in most conversations in the academy and, of even more importance, in the church community.

> Though modern thinkers mentioned generally overcame the crudely dualistic dichotomies that characterized the orthodox tradition—body and soul, individual and society, sacred and secular—they did not offer a fully viable anthropology because of their failure to understand how the dynamics of personality operate in relationships, and because they lacked a comprehensive grasp of the reality of nature of which man is a part.[1]

The marks of the church's decline due to its inadequate anthropology were then, at the time of Lapsley's book, as they are now, not hard to find: declining memberships, churchwide programs that arise in fits and starts seemingly more tied to the latest crazes and fads of our culture than to thought-out biblical and theological precepts, and the decline of clergy morale and, it seems, morality. Then, as now, although programs of evangelization and stewardship, campaigns for gender equality and sexual ethics, and statements about social and ecological crises were signs of life in the church, they were just that, signs, and they were not enough. Without a viable and clearly articulated notion of what human nature is and what human destiny is about, the church could continue to collapse under the weight of busyness and frustrations. Without a theory of what it is to be human and in relation with God, practice becomes hollow and alienating for the practitioner, lay and clergy alike. We must not only know *how* to do things, but we must also know something about what criteria there are for deciding *what* to do and *why*.[2]

Although I do not want to outline the sequence of Lapsley's tightly packed answer to the crisis, there are several aspects to the book on which I would like to comment in order to continue the discussion begun by my teacher and friend. As an aside before moving on in the discussion, I do want to say that I am somewhat puzzled that Lapsley's work did not gain more of a reading than apparently it did. Possibly, the book is too tightly packed (it is only 172 pages). Possibly, process theology was not explained fully enough to capture the imaginations of its intended readership— parish ministers rather than just professors or specialized practitioners. Lapsley was the first pastoral theologian who took process theology a step beyond even Daniel Day Williams' attempt to make it practical. We must remember, however, that most of his readership were immersed in Tillich, Barth, Bultmann, and the Niebuhrs, and not Whitehead or his theological disciples such as Cobb and Ogden. In this sense, Lapsley was ahead of his time. Although Hiltner, Jackson, and recently Poling have written in a process vein, process theology has never really caught on in practical theology. This is a shame. Lapsley's diagnosis, however, is still on target; and in ever more trying times, such as the present, his diagnosis still needs a vigorous response.

The key to Lapsley's project is to investigate the connection between salvation and health. Salvation is understood not as an escape from divine punishment but as a deliverance from both personal and corporate evil and sin.

> In the view being set forth here, salvation is from the perishing of time and from evil and mutual destructiveness. . . . Salvation means

a progressive response to the lure of God toward the realization of beauty, and the peace which is the preservation of beauty.[3]

Health is seen in a relational dimension. It cannot be reduced to just the absence of physical or biological loss, trauma, or disintegration. "Health generally refers to the relatively active potential for appropriate functioning which any individual possesses at any given time."[4] Appropriate functioning is always understood as the degree in which the person can participate in the salvatory process. It has an enabling function in persons, albeit by degree depending on the context, and it generally relates to the engagement of the person with the rest of creation in some form or another. Although Lapsley speaks of health as the health of the particular individual (and is used in the discussion of groups only analogically), he also speaks of it in relational terms because the individual's health is always tempered by the individual's group membership.

Lapsley's project is an ingenious one. His notion is that the interlocking processes of life that indicate the relationship between salvation and health entail a schema of hierarchies that illustrate a dynamic of factors (development, maintenance, and participation) potential in levels of interaction (in six levels). Level one is dominated by maintenance with little or no development and participation with minimal salvatory participation. Level two is full of development, which may or may not entail salvatory participation. Level three entails compensation (a kind of maintenance) again with ambiguous signs of salvatory participation. Levels four, five, and six are levels of more and more participation, level six being identified by participation for participation's sake with little or no maintenance functions. These last three offer the most potential for salvatory experience. Of course, as any reader of the book knows, things are not so neat and clean, and Lapsley does warn the reader to avoid any kind of value rating of the hierarchy, as difficult as that might be for most of us. Lapsley is always ready to warn the reader about the moral and theological ambiguity resident in each stage of the relationship between salvation and health. In level three, he discusses prejudice and its relationship to maintenance and compensation. In level five, there is an extended discussion of Robert E. Lee, a man of great potential, courage, and participation, who also aligned himself with the Virginia aristocracy at the cost of participating in the cause for slavery during the Civil War. In other levels, Lapsley discusses such practical matters as marriage, child rearing, vocational choices and crises, and political activity. As complicated as his description can be in this hierarchical schema, it is ultimately practical in its descriptive force and in its theological integrity.

THE LIMITS OF LAPSLEY'S MODEL

It does seem to me that the model Lapsley proposed is limited in two very important ways. First, Lapsley's model for situating his anthropology is heavily psychological. Although this is understandable given the dominance of psychological models of humanity that was, and may still be, primary in most pastoral theologies, it is still limited. It is also understandable in regard to the process understanding of the human person, which views humans as the most complex organism that has feeling and can articulate that experience of feeling within the notion of prehension and the aesthetic concept of beauty. So far as it goes, some sort of psychological model of humanity works well, as is attested by its usefulness in clinical pastoral education, pastoral counseling, and group theory in conflict management and Christian education. It is limited in that the psychological model (be it personality theory based on conflict theory or ego psychology or humanistic psychology) seems to understand what it is to be fully human and, therefore, have greater potentiality to participate in salvatory events, at least in individuals who are roughly speaking in midlife. Lapsley's model seems dependent upon understanding what it is to be human in terms of midlife cognitive, emotional, and physical maturity. Levels four through six seem to describe optimal functioning in people who are well into their working life, family life, and possibly their mature spiritual life. It is significant to note here that the two extended case studies discussed in the book are that of the American Quaker John Woolman and the military statesman Robert E. Lee. Both of these case studies center on their midlife (and late midlife) contributions. Although Lapsley is concerned with the very young and those in later life (as we see in his recent book *Renewal in Late Life through Pastoral Counseling*),[5] his model does seem to minimize the place of the very young and the elderly. I wonder if there could be more study of the so-called boundary edges of humanity: the neonate and the near dead (in our culture often the very old) and the comatose (or those in persistent vegetative state).

The second limitation of Lapsley's schema is that its primary concern is with the participation of the individual as the main locus of the action to the neglect of the community of actors in which so much of what it means to be human is, in fact, negotiated and actualized. Lapsley does address this criticism in his references to Thomas Szasz and Theodore R. Sarbin. He acknowledges that mental disturbances can be diagnosed culturally and that "their association with notions of illness is due to historical accidents rather than to any intrinsic relationship, and is perpetuated by the medical profession, who have a vested interest in it."[6] The issue is not whether the antipsychiatric theorists are correct in their assessment of mental disturbance as "myth," but that they might well be on to something important about how cultural, political, and economic factors do, in fact, influence how we understand persons as either fully human, fully participatory, and, therefore, part of the human community—God's creation. To put the matter another way, can we understand what it is to be human not only on the basis of what the individual actor is able to do but also on what the human community does with individual actors who may act only minimally, if at all? I have mentioned that in terms of individual psychology, certain boundary examples of persons—the neonate and the comatose, for example—are difficult to talk about when their level of participation is nil due to a lack of either physical and psychological maturity or to unconsciousness (either by disease or accident). These same persons on the boundary, however, can be responded to, even if only abstractly (though dealing with people in the abstract itself borders on not dealing with them at all) by others, who through their attitude or treatment of them, therefore define what it is to be human.

There is a theological problem for both Lapsley, to some extent, and for me in the way I am now placing my objections. In the final analysis, we all are dependent upon God and not ourselves for salvation—for our being freed from the perishing of time and destructiveness. We cannot save ourselves by ourselves. On the other hand, I do agree with Lapsley that the traditional theological antagonists—the Armenians and the Calvinists—both have points in their favor. The Calvinist and neoorthodox position of God's otherness (if not dominion) should temper any smugness about our ability to usher in the kingdom on our own. Sin may be easier to demonstrate empirically than sanctification. Even so, in our relative freedom we can participate in the signs of the coming kingdom when we carry another's burden (Gal. 6:2) and treat strangers with hospitality, thereby entertaining angels unawares (Heb. 13:2).

The Impact of Recent Developments in Medicine

Some recent developments in medicine and medical ethics may give us some better handles on developing a broader theological anthropology than Lapsley's model does. By looking at boundary situations discussed in modern bioethics, we might overcome the two limitations of his model I have discussed. What I am suggesting here is not a full-scale revision of the model, which all in all is not only helpful but profoundly descriptive, but rather an addition to it that incorporates the boundary examples of what it is to be a human, thereby cutting through the psychological limitation as well as the restrictions of the model's individualistic slant.

In the twenty or so years since Lapsley published his book, modern medicine has taken leaps and bounds in its ability to sustain biological life. Neonatologists now have the ability to reduce minimum gestation time for the viability of the fetus to twenty-eight weeks and less. Children born with severe physical abnormalities can be sustained for months in highly technological environments. Although there is a high mortality rate, some do leave the hospital (though many who do have guarded prognosis for "quality of life," a term that is itself ambiguous). Children can be born with drastically limited neurological systems as well as physical abnormalities. The physical systems can be surgically repaired, leaving them neurologically, mentally, and emotionally highly dependent on others for the rest of their lives.

In a somewhat similar vein, older persons who have suffered disease or trauma can be organically and physically supported when their own systems cannot do so. Persons with only brain stem functions due to the destruction of higher brain functions (through trauma, oxygen starvation, and stroke) can be supported with food and water and sometimes with artificial ventilation so that in hospital intensive care units and in long-term skilled nursing care units, one can hear house officers say, "The front porch lights are on but nobody is home." Even if the older person is in and out of consciousness and organ systems begin to collapse, resuscitation procedures can revive a patient who under other circumstances would die. For some there is a genuine concern that life can be sustained beyond tolerable limits, and the issue of "quality of life" becomes a common category with its polar opposite, "quantity of life."

These problems, I contend, are not problems that have been created by medical technology alone. They are problems that have very complicated origins and involve public policy decisions, legal precedents, and economic—and often times—religious and philosophical implications. My concern here is to go into these issues only in one particular area: what does this situation, when persons are organically alive but have no objective or knowable subjective participation with others, tell us about what it is to be human? This question is not just an academic exercise. Benchmark "cases" such as those of Karen Ann Quinlan, Dax Cowart, Nancy Cruzan, and the Baby Doe directives clearly illustrate that what we *think* about what humanity is or does or has potential to become leads in each of these cases to what we *do*.

Currently, there are various efforts to make public policy in regard to such boundary situations. Advanced directives are encouraged, though in the heat of rapid emergency situations, they are often neglected. Several states have had referendums calling for making euthanasia a legal act. Other states have called for the voters to decide whether physician-assisted suicide should be legalized. Although at the time of this writing the initiatives have failed, one survey has indicated that between 55 and 65 percent of the public would favor the legalization of assisted death.[7]

Medical ethics has begun to address these issues, though it has found itself largely unprepared to do so with any uniformity. This is in part because the field of biomedical ethics is a discipline in its infancy, and also because the rapid advance of technological medicine makes it almost impossible for the philosophers, ethicists, and theologians to keep up. However, various voices have been raised. Some believe that "thou shalt not kill" is part of the Hippocratic foundation of medicine that directs physicians first to do no harm. The physician's job is healing; and when healing is not possible, there is no warrant to kill. This position is somewhat equivocated by another Hippocratic precept that the physician should not perform medical procedures that do no good. This would include the cessation of medical interventions if it could be argued that the possibility of healing was past. Death, in this instance, would not be the intention of the medical worker but would be the result of the natural course of the disease. The cessation of life support or medical intervention in these cases would also demonstrate a kind of benevolent care in that the patient would not have to undergo undue suffering as a result of the medical procedure; nor would the patient, the family, or society have to bear the financial burden.[8]

Still others argue that more aggressive steps be taken with persons in boundary situations. With advanced directives, persons can choose, when they are of sound mind and competent to do so, to dictate what procedures they want and do not want, knowing that without them death will come. Others argue that if the person gave no advanced directives (either because of mental incompetency or legal incompetency due to young age), then what the law calls a substituted judgment could be made. A substituted judgment is a legal device by which family or a legal surrogate can decide what treatment should be initiated or withdrawn.[9] There are others who believe that advanced directives should also provide for the provision that, under certain circumstances, active euthanasia and physician-assisted suicide be employed.

THE NARRATIVE PERSPECTIVE

What are the arguments for more active facilitation of patient death? It is of interest that the most powerful arguments are from a narrative perspective. James Rachels proposes that there is a distinction between biological and biographical life.[10] Biographical life is defined by Rachels as the narrative anyone can tell about his or her life including accomplishments, relationships, aspirations, goals, and an assessment of these very things. It is now possible to be biologically alive, due to medical interventions, yet have no capability to form narratives out of the elements of biographical personhood. Rachels would say something similar about a severely handicapped newborn who cannot even begin a biography. When the ability to form a narrative has been lost or when there is no potential to form a narrative, Rachels suggests that what is distinctive about being human is not to be found and that, therefore, considerations about active forms of euthanasia are morally well founded.

The line of argument that Rachels makes, that narrative is based on the capacity to make sense of experience (in terms of past, present, and projected future), is in many ways consistent with other narrative theorists who are not necessarily working in the field of biomedical ethics. Alasdair MacIntyre, for instance, claims that "all attempts to elucidate the notion of personal identity independently of and in isolation from the notions of narrative, intelligibility, and accountability are bound to fail."[11] MacIntyre goes on to say that a narrative must have the property of unity, and that when a narrative of a person is challenged or rendered incoherent, then a new unified narrative is created out of the epistemological crisis. "What is carried over from one paradigm to another are epistemological ideals and correlative understanding of what constitutes the progress of a single intellectual life."[12] The implication seems to be that when one has lost the narrative ability either through epistemological crises (possibly such as Paul's conversion experience?) or through the inability to think narratively, then one's personhood, one's sense of accountability, is lost. He says as much in his comment on suicide:

> When someone complains—as do some of those who attempt or commit suicide—that his or her life is meaningless, he or she is often and perhaps characteristically complaining that the narrative of their life [sic] has become unintelligible to them, that it lacks any point, any movement towards a climax or a *telos*. Hence the point of doing any one thing rather than another at crucial junctures in their lives seems to such a person to have been lost.[13]

Other narrative theorists seem to echo Rachels and MacIntyre. Persons have stories or narratives that are typified by coherence and unity. For this to be so, the person must have memory, a sensory and cognitive present, and a sensed future or telos. The question is, What do we make of persons who cannot form such unified stories? Can people be incoherent and still be persons? Is the narrative solely dependent on the person telling the story about the self, or can stories also be told by others for others? If this is so, can they constitute stories that tell us what it is to be human? Of more importance, can these stories told by others tell us something about what we are to *do* as well as to *think*. Can communal stories include our care for the storyless? Finally, what does this tell us about those with no stories in terms of salvation? In order to answer these questions, we must (1) temper the individual/psychological paradigm with its dependence on subjective human consciousness and intentional action and (2) add a communal notion to narrative theory.

My colleague and narrative theologian George W. Stroup may give us some clues to answering these questions. In his essay "The Coherence of the Gospel in an Incoherent World," Stroup argues that narrative theologians deserve criticism on some important points.[14] First, they should not assume that personal and communal identity must have a unity and a coherence. There are lives that are so full of chaos and meaninglessness that to deny their existence is to ignore the reality of suffering in lived experience. Second, narrative theologians often assume that there is a unity and coherence in the Bible, and, therefore, gloss over the important element of the apocalyptic in which chaos and incoherence are a reality. Finally, narrative theologians often confuse the categories of unity and coherence.

> One interpretation of "coherence" would suggest something like the reconciliation of different and perhaps even contradictory events, while "unity" might be understood to mean not the reconciliation but the dissolution and even the denial of contradiction. In other words, do narrative theologians compound their mistakes about the unity and coherence of both life and the Bible by suggesting that the Bible provides a unity that denies life's experience of evil?[15]

Stroup argues that some understanding of the gospel story of Jesus may involve a profound notion of incoherence that is important to the gospel itself and to which narrative theologians have turned a deaf ear in their desire for notions of unity and coherence. He discusses the example of the "little apocalypse" in Mark 13 to show that the meaning of the connection between the ministry of Jesus and Jesus' passion and death cannot be found within the story itself but that the final meaning must be found *outside* the story. Without the "little apocalypse," the movement from Mark 1–12 to Mark 14–16 would constitute the literary genre of tragedy. There is scant reason in tragedy for the call to discipleship that is central to Mark's Gospel. Mark tells the reader that the incoherence of the story is resolved by the apocalyptic activity of God. He then informs the reader in a very personal way in 13:14 that her or his life too will be filled with chaos, suffering, and the reality of evil, and only after the time of suffering will the Son of Man come in clouds of power and glory to collect the faithful.

> Mark 13 occurs where it does in the Jesus story not primarily because of the content of Jesus' apocalyptic discourse, but because the fissure in the Jesus story cannot be overcome within the story itself. In this sense, it is fitting that Mark's gospel ends at 16:8, because this so-called shorter ending, as well as Mark 13, tells the reader that the ending to the gospel story is outside of and from beyond the story.[16]

The implications of the apocalyptic in the gospel are many. Although there may be some kind of coherence in personal identity, this does not require that there exist a unity that creates the resolution of contradictions. There may be no unity in our lives in the face of irrevocable contradictions. Narratives that are unified and fully coherent would in some analysis be a-theistic narratives in that they are self-contained and require nothing beyond themselves for completion. In addition, the apocalyptic reminds us that we must be realistic about the presence and ubiquity of evil and suffering in the world. It is significant that the gospel affirms the reality of evil by making it central to the story of Jesus' ministry— a ministry in which it is the demons in Mark 1–12 who recognize Jesus for who he is. This does not mean that Christians can read only the passion and resurrection story without also taking seriously Jesus' ministry and call to discipleship. But it should also be remembered that our ministry of and for the suffering are only the signs of the triumph of God and not the triumph itself. Finally, the apocalyptic points to the critical theological claim that the meaning of human existence is not to be found within human existence alone. The meaning of human existence is ultimately to be rooted in God.

> More so than any other theme in the biblical story, Pauline [and Markan] apocalyptic affirms not only the transcendent otherness of God but also the transcendence of human identity and destiny. . . . Over against everything in contemporary society that insists that the meaning to human life is to be found within life itself, Pauline apocalyptic is a reminder and a promise that the final meaning to life—when we see "face to face"—is an eschatological and apocalyptic event.[17]

HUMANITY IN THE BOUNDARY SITUATIONS

What now do we say about the humanity that is humanity in what I have called the boundary situations? First, it seems that we cannot rely on notions of the intelligibility of the narratives, if there are any, in the first person alone. Our personal narratives, as important as they are, are not the self-contained narratives we may think that they are. Our existence, no matter in what condition, is to be found within a larger narrative that achieves its conclusion from outside our personal stories. It is not only a theological error but also a categorical error to deny personhood to those who have no narratives to tell. All of our stories are incomplete, and we are called to live in the tension between Jesus' ministry and God's final activity. Mark's Gospel seems to be telling us that it is a mistake to fixate on the passion and resurrection of Jesus without the call to discipleship that entails the ministry of tending to the sick, the suffering, and the powerless. The stories of boundary humanity are part of our story. Where there is minimal participation on the part of one, there is a call to increase the participation of those who are able. Although there may be no unity, there is still coherence.

In a sense, persons can have stories that begin even prior to their conception. Couples who are struggling with infertility often begin a child's story as they attempt, often with medical intervention, to conceive. Rooms are prepared, names are chosen, fantasies are created and given some kind of concreteness. If conception does not occur, many couples pass through a grief process, thereby mourning the loss of a story that was beginning. A person is not a person only because of his or her own biography, in such cases, but is a person because a projected biography is given to him or her. Should there be conception and birth, the child is given a story from the beginning; and though there can be a conflict between stories, one given by parents and the other enacted and created by the child, as the child develops his or her own biography, coherence is possible in integrating these biographies. Although often conflictual, it is nevertheless a narrative process.

In a case study, Warren T. Reich has reported a moving example of attributed biography; that is, a narrative that, in part, is imposed on a person but is also played out by the person.[18] Reich was called for an ethics consultation at a pediatrics hospital. The subject of the consultation was a twenty-one-year-old man who, because of severe birth defects, had the physical age of a seven-year-old and the mental age of a two-year-old. His birth was a difficult one. He had severe lung dysfunction and was required to undergo intensive neonatal care for several months. Upon recovery, his parents placed him in a state facility because they were emotionally and physically unable to provide the attention and intensity of care he would require. The child lived in the retardation hospital, but due to his fragile pulmonary function, he suffered frequent pneumonias and pulmonary crises that necessitated multiple hospitalizations.

Reich was called on to help the staff and the hospital administration discuss two issues. First, should the man be continued on antibiotic treatment for his chronic lung problems, and should he be resuscitated if he were to have cardiopulmonary arrest? The second issue involved deciding whether hospital policy should provide "extraordinary" means of treatment for such severely birth-defected neonates in the future. Such care is expensive and the results mixed.

The man spent his days in bed usually curled in a fetal position. He could not control his bowels or his bladder and had to be fed by staff. He could not walk or talk. His parents did not visit him either at the retardation center or at the hospital during his medical crises.

Reich first spoke to the resident physician about the young man. He collected the necessary medical history and the report of his social and psychological functioning. He also asked the resident physician and several nurses about him. He asked not just medical questions but questions that would elicit the story. He found that the physicians had mixed feelings about the man. Some felt that the medical interventions were of questionable value but that perhaps it was their duty to do them well. When Reich asked one physician what he felt about the man, what distinctive nonmedical feelings he had, the resident said some important things about the man. First, whenever he went into his room, the man would give him a big smile, a beautiful smile, that pleased him even though he knew the man did not recognize him or "know" him in any common sense of the term. Second, he talked about the man's habit of what the resident called "finger ballets." "Finger ballets" were what the resident called the man's playing with his hands and fingers much as young children do with "here's the church, here's the steeple." He said that the man did this with such grace and concentration that it reminded him of the intensity he had seen in concert pianists. The resident also said that surely the man could not have the same meaning in his finger play as does the skill of a Horowitz. Finally, the resident talked of the man's playing with the wheels of a toy tractor somebody had given him. He could lay in his bed spinning the wheels of the tractor for hours on end with great concentration.

When Reich asked the resident what he felt about all of this, the resident said that it frightened him because the man seemed so alien. The resident was moved and sometimes frustrated. At last Reich asked to see the man. Reich watched as the resident took his stethoscope to listen to the man's chest. Reich saw the man holding the end of the instrument along with the resident's hand. Reich observed the man's large smile and expression of what some might call gratitude.

This story can be seen as overly sentimentalized. It can also be evaluated critically as another example of the health care professional denying the voice of the patient. Reich and the resident can be accused of making attributions about the man that the man did not and could not make for himself (such as gratitude or concert pianist concentration or calling random hand fidgeting a "ballet"). Nonetheless, here is a story about a storyless man that called for some kind of reaction. A reasoned ethical decision could indeed be made not to use extraordinary means should the man go into a medical crisis. Yet the call for the palliative care of the man through the crisis was clear, because the man was known in part through the story given by the community and in part by his own behavior.

Another kind of boundary situation deserves further attention. In a very recent large and detailed survey, it has been shown that, with the possible exception of small hospices, our health care institutions do not do well in the care of the terminally ill.[19] This study surveyed hundreds of physicians and nurses to assess the care patients received near the end of life, and to learn whether physicians and nurses were aware of and in agreement with national recommendations concerning a patient's right to deny life-sustaining treatment while at the same time receiving adequate palliative treatment. The most troubling conclusion of the study was that between 86 and 91 percent of the physicians and nurses thought it was possible to control pain in dying patients, yet between 78 and

85 percent of the health care workers thought that the most common form of narcotic abuse was undertreatment and not overtreatment. There seems to be a chasm between the theory and the practice of pain control in end-of-life situations. Perhaps there is too much emphasis on curing in our medical expectations and not enough emphasis on caring. Perhaps we need to listen more than we do.

The discussion about physician-assisted suicide is relevant here. In terms of physician-assisted suicide and in light of the research mentioned above, we might be able to agree with Ron Hamel when he says:

> Despite all the talk about advance directives and a national consensus about forgoing life-sustaining treatment articulated in widely publicized guidelines and policy statements, a wide gap between theory and practice in end of life decisions remains. Can physician-assisted death be seriously proposed as a "last resort" while that gap continues to exist? In theory there may be a broad continuum of options for care of the terminally ill, but in practice that continuum is truncated. In this case, physician-assisted suicide is not truly a last resort.[20]

The issue is not so much the morality of physician-assisted suicide, which can be a caring response to a reasoned request. The issue that needs to be addressed is something else: Is physician-assisted suicide (which is ethically quite different from advanced directives to forgo medical treatment) an avoidance of our responses to persons in pain because they represent our medical limitations without testing and challenging our ability to care in the midst of pain, suffering, and evil? Could we even see the desire legally to sanction physician-assisted suicide as our attempt to impose an apocalyptic solution from below as opposed to caring through the suffering in anticipation of the apocalyptic solution from beyond? To put it in terms that Paul Ramsey once used, Are we asking modern medicine to relieve the human condition of the human condition?[21] If so, then we are a-theists in our notion of human destiny, and we are negligent in our response to the reality of suffering and our call to care.

In addition, there are issues that we must face in our inclination to "medicalize" death, thereby privatizing it, denying it, and isolating those who are dying from our community. Finally, it is not clear to me that we must exclude a person's unconsciousness from his or her biography. As John Kleinig has said: "Karen Ann Quinlan's biography did not end in 1975, when she became permanently comatose. It continued for another ten years. That was a part of the tragedy of her life."[22]

Probably, I am a little less Arminian than is Lapsley, but only in degree and not in intention. I have argued that Lapsley's hierarchical model of the relationship between salvation and health is too focused on the psychological ability of the individual for salvatory participation, and too neglectful of the communal aspect of salvatory expression. Yet, in another sense, I have come full circle in some real sense to Lapsley's position. Through God's grace (and, dare we say, some luck?), we who have been nurtured in salvatory participation are called to include those who have no stories of their own or whose stories are closing according to our understanding of human value and destiny. Possibly, what I am proposing could be pictorially illustrated. In *Salvation and Health*, Lapsley gives schematic representation of his salvation-health model. In this representation, the various stages are connected by lines denoting either major, minor, or minimal flows of energy toward or from the categories of maintenance, development, and participation. Perhaps there could be lines denoting energy flow between the stages themselves. Level six can flow to level one and so on. In this adaption of the schema, the communal narrative quality of human existence can temper the individualistic inclination.

Whose participation are we speaking of? The participation of *all* of us as an ethical and narrative participation. Whose humanity are we? Finally, we are God's, and God will write the final chapter of our book.

Notes

1. James N. Lapsley, *Salvation and Health: The Interlocking Processes of Life* (Philadelphia: Westminster Press, 1972), 21.

2. Ibid., 17–19.

3. Ibid., 36.

4. Ibid., 71.

5. James N. Lapsley, *Renewal in Late Life through Pastoral Counseling* (New York: Paulist Press, 1992).

6. Lapsley, *Salvation and Health*, 66.

7. Howard Brody, "Assisted Death—A Compassionate Response to a Medical Failure," *New England Journal of Medicine* 32 (November 5, 1992): 1384–88.

8. For further reading on the subject of active euthanasia and physician-assisted suicide, see: *Journal of Medicine and Philosophy* 18, no. 3 (June 1993); Ron Hamel, ed., *Choosing Death, Active Euthanasia, Religion, and the Public Debate* (Philadelphia: Trinity Press International, 1991); *Trends in Health Care, Law and Ethics* 7, no. 2 (Winter 1992); *Hastings Center Report* 22, no. 2 (March-April 1992); President's Commission for the Study of Ethical Problems in Medicine and Biomedical and Behavioral Research, *Deciding to Forgo Life-Sustaining Treatment* (Washington, D.C.: Government Printing Office, 1983). The journals cited are special issues devoted to the topic.

9. Alexander Morgan Capron, "Substituting Our Judgment," *Hastings Center Report* 22, no. 2 (March-April 1992): 58–59.

10. James Rachels, *The End of Life* (New York: Oxford University Press, 1986). For another treatment of narrative biomedical ethics, see Howard Brody, *Stories of Sickness* (New Haven: Yale University Press, 1987), and *The Healer's Power* (New Haven: Yale University Press, 1992). Although Brody does not deal specifically with physician-assisted suicide in these books, he does make the observation that narrative theory offers the moral agent an opportunity to think in terms other than in those associated with midlife or those capabilities of so-called competent persons. Brody argues that most thinking about advanced directives, patient autonomy, and the like is modeled on midlife, leaving no voice to those who have either no stories or only the potential for stories (or biographies) and to those for whom the present marks the last part of the last chapter of their biography. Brody has considered physician-assisted suicide in "Assisted Death—A Compassionate Response to a Medical Failure," and in "Causing, Intending, and Assisting Death," *Journal of Clinical Ethics* 4, no. 2 (Summer 1993): 112–17. Brody is far more cautious about physician-assisted suicide than is Rachels, and sees it as ethically permissible when associated with medical failure; that is, when medical intervention increases pain and suffering beyond palliation. Then, and only with full patient desires for suicide and a review by medical and ethical personnel, would it be possible.

11. Alasdair MacIntyre, *After Virtue: A Study in Moral Theory* (Notre Dame: University of Notre Dame Press, 1981), 203.

12. Alasdair MacIntyre, "Epistemological Crises, Dramatic Narrative, and the Philosophy of Science," in *Why Narrative? Readings in Narrative Theology*, ed. Stanley Hauerwas and L. Gregory Jones (Grand Rapids: Wm. B. Eerdmans, 1989), 140.

13. MacIntyre, *After Virtue*, 202.

14. This essay will appear in a *Festschrift* in honor of J. Christiaan Beker, Professor of New Testament Theology at Princeton. The essay was shared with me by the author, and I am citing him with his permission.

15. Ibid.

16. Ibid.

17. Ibid.

18. Warren T. Reich, "Caring for Life in the First of It: Moral Paradigms for Perinatal and Neonatal Ethics," *Seminars in Perinatology* 11, no. 3 (July 1987): 279–87.

19. Mildred Solomon et al., "Decisions Near the End of Life: Professional Views on Life-Sustaining Treatments," *American Journal of Public Health* 83 (January 1993): 14–23.

20. Ron Hamel, "Physician-Assisted Suicide: Putting the Cart Before the Horse," *Second Opinion* (July 1993): 86.

21. Cited in Courtney S. Campbell, "Religion and Moral Meaning in Bioethics," *Hastings Center Report* 20, no. 4 (July-August 1990): 6.

22. John Kleinig, *Valuing Life* (Princeton: Princeton University Press, 1991), 201.

8
Immanence and Transcendence in Pastoral Care and Preaching

DON S. BROWNING

When I consider the relation of pastoral care to preaching, my mind goes back to my earliest student days at the Divinity School of the University of Chicago. In those years of the late 1950s and early 1960s, when James Lapsley and I were fellow students, the two dominant intellectual influences were the two Carls—one Karl Barth, who spelled his name with a *K*, and the other, Carl Rogers, who spelled his name with a *C*. One was the towering Swiss theologian of the word, Karl Barth. The other was the American psychologist whose theory of client-centered and non-directive counseling was the single most powerful influence on mainline Protestant pastoral care and counseling from the 1950s to the 1970s and possibly even until today. It never occurred to us students during those days that either of them had anything in common. We totally overlooked the fact that they shared at least the same first name.

At the University of Chicago, the tension between these two figures was felt with particular sharpness. On our faculty at that time as Professor of New Testament was Marcus Barth, the son of Karl Barth. At the same time, we also felt the considerable presence of Seward Hiltner, the single most important interpreter of Rogers' psychology to the American religious community. In addition, Hiltner was associated with the Counseling Center of the University of Chicago, which had been founded by Rogers himself. Rogers had left for Wisconsin before I arrived as a student, but his spiritual presence lingered. Almost all students who earned their Ph.D.'s in the field of religion and personality in those days did much of their clinical work in the counseling center that Rogers had founded.

Seward Hiltner and Marcus Barth were perceived to present totally different religious worldviews. Marcus represented his father to a fault. Hiltner's representation of his symbolic father, Carl Rogers, was more nuanced but still quite forceful. From the two Barths we heard a theology of the transcendent Word of God. It was a theology of proclamation and a theology that appealed to many of us when we thought of preaching. It was a theology which said that God revealed himself (and in this case, the male pronoun was always used) in the figure of Jesus and in Paul's theology of justification. Humans were totally and completely dependent upon the initiative of God—on God's action from the outside—for their salvation. It was completely a matter of God's justifying grace.

God for Barth could not be found in any of the anthropological realms where modernizing theologians and philosophers had tried to locate the Divine.[1] God could not be found in our feelings, as Schleiermacher had believed. God was not an implication or postulate of our moral consciousness, as the Kantians had argued. God was not a postulate or inference of our theoretical reason, as some Catholics and natural theologians had held. To say that God was discoverable in any of these realms was to suggest, according to Barth, that humans owned something and had control of something upon which they could stand and perhaps climb as they made their way to God. All such claims, according to Barth, were efforts on the part of humans to justify themselves rather than to submit to the complete justifying determinations of God as revealed through God's Word. In the drama of salvation, God was everything; humans were nothing. Because this was a theology of proclamation—the proclamation of the justifying Word of God—when we thought of preaching, many of us thought of Barth. To preach was to proclaim and to proclaim was to preach Barth, or at least his version of the gospel.

But these were very schizophrenic days. There was another side to our theological and ministerial psyches. This was the part formed by Hiltner and Rogers. For Hiltner, revelation was to be found in experience. Marcus Barth could never understand Hiltner's fascination with the verbatim interview and clinical experience. When Hiltner replied that it was because they were sources of revelation, Marcus, we were told, was speechless. For him, and for his father, this was locating God in an anthropological realm and the most disrespectable realm at that—the realm of subjective experience. In addition, Hiltner, as did Rogers, believed in the curative power of listening.[2] In the Rogersian view of counseling, one did not listen first in order to say something or proclaim something later. In the Rogersian method of counseling, listening was an end in itself.[3] The counselor listened because it helped troubled persons listen to themselves. In listening to themselves, clients and parishioners came into contact with the curative powers that were within themselves.

It would not be fair to Hiltner to say that he associated God with the inner, recuperative, and self-actualizing powers of each person. But he came close to this. As a Whiteheadian, he believed that God placed before every actual entity's subjective aim the most relevant possibility for that entity's move toward completion. There is little doubt that Hiltner believed that there was a close association between a person's inner press toward self-actualization and the relevant possibility that God placed before that person. The spacial metaphors separating Hiltner from Marcus Barth were clear and dramatic. When you were around Hiltner and thought of counseling and care, you looked inward, downward, or at least horizontally. When you were with Marcus Barth and thought about preaching, you looked upward, outward, and beyond.

For most of us, proclamation and counseling were finally matters of either/or. They may have been similarly dichotomized for the entire generation of mainline ministers educated in the late 1950s and early 1960s. For many of us, it seemed impossible to bring these two worlds together. To care and counsel was to listen to the other person, remove your own witness, and indeed protect the counselee from the external pressures of the transcendent gospel. To preach was to open others to that pressure, to proclaim a message that transcended all aspects of human experience, a message that robbed our hearers of any place to stand and that totally determined them from without.

The controversies between Seward Hiltner and Marcus Barth were more than polite discussions. Thunderous rumbles sounded forth from the committee rooms and conference tables of the Divinity School during those years. You will not be surprised to hear from those of us who knew Hiltner that he did not only listen and that Barth did not only proclaim.

MEDIATING MODELS: THURNEYSEN AND ODEN

However, within a few years, models for bridging these two worlds began to appear. The first was from Eduard Thurneysen.[4] Thurneysen was a Barthian who brought the Barthian theology of proclamation directly into the sphere of pastoral care. Pastoral care, for Thurneysen, was primarily a matter of deepening a troubled Christian's sense of justification. For Thurneysen, behind all human problems was the sin of self-justification. The source of all human spiritual difficulties was the drive to earn one's own salvation, one's own justification—either before other humans, before oneself, or before God. Care and counseling was a relentless process of pronouncing, yes, proclaiming in the intimacy of a caring relationship, that all justification comes from God and must be received in faith. In Thurneysen's formulation, the dichotomy between inner and outer, immanence and transcendence, became more of a dialectic. God's justifying grace came totally from the outside. Rather than hurled like bolts of lightning from some elevated pulpit, however, it was now gently and persistently communicated within the confines of an intimate conversation.

I must admit that at times we questioned whether his theory of counseling was psychologically sound. Those of us with training in psychotherapy knew how a loss of sense of self-worth was central to so many human problems. We knew that such a loss led to a variety of self-justifying measures. We began to wonder whether there was a link between a Barthian theology of proclamation and the requirements of care and counseling. Maybe a persistent and quiet witness to God's justifying grace was precisely what so many people needed who were destroying themselves with their self-justifying maneuvers. If it is true that we know ourselves as we are known by others, maybe a Barthian perspective on pastoral care and counseling, as Thurneysen represented it, was just what was needed. If this were true, the earlier perceived tension between pastoral care and proclamation, some thought, may have been an illusion and a false dichotomy.

Barth, it seemed for a moment, may have been right about both pastoral care and preaching. In both places, we proclaim the justifying grace of God against all efforts at self-justification. In preaching, we do it publicly from the pulpit; in pastoral care, we do it gently but persistently in the intimacy of the one-to-one or small-group conversation. In both places the flow is from outside to inside, from the minister's witness to the justifying determinations of God downward to the inner restructuring of a person's selfhood.

Thurneysen's perspective was soon reinforced by the creative early writing of Thomas Oden.[5] Oden turned the Barth-Rogers discussion upside down. But in doing so, he made Barth, not Rogers, the victor. Oden tented a hidden ontological assumption in the Rogersian perspective. He noticed, quite correctly, that Rogers believed that the counselor's active listening to the client was a way of communicating respect to the client. But the word *respect* was actually too weak for what Rogers had in mind. In his early work, he used the word *acceptance* instead of the tamer word *respect*.[6] In his later work, he coined the exotic terms *unconditional positive regard* and *prizing* to communicate what he thought careful and consistent listening conveyed to clients.[7] Good, careful, and constant listening to all of a person's feelings and verbal communications conveyed, Rogers thought, a sense that the troubled person was a being of unconditional worth and value.

Oden detected a hidden ontological assumption in this therapeutic attitude for which secular psychology itself could not account. If the counselor was to convey an attitude of unconditional positive regard to the client, Oden believed that the counselor had to assume that the client was indeed of unconditional value, not only to the counselor, but to something beyond both client and counselor. Oden held that the secular counselor's belief in the worth of the client assumed an ultimate structure or framework of valuation—a structure that Oden believed only God could provide.

Hence, Oden believed that the Barthian view of God as *Deus pro Nobis* (God for us) provided an explicit clarification of what the Rogersian counselor assumed but could not explicitly articulate. The reason the counselor could assume the unconditional worth of the client was because God in God's *being for us* (*Deus pro Nobis*) had already assigned to all humans this worth.[8] The counseling process, to Oden, was a long and protracted implementation of this ontologically grounded attitude into the psyche and the experiencing of the client, thereby overcoming the client's own idolatrous conditions of worth—the client's own efforts to justify herself or himself.

Once again, as in the case with Thurneysen, counseling needed Barth and proclamation more than the reverse. The accent was still, as it was for Thurneysen, from the outside in and from above to below. Counseling could indeed free the troubled person, but it was a freedom that was bestowed from the outside and from above. Counseling was a form of proclamation just like preaching. In preaching, the minister declared the gospel of *Deus pro Nobis* explicitly and intentionally. In care and counseling, ministers witnessed to the same message implicitly in their attitudes and in the quality of their relations.

Those readers who know something of this story will remember that Oden and I hit on much the same insight at about the same time—he from a Barthian perspective and I from a process theology and Hartshornian perspective.[9] Oden believed it required the explicit revelation of God in Jesus Christ to make manifest the hidden assumption behind the basic attitudes of all good counselors. I argued that, in addition, the reality of God's attitude toward humans could be sensed in the thickness of our ongoing experience.

Oden and I knew that behind both Barth and Hartshorne was Anselm and his formulation of the ontological argument for God. Both Barth and Hartshorne held that our particular, concrete judgments about the good and the true are surrounded by larger assumptions about the really good and the truly true. We were both, in different ways, trying to unpack the larger assumptive world implicit in secular formulations of the counseling process. We were both certain that the assumptions that animate the secular psychotherapeutic process do not stand on secular foundations, and we were trying to determine what they in reality did stand on. Neither of us, at that time, investigated more hermeneutical models for uncovering those deeper assumptions undergirding both secular and religious counseling. This is a resource more available today and one to which I will now turn.

HERMENEUTICS VERSUS REALISM IN RELIGIOUS EPISTEMOLOGY

Barth was an epistemological realist. By this I mean he believed that we humans know something when our minds are completely conformed to the object we are trying to grasp. This is the way we know things in the finite world, he thought, and it is also the way we know God. God is known when our minds are conformed to God's determination of us. To know God is, in many ways, to get rid of ourselves and denude ourselves of the constructs, hopes, aspirations, and distortions we bring to the rest of experience. Preaching witnesses to God's determination of us. In preaching, ministers should remove their own wants, hopes, and aspirations from the process of proclamation. In hearing the gospel, the listener should do the same.

A Barthian view of care implied the same thing. If Oden and Thurneysen were right, the emphasis in care was so much on God's justifying love coming from the outside it seemed at times that the counselee's experience and selfhood brought only distortion and self-justification and never strengths. Epistemological realism stood behind both a Barthian view of preaching and a Barthian view of care. Solving the split between care and preaching with the Barthian realism of Thurneysen and Oden seemed attractive for a time but soon grew problematic, as James Lapsley pointed out to me in both written and spoken communications.

It took years for some of us to realize that the problem lay with the inadequate epistemologies on both sides—the side of Rogers and the side of Barth. If Barth was an epistemological realist, Rogers was a radical epistemological constructivist; meaning for him came from shaping the world to fit needs and tendencies that come from within. It gradually dawned on some of us that neither epistemology was adequate. We could not be epistemological realists while preaching and radical constructivists while counseling. Nor should we reduce care and counseling to the epistemological realism of Barth. Finally, we certainly should not reduce preaching the gospel to the radical constructivism of Rogers.

UNDERSTANDING AND THE HERMENEUTICAL MODEL

The differences between Rogers and Barth were not just that one was a humanist and the other a Christian. There was that difference, but there was something more. The difference was in their general epistemology—their general theory of understanding. Rogers's constructivism made him more Platonic; knowing the truth was a matter of looking inward and bringing what was inside outward and into the center of the personality. Barth was more like the naive realism of Descartes or Locke; knowing was like constellating the tabula rasa of our consciousness with the impressions of the outside world.

Gradually, another model of understanding began to gain the attention of scholars in a number of fields. It was called a hermeneutic model of knowing or understanding. It had implications for how people go about understanding the Christian gospel. It had implications for how understanding and transformation take place in all forms of care and counseling, including Christian care and counseling. Although several of us saw the potential of this model of understanding in both theology and care, Charles Gerkin saw its potential in counseling more profoundly than most.[10]

The word *hermeneutics* is a frightening word. It seems to be an un-American word—foreign to our intellectual traditions and familiar terminologies. In many ways it is foreign. It is a word used in European intellectual circles more than it is used in the United States, although we have our own rich American traditions of hermeneutics. Hermeneutics is the theory of how humans come to understand or interpret the gesture, words, and meanings of other humans, especially when these words and gestures are written in texts. More specifically, it has to do with how we understand human gestures and words in contrast to comprehending things and objects in the natural world.

In recent decades, thanks to the work of Martin Heidegger, Hans-Georg Gadamer, Paul Ricoeur, and many others, this process of understanding has more and more been seen as a kind of dialogue or conversation.[11] The words *dialogue* and *conversation* most likely make us feel much more comfortable than does the word *hermeneutics*. The theory of understanding—the theory of hermeneutics that I am describing—makes the simple yet very profound point that all attempts to understand another human communication are like having a conversation. It is possible to go another step and say that reading a biblical text is like having a conversation. One can go further and say that counseling and caring for another person is like having a conversation. If I say, "Preaching is like having a conversation," the reader may respond, "Certainly not, at least not when my minister preaches—it is anything but a conversation. It is more like a monologue." In spite of your initial incredulity, I think that I can make my point. When they are done well, all of these examples are like conversations even though they are slightly different kinds of conversations.

To understand a human message, spoken or written, is to have a conversation. Because this is true, when understanding is profound and honest it leads to transformation. According to Heidegger and Gadamer, understanding a human communication is not like holding a scientific experiment or making an empirical observation. That is the most common misconception of understanding that Gadamer would have us set aside. Furthermore, understanding is not a long and extended act of empathy, like Dilthey thought it was in historical understanding and, indeed, Carl Rogers thought it was in counseling. It is not, as they believed, just a matter of getting as far as possible into the meanings and feelings of another person and removing, as nearly as possible, our own meanings and feelings. Rather, in contrast to these models, understanding another is like having a conversation.

According to Gadamer, good conversations have the following elements. First, people who converse are located in particular social and historical locations. They have particular concerns and unique experiences and questions. They bring these situated experiences and questions into the conversation. Second, people in conversations generally share something in common; it may be their common humanity, but it is also likely to be some shared historical experience to which they both can make reference. Third, conversations have a give-and-take quality to them; they are in this respect almost like play. Fourth, people in conversations also have to listen to the other in openness and be willing to take the risk that the other may have something important—possibly even transforming—to say. Being open to this transformation does not mean we suppress our own experiences, questions, and concerns. In fact, it is likely that the truth the other speaks will be understood as meaningful, real, relevant, and indeed revelatory only in light of our concerns and questions.

Gadamer uses this analogy of the conversation to describe what it means to understand a classic text, be it a philosophical text or a religious text such as those that contain the gospel message. Interpreting these texts is also like a conversation. It is a very practical conversation, as all genuine conversation really is. It is a conversation in which a concern for practical application dominates the conversation from the beginning. When we attempt to understand our Christian texts, we must be open to the practical concerns that bring us to the texts, and we must be willing repeatedly and seriously to take the risk of letting the text address these concerns. Understanding these texts is always a fusion between the questions we bring and the manifestations of truth in these texts that address our questions.

Both preaching and pastoral care are conversations with all of these features, but the mix of these elements in the two classes of acts is different. In addition, preaching and care in a Christian context always entail a third element—indeed, a third party. This third party is Jesus the Christ, who is thought to be most decisively revealed in a text that we call the New Testament, but who is also thought to be alive as Spirit in the life of the church.

So what does this model of understanding as conversation have to say about preaching? How can preaching be thought to be a conversation when in almost all cases it is done by a single person talking to a congregation? First, let me remind the reader that when I use the word *conversation,* I mean a hermeneutically conceived conversation in the strict sense that I have just proposed. In this sense, preaching is at least three conversations. First, it is a conversation that the minister conducts between the congregation and the text that is being preached. Second, it is a conversation between the preacher and the text. And third, it is a conversation between the preacher and the congregation. I am assuming that insofar as the sermon is a Christian sermon, the text in some way witnesses to the meaning of Jesus the Christ.

The first conversation is the preacher's principal task. To conduct this conversation, the minister must perform a twofold act of representation. The minister must represent the deepest, most human, and most pervasive concerns and questions of the congregation. At the same time, the preacher must attempt to represent the most authentic and most truthful response that the text makes to those questions. Here is the first point of intersection between preaching and counseling. To represent the questions of the congregation, the minister must be deeply involved with the life of the congregation and the individuals who make up this life. A ministry of care and counseling facilitates this involvement. In most good sermons, after the subject of the sermon is stated and the general direction of the sermon is announced, the minister attempts a careful description of the life experiences of the congregation and the wider society that have gone into the formulation of the question the sermon addresses. If this description of the question is not rich, nuanced, and differentiated, if the individuals in the congregation do not in some way recognize themselves in this description, the preacher probably will never carry them to the text, let alone help them to hear it. Yet I am amazed at how many sermons never describe the human experience behind the question.

I equally am amazed at how many sermons never get beyond that question, never really return to the text, never really listen to it, and never really take the risk of hearing from the text a Word that will transform. After the question is described in all its richness, the Barthian moment of the sermon begins. The otherness of the text must be allowed to shine forth. This otherness of the text must be permitted to go as far as it will—even so far as to reveal the inadequacies of the very question that was first posed to the text. For this exposure to be effective and to be heard, it must be aimed at the original question—the question that these people, this congregation, originally asked. Even to recognize that the question asked was the wrong question, the congregation must recognize it as *their* original question.

The sermon as conversation should be conceived also as a conversation between the minister's own questions and the text and, finally, a conversation between the preacher and the congregation. The individuality of the preacher can come forth only after the representative nature of the sermon has been duly satisfied. Here the minister's experiences and questions can emerge as a variation of the experiences that the congregation recognizes. The minister's response to the text becomes a possible illustration of a response that the congregation may have as well.

Finally, in really great sermons, the conversation between question and text is a critical conversation. Not all sermons achieve this, and not all preachers have the skill to do this honestly and openly. In hermeneutic theory, there is a debate between those who see understanding as primarily a fusion between the question and the response of the text and those who believe that the response of the text should in some way be tested and further defended.[12] Sermons are not systematic theological treatises; but some great sermons, after staging the initial encounter between question and response, permit new questions, new doubts, and genuine skepticisms to come back into play. A critical conversation emerges. The scriptural text does not get the last word so easily. A struggle ensues. Additional appeals are brought into play—appeals from experience, from reason, from other parts of the tradition. Although definitive closure may not be achieved, good reasons are further advanced that support the plausibility and truth of the scriptural response.

Such a sermon goes beyond the constructivism of Rogers but still attends to the experience of the congregation in forming the question. Such a sermon tempers the epistemological realism of Barth, acknowledging that the meaning of the gospel is only a meaning in light of the questions and human experiences that are brought to it.

Care and Counseling

Pastoral care and pastoral counseling are conversations as well, but the various components of the conversation are weighted differently than in preaching. Here, too, the conversation is a three-way conversation between text, counselor, and the troubled person. In all forms of care and in more structured counseling, however, concern with the questions and experiences of the troubled person are of even deeper interest. The preacher describes the questions of a congregation, the questions of the larger society, or the general questions of human existence. The counselor and caregiver, on the other hand, try to describe the questions and experiences of this concrete person. Not only does the counselor describe this person, but the counselor tries to communicate this understanding back to the troubled person.

Increasingly, pastoral counselors use two interpretive perspectives to understand the experience of a person. One is a genetic perspective that uses psychological developmental categories to see experience in terms of its origins and developmental history. Insofar as the caregiver is a Christian, the other more dominant interpretive perspective is the Christian message itself and what it reveals about the past and present as well as for the possible future of the person.

Most counseling theory concentrates so much on hearing the questions the troubled person is asking that it fails adequately to attend to the pastoral responses that make care a conversation. The reverse, as we saw, is true of preaching. Sometimes preaching so concentrates on the response of the gospel that we cannot discern the question that makes it a conversation.

In counseling and care, the person of the counselor plays a slightly different role than in preaching. In preaching, the preacher tries mostly to stand aside and conduct a genuine confrontation between congregation and text. In counseling and care, the actual person of the counselor plays a greater role as a metaphorical representative of the Christian texts. The texts themselves may or may not play a direct role in counseling and care. This depends on the troubled person, the context of care, and the permissions that both troubled person and institutional context give for the introduction of the scriptural text. Whether the text is present or absent, the person of the counselor must be a metaphor of the gospel message disclosed in the text. The interaction between counselor and troubled person is still very much a conversation between the questions and the old answers of the troubled person and the answers and new questions disclosed by the gospel, sometimes through the person of the counselor as metaphor. Now the gospel must be embodied in the attitudes of constancy, affirmation, acceptance, forgiveness, and grace reflected, and yet never fully captured, in the person of the counselor.

The counselor is not Christ, but a metaphor for Christ. I use the word *metaphor* because even more than symbol, it communicates the broken and fragmented way in which the pastoral counselor represents the love of God in Christ, for there are many ways in which Christian counselors are broken themselves. For this reason, their own love, acceptance, and constancy are flawed. The genius of Christian counselors is their capacity to communicate a love, constancy, and acceptance that is not their own. Their love and constancy assumes a text, a story, and a structure of meaning that transcends and yet grounds their own love and constancy.

Because in Christian care the person of the caregiver is simultaneously so important yet so limited, the conversation in this context must be allowed to have a critical moment. Doubts must be allowed to surface. Rebuttals from the client must be heard. Negativities and new questions must be allowed to express themselves. The finitude and brokenness of the counselor must be acknowledged. The explicit or implicit witnesses of the gospel must be permitted to be tested. The subtle testimonies of reason and experience must be allowed into play. If the truth of the gospel is to prevail, all enemies to it must be allowed to register their complaints, even in the counseling relationship.

The constructivism of Rogers and the realism of Barth are both transcended. The experiences and questions of the client are permitted into the conversation, but they do not produce their own answers in the way Rogers envisioned. The answers of the gospel are permitted to come forth, but never quite in the monological way Barth envisioned. In the end, in many ways every preacher is, in the act of preaching, a counselor just as is every Christian counselor a witness and proclaimer of the gospel.

NOTES

1. Karl Barth, *Church Dogmatics*, vol. 1, pt. 1 (Edinburgh: T. & T. Clark, 1936).

2. Seward Hiltner, *Pastoral Counseling* (Nashville: Abingdon Press, 1959), 28–33.

3. Carl Rogers, *Counseling and Psychotherapy* (Boston: Houghton Mifflin, 1942); and *Client-Centered Therapy* (Boston: Houghton Mifflin, 1951).

4. Eduard Thurneysen, *A Theology of Pastoral Care*, trans. Jack A. Worthington and Thomas Weiser (Richmond: John Knox Press, 1962).

5. Thomas Oden, *Kerygma and Counseling* (Philadelphia: Westminster Press, 1966); and *Contemporary Theology and Psychotherapy* (Philadelphia: Westminster Press, 1967).

6. Rogers, *Counseling and Psychotherapy*, 113.

7. Carl Rogers, "A Theory of Therapy, Personality, and Interpersonal Relationships," in *Psychology: A Study of a Science*, vol. 3, ed. Sigmund Koch (New York: McGraw-Hill, 1959), 196–230.

8. Oden, *Kerygma and Counseling*, 115–45.

9. See the similarities and differences between Oden's *Kerygma and Counseling* and my *Atonement and Psychotherapy* (Philadelphia: Westminster Press, 1966).

10. Charles V. Gerkin, *The Living Human Document: Revisioning Pastoral Counseling in a Hermeneutical Mode* (Nashville: Abingdon Press, 1984).

11. Martin Heidegger, *Being and Time* (London: SCM Press, 1962); Hans-Georg Gadamer, *Truth and Method* (New York: Crossroad, 1982); Paul Ricoeur, *Hermeneutics and the Human Sciences* (Cambridge: Cambridge University Press, 1981).

12. For a revised correlational (sometimes called "critical" correlational model of hermeneutics), see David Tracy, *Blessed Rage for Order* (Minneapolis: Seabury Press, 1975) and my *A Fundamental Practical Theology: Descriptive and Strategic Proposals* (Minneapolis: Fortress Press, 1991).

9
We Belong Together:
Toward an Inclusive Anthropology

E M M A   J.   J U S T E S

In his 1986 article in *Pastoral Psychology*, "The 'Self,' Its Vicissitudes and Possibilities," James Lapsley restates a call he made in *Salvation and Health* in 1972, a call for a more adequate theological anthropology. Lapsley's call still seeks an adequate response. We are still without an adequate anthropology that would better inform pastoral care. One of the ways in which theological anthropology can become more adequate involves the inclusion of those voices that would be considered to be "different."

Theological anthropology has been developed from a limited perspective. The voices of women, people of color, and people of varied languages and cultures have been underrepresented in the shaping of theological anthropology (and consequently, in the shaping of pastoral care and pastoral theology).

Instead of the voices of "different" people being heard in the shaping of anthropology, anthropology has had a role in shaping the people. How we have interpreted who we are, under God, has influenced how we have understood those who are neither white nor male. How we understand ourselves and are understood by others leads to what we do and believe and what is done to and with us in families, in churches, and in societies. Although anthropology has been tacitly understood as universal, it has failed to be inclusive.

This essay focuses on the role that our perception of difference has had in our understanding of both ourselves and others. It addresses our relationships and the development of the structures within which our relationships exist. My premise is that for adequate pastoral care to be developed, different voices must be heard and incorporated into our understanding of theological anthropology. Difference need not divide. Rather, differences may enhance our understanding, not only of the whole of humanity, but also of ourselves individually and of God. With an expanded worldview, brought about by the inclusion of different voices, pastoral care itself will be different.

In 1968 at Princeton Theological Seminary, Jim Lapsley, after making a point in a lecture, turned to me (as I remember it, the only woman in the class) and asked me whether the point he had made checked out with my perception as a woman. No one in my education thus far had ever suggested that a woman's voice was a "different voice" that was missing. Lapsley's point was made. He was not accepting of the universality of thought or theory that came from an exclusive point of view. I realize now that this was not a momentary divergence from the agenda of the day, but was consistent with Jim Lapsley's work. He saw the need for, and attempted to include, underrepresented voices. We do well to follow in his footsteps. The attempt he began will be taken further in this essay.

I will begin with an overview of some of the problems that are created in relationships within church and society by hearing a singular voice for the shaping of anthropology. We will see that when only a singular voice is heard, true differences among people are both ignored and overemphasized. Then I will present alternative ways to look at some theological roots for the development of anthropology. The alternatives proposed are meant to be more suggestive than conclusive. Finally, I will offer some possible implications for the functioning of pastoral care in light of this wider anthropological perspective.

An Interpretation of Who We Are: The Problem

Difference has become defining. Dividing has become our mode. Jean Baker Miller raised a question at the very beginning of *Toward a New Psychology of Women* about what we do with people who are different from us.[1] This question is of vital importance to the practice of pastoral care.

What we tend to do with people who are different is to create hierarchy. Every difference we perceive can be interpreted as a base for decisions about better or worse, right or wrong. In a hierarchical societal context, one has to be either one-up or one-down. We do not easily accept difference as merely difference. Difference always has more meaning. Difference is at the heart of "Us-Them" thinking and believing, of building dualisms and dichotomies and creating divisions.

Difference readily becomes adversarial. We come to see ourselves as "opposite" sexes, and we discover ourselves enmeshed in a "war between the sexes." Men wonder and ask, "What do women want?" and "What are women like?" from interpersonal, psychological, and theological perspectives. It is clear who is the speaker and who is the "other" when these questions are raised. Similar questions are raised regarding differences in race and culture. "We" are not sure what "they" are like or what "they" want. In this position, we become opponents, adversaries, and, perhaps most important from a theological perspective, we become alienated.

Emphasis and focus on what is different about us has, in turn, created greater difference. Expectations developed according to gender and race lead to perception and socialization that create and reinforce difference. For example, we develop different gifts as strengths as women and men within this matrix. Different human characteristics are expected, encouraged, and sustained for women than for men. Consequently, we see those characteristics in women that we expect of women and those in men that we expect of men. Differences emphasized as we develop in different directions drive us further apart. Our ability to see one another clearly is further dimmed as we view one another across an expansive gulf.

Social constructions reflect separateness and brokenness. We divide ourselves according to gender, race, class, culture, sexual orientation, tribe, language or dialect, nation, level of education, age, abilities, faith, political party, gang, and so on. The list is almost endless, for we continue to discover ways to "break down" humanity into various parts. We divide over and over again according to ideologies and over issues that are of importance to us. Standing in separate "camps," the distance is emphasized, and others are seen only through an image we carry of them and not face to face as they really are. The divisions we create in the ways we see one another often become dualisms, and "the other" is viewed as being at the far end of a particular spectrum. In these divisions, humanity fails to see itself as one. In this failure to see ourselves as one, we experience alienation, and hostility thrives.

The differences perceived and created by our perceptions may tend to become invisible to us when we examine ourselves psychologically or theologically. For example, an understanding of the meaning of "self" has been an issue in anthropology. Jim Lapsley discusses characteristics of the self as inclusive of self-esteem and a sense of identity.

This understanding of self has been determined from a singular perspective of those who are in power. Self-esteem and identity remain central struggles in the experience of women and all who have been considered to be the "other." For women to have a sense of identity apart from identification that is attributed to women by their relationships with men has not been expected or desirable (we may imagine that this has changed in recent years). The fact that for women, attaining adequate self-esteem continues to be a battle against theological tradition as well as social convention is one example of how differences among us, unaddressed, distort any creation of an adequate anthropology. (See Linda Tschirhart Sanford and Mary Ellen Donovan's *Women and Self-Esteem*.[2] The use of this book in seminary classes has brought out powerful recognition from women students aware of the struggle for self-esteem for themselves and for women they know.)

In thinking about difference, we also confront the issue of race. We assume that differences in races are "given." Ashley Montague in 1964 challenged this accepted view of humanity when he wrote about race as "man's most dangerous myth." Regarding slavery in America, he wrote:

> The idea of "race" was, in fact the deliberate creation of an exploiting class which was seeking to maintain and defend its privileges against what was profitably regarded as an inferior social caste. . . .
>
> [The slaves'] different physical appearance provided a convenient peg upon which to hang the argument that this represented the external sign of more profound ineradicable mental and moral inferiorities. . . . [T]he obvious difference in their social status, in caste status, was equated with their obviously different physical appearance, which, in turn, was taken to indicate a fundamental biological difference. Thus was a culturally produced difference in social status converted into a difference in biological status.[3]

Even though slavery elsewhere existed prior to slavery in America, previously it had not been based on the perception of an entire "race" of people being inferior. In order for slavery to exist in America, this had to be the route taken. The declaration made that all men were created equal with rights to liberty and justice had formed a foundation that had to be circumvented in order to enslave human beings.

Montague quoted the Reverend Samuel Stanhope Smith, a Presbyterian clergyman, who wrote:

> If we compare together only those varieties of human nature by which the several sections of mankind differ most widely from one another, the difference is so great that, on the first view, it might very naturally lead to the conclusion that they must belong to distinct species. But, when we come to examine more particularly the intermediate grades which connect the extremes, and observe by what minute differences they approach, or recede from, one another; and when we observe further, that each of these minute gradations can be traced to obvious and natural causes, forming so many links, as it were, in the great chain connecting the extremes, we are ready to call into question our first impressions.[4]

What has come to appear to be so natural in our views of humanity may be more our creation than a "natural condition."

The experience of South African Blacks today may be another way to illustrate the mythical nature of our concepts of race. The South African government has "created" a race designated as "coloured" (referred to in South Africa by many folks as the "so-called coloured" race). The "so-called coloured" are supposedly those who are of mixed black and white races. Differences in appearance or ability, even genetics, do not determine this designation. To be "coloured" is to have a European surname, regardless of the shade of one's skin or other physical characteristics. This designated "race" has been a source of further alienation and division among people of color in South Africa, to the clear advantage of the Whites who are in power.

We assume that we can "see" what race a person is without awareness that within each of the designated racial groups there is as much variety as there is from one racial group to another. Our perception of ourselves as God's human community has seen us as divided into races only since the eighteenth century, when the exploitation of people of other colors became economically expedient.[5]

Although we have placed great importance on separating ourselves according to differences within humanity and have structured societies accordingly, theologians have proceeded often without regard for the existence of differences. This is as great a problem as our perpetual dividing of ourselves. When actual differences are not recognized, theology does not address those whose voices have not been heard in creating the theology. We have tended, on the one hand, to presume that there are no differences and that a particular theology is relevant for every person. On the other hand, we tend to make more of the differences than we should.

WHO WE ARE AS GOD'S HUMANITY:
A BASE FOR THEOLOGICAL ANTHROPOLOGY

An approach to theological anthropology includes a list of assertions about ourselves that appear to be contradictory. We know ourselves as having been created in the image of God. We enjoy a special place as the children of God. As part of God's family, created in God's image, we both bear the image of God and remain part of the created order. We also know ourselves as fallen creatures who have failed in obedience and faithfulness to God and thus experience alienation from God and one another. We may live out our theology experiencing ourselves as alienated from God and struggling to gain God's favor or avoid God's punishment.

Further, we know ourselves as redeemed humanity, restored to relationship with God and one another through Jesus Christ. We may be comforted by an understanding of Christ suffering with us, while at the same time we can see both those who suffer and ourselves when we suffer as somehow demonstrating the results of God's judgment. When we are not suffering, we see ourselves as blessed by God. At times we may think that the less we suffer, the closer we are to God, even as we may remember and tell one another that Christ is present in our suffering.

We are both good and bad; fallen and redeemed; sinners and saved. Although we experience ourselves as individuals—separate, loved by God as individuals, and in a personal relationship with God—we also experience our separateness and, at times, our alienation from one another. We know ourselves as redeemed through Jesus Christ to a relationship of being one in Christ. We are both separate and united with others. We are created in the image of God as both female and male, as a human community of diverse individuals. We are both unique and alike within this diversity.

Theology is full of assertions that seem to be ambiguous, contradictory, or "both/and" as this list demonstrates. Somehow we manage to hold these ambiguities in tension as we think about ourselves as God's human creation. Whenever our theological reflections and assertions favor one side or the other of these contradictions, our anthropology becomes distorted. When we feel we must decide whether humanity is basically good or bad, whether we are being or going to be punished, or whether we are saved and secure, we are in the midst of making decisions about difference. We do not rest comfortably in the midst of ambiguities, so we seek clearer images of humanity that can tell us precisely how things are. For example, we want to know exactly what it means that we were created as female and male.

Theological anthropology has developed under the pretense of being inclusive of and relevant for all of humanity. I am suggesting that our difficulties with the inadequacy of theological anthropology begin with how we perceive difference, how we interpret it, and how we act on it. Without attention to valid differences and without effort to keep them in perspective and not create differences where none exist, we cannot adequately perceive what it means to be human.

Valerie Saiving Goldstein has suggested that there has been a predominant traditional view of sin that may be understood as reflective of the singular nature of the origins of our traditional theology. She has suggested that humanity's temptations to sin have been shared unequally by women and men. Man has had a greater temptation toward pride and woman toward sloth.[6] The traditional emphasis on pride has ignored the different inclination of women. Women have been the hearers of sermons warning them against being prideful while they struggled to have a positive sense of self-esteem. Theology has been developed and presented as though it is relevant equally for all humanity, in this case, under the assumption that all human beings are equally tempted to be prideful. At the same time, there have been expressions of concern regarding the differences between genders and races of people. When questions of the particularity of the place of women emerge, the difference between female and male has been exaggerated, claiming that women cannot be leaders and cannot serve in God's ministry as pastors.

A reading of the Genesis accounts of creation may be used to illustrate how gender difference can be both ignored and over-emphasized. In Genesis 1, even though the female and male are created simultaneously, both are addressed as created in God's image, and both are given dominion over the rest of creation, the point has often been ignored that dominion was given to the woman as well as to the man (Gen. 1:28).

The creation story in Genesis 2 begins with a unified humanity, referred to by Phyllis Trible as a "sexually undifferentiated earth creature."[7] We witness Adam as he discovers the presence of Eve for the first time. "Aha!" he exclaims (the author's interpretation). "Bone of my bones and flesh of my flesh." Adam first recognizes the sameness—face, arms, legs, hands, feet, elbows, knees, shoulders—all of these parts and many others that they had in common. He first sees similarities. This one is not like the others he has seen but is more like himself. He expresses delight for the ways in which she is like him as no other creature has been in all of God's creation. Secondarily, he notices the difference.[8] She is not exactly like man; instead he identifies her as woman.

Throughout our theological history, we have leaned more heavily on the second response than on the first. This inclination has created a distorted theological anthropology that has emphasized difference without also valuing sameness and has ignored the oneness of our origins.

When we look at the Fall, we might consider a related interpretation. When Adam and Eve eat of the fruit of the tree of knowledge of good and evil, their eyes are opened and they suddenly notice their nakedness and are ashamed (Gen. 3:7–11). Prior to this point, they were aware of the difference, but not until this point does it become a matter of shame (see Gen. 2:25). This new sense of shame suggests to me that we might interpret the entry of sin into the human experience as a point at which difference was made too much of. Adam and Eve saw their differences as something to hide, as something that was alienating rather than as gift. Might not it be at the very heart of our sinfulness that we make too much of our differences?

A theological base for the establishment of apartheid in South Africa has been an understanding of God as being the one who separates and divides. At creation God separated the light from the darkness and the land from the water (Gen. 1:4–10). God's desire to separate is understood as being the essence of God and what God aims for. Looking at South Africa, we can see what anthropology looks like from that starting point. We see a humanity divided by race, and these divisions of race made the grounds of oppression.

In some ways, I am able to look at this interpretation and see it as an interpretation that could be valid. There is a base in scripture. Yet when I turn to Jesus of Nazareth, identified as the Christ, what I see is a drawing together. He drew people to himself and drew people together from widely separated societal strata, with national, religious, and cultural differences. He included, rather than excluded, women, refusing to divide them from men. When he was confronted by a woman for taking a position that reinforced division, he welcomed her criticism and came to a new awareness as a result (Matt. 15:22–28 and Mark 7:24–30).

Humanity, existing in our constructed divisions of culture, race, and gender, has been made one in Jesus Christ (Gal. 3:28). What is divided is restored. What was encompassed in the human creation has become one again in Jesus Christ. Our difficulty in realizing this oneness is demonstrated in the urgency expressed in the question "Who are we without these divisions that give us identity?"

The most powerful message regarding the overcoming of difference and division comes in the form of incarnation, God made human flesh to dwell among us. We can begin to look at creation not as separate from redemption. The understanding of the two comes together in a new way when we view them from the perspective of overcoming difference. What this new perspective leads to is not a small or simple shift in self-perception.

The overcoming of our divisions requires nothing less than transformation. It is a transformation that can come about when we are liberated from the oppression that comes through our hierarchical divisions of humanity into multiple identities and oppositions. This transformation comes both through our restoration to the oneness of our created nature and our redeemed nature in Christ, and participates in this restoration. Jesus Christ, who demonstrates to us the willingness of God to break down barriers as he becomes God With Us, is the source for the interactive process of liberation, restoration, and transformation.

We are called to a liberation from the bonds of division that become oppressive as they limit our access to the full range of human gifts and subject us to perspectives on one another that diminish the value of some human beings. We are called to a transformation of the social structures within which we live as they deceive us into thinking that the way it is is the only way it can be—that humanity in its divisions is God's will for us and the only way we can live and work together. We are called to a restoration of oneness within humanity that was ours at creation and has been restored to us through Jesus Christ.

What We Can Do as God's Caregivers: A Direction

As pastoral caregivers and pastoral theologians, we examine the implications of any view of humanity, looking for what it signifies about our understanding of people and our care for them. An experience with a particular teaching occasion will present what can result when we bring ourselves together rather than divide ourselves from one another.

I was teaching two Doctor of Ministry classes concurrently. Both were sections of a pastoral theology course. In the process of the two classes, we discovered that the time for presentation of case materials was too short for everyone to have class time to make an individual presentation. In one class the students chose to determine who would present on a first-come-first-serve basis. Those who volunteered first got to present, and the others would learn from the presentations of their classmates and not from presenting their own case materials.

In the second class something quite different occurred. The students decided that everyone would present and that the time for presentations would not be cut short or expanded. The students decided to examine the subjects of their case materials to see where there would be common threads and then to group themselves together to make joint presentations around these common themes shared with their copresenters. There was no model for these students to follow. They had to create the model themselves. What this meant for the students in this class was that they had to work very hard to figure out what common threads there were without doing a disservice to the cases they chose to present anywhere along the way. They then had to work even harder to try to make a coherent presentation from three or four different case situations. The results were astounding! The students acquired more comprehensive understandings of their own cases and significant ownership in the cases of others. It worked, and what the students gained from these shared presentations far exceeded their expectations, and mine as well.

We can examine the work of the students who decided to create joint presentations to find some directions for the practice of pastoral care. First, one must honestly acknowledge that it becomes harder work to come together than it is to divide. Our experience has been extensive in dividing. We have much less success in getting together. Second, their experience says that we do not have to assume "either/or" circumstances, even when situations seem to present this as reality. They could have said, "Either you get to present, or I get to present." Instead, they chose the alternative that said, "None of us will be left out, and we will all present." They chose for mutuality and community rather than individuality and independence.

Third, their struggle was one of creating a synthesis along with doing an analysis. They had to examine the pieces of their individual cases to see what was there in order to come together with a common theme. They also had to see together how their pieces would fit into a unified theme. Because they were "working against the stream" and not in the usual way expected, with an individualistic and hierarchical first-come-first-served model, they had to struggle much harder than the students in the other course who simply worked out, individually, the presentation of their cases.

Fourth, the students who participated in shared presentations discovered that this work required a greater intimacy among the members of the presentation teams. Their choice functioned to minimize differences rather than to value status. Deborah Tannen writes:

> Intimacy is key in a world of connection where individuals negotiate complex networks of friendship, minimize differences, try to reach consensus and avoid the appearance of superiority, which would highlight differences. In a world of status, independence is key.[9]

The work of the second group could not be done in isolation. Their work demanded that they function in partnership, which, like intimacy, diminished distances between them. As partners working on common themes for presentations, they saw their own case situations in the cases of others. This process not only helped them to understand and participate with one another, but also enabled them to have a fuller understanding of their own cases.

The second group of students were freed from old hierarchical models of doing course work. They experienced a restoration to oneness as God's people. They came together from across the whole American continent, from California to Massachusetts, and from around the world, including Korea and Germany. They were, it is interesting to note, all women. Their work in the course and their ministries underwent transformation.

The choices that these students made and the process that they followed suggest benefits in the use of analysis and synthesis together. The tendency in Western thinking is to honor analysis as the way to arrive at understanding. In African thought, synthesis is given greater value. We can use both of these modes to focus on how we fit together, how we make up the whole of humanity, as well as what the pieces are of which we are made.

Bonganjalo Goba, a South African theologian, looks at human anthropology from a perspective of the need for healing of human brokenness. He makes a case against the "privatization of faith." When faith is a matter of private concern between me and my God, a matter of my relationship with Jesus Christ, it fails to consider the circumstances of society and those around me who suffer and who may be suffering under my oppression. Such faith contributes to brokenness rather than to the healing that God desires for humanity: "[T]he emphasis is on the salvation of the individual, a highly spiritualized notion of salvation which refuses to incorporate a political understanding of salvation."[10]

Goba says that pastoral theology "should reflect a theological self understanding that is thoroughly aware and critical of the existing sociopolitical context."[11] Privatization of faith compels division and fails to move us toward oneness in Christ. Its impetus is individualistic, and it does not contribute to the dissolution of barriers that divide humanity. Pastoral theology must take this into account when it seeks an adequate anthropology.

Conclusions

In our search for an adequate theological anthropology, we will need to take dramatic steps away from some of the distortions our theological traditions have engendered. A focus on the created and restored oneness of humanity gives us a direction that can lead us away from the social and theological constructions that divide humanity into multiple and alienated segments.

Movement toward the perception and the realization of our oneness as humanity can be aided by relying on synthesis as well as analysis to understand ourselves and one another. We can begin to take the reality of the incarnation seriously as it demonstrates the dissolution of perceived barriers within and among us. Just as Jesus was both human and divine, we are both human and bear the image of God. We can begin to see that many instances of "either/or" are neither but are rather "both/and." The problem and the solution are both present in the situation, and one is not found outside of the situation (whether it be the problem or the solution that we seek outside).

Greater intimacy can develop when we are not bound by patterns that divide us from one another. We must be able to understand intimacy in a theological context and to tolerate the vulnerability it places on us as caregivers. When we cling to a dividing status that creates classes of helper and helpee, we work against the development of intimacy.

A willingness to become more intimate can mean that we will be drawn away from making too much of our differences. Being closer to one another, we are enabled to see one another more clearly rather than through the lenses of stereotyped images of one another that we have been given and have participated in creating.

The creation of a new anthropology involves a transformation of perceptions that we hold and structures that limit our perceptions. This transformation involves liberation and results in restoration. We look toward a restoration of our oneness in Christ. We belong together as God's humanity.

Notes

1. Jean Baker Miller, *Toward a New Psychology of Women* (Boston: Beacon Press, 1976), 3.

2. Linda Tschirhart Sanford and Mary Ellen Donovan, *Women and Self-Esteem: Understanding the Way We Think and Feel about Ourselves* (New York: Penguin Books, 1984) is a helpful resource in examining the struggle for self-esteem that women have been and are still experiencing. Through reading this book, the women and men in seminary classes recognize their own struggle and those of the women they have known.

3. Ashley Montague, *Man's Most Dangerous Myth: The Fallacy of Race* (New York: World Publishing Co., 1965), 50, 54.

4. Ibid., 48–49.

5. Ibid., 46.

6. Valerie Saiving Goldstein, "The Human Situation: A Feminine View," *Journal of Religion* 40 (1966): 100–12.

7. Phyllis Trible, *God and the Rhetoric of Sexuality* (Philadelphia: Fortress Press, 1978), 98–99, 101–3.

8. Ibid., 99.

9. Deborah Tannen, *You Just Don't Understand: Women and Men in Conversation* (New York: Ballentine, 1990), 26.

10. Bonganjalo Goba, "The Role of the Black Church in the Process of Healing Human Brokenness," *Journal of Theology for Southern Africa* 28 (September 1979), 9.

11. Ibid., 8.

10
Incisions from a Two-Edged Sword: The Incarnation and the Soul/Spirit Relationship

JAMES E. LODER

This essay, written in appreciation of Jim Lapsley's friendship and scholarship, is focused on two points of common interest that he and I discussed periodically during our thirty years together as colleagues. The original concern was interdisciplinary methodology in practical theology, and the second was the concept of spirit, a latter-day topic on which we once considered writing a book. I have greatly appreciated his contributions both to me personally and to theological education.

My aim in this essay will be to set forth an interdisciplinary discussion that will bring the spiritual quality of human existence into focus as a foundation for practical theology. As a way of focusing the essay, I will construct it as an interpretative response to the text in Heb. 4:12–13, particularly the phrase underlined below. The reason for selecting this particular text is twofold. First, it is the *locus classicus* for claiming that the New Testament distinguishes between the soul and the human spirit. Second, it became a focus of faculty discussion related to a paper that Jim Lapsley once presented to the Princeton Seminary faculty. Although the phrase—what it means and what it might imply for theological anthropology—has nettled my thoughts ever since, I do not pretend that this essay in any way reflects either Jim Lapsley's or the faculty's part in that discussion.

Indeed, the word of God is living and active, sharper than any two-edged sword, piercing until *it divides soul from spirit*, joints from marrow; it is able to judge the thoughts and intentions of the heart. And before him no creature is hidden, but all are naked and laid bare to the eyes of the one to whom we must render an account (Heb. 4:12–13).

BACKGROUND

Without extensive historical and critical comment, it can be said that the letter to the Hebrews was written to Jewish Christians who were in danger of committing apostasy and returning to their Jewish origins. It is evident that the argument is predominantly concerned to demonstrate the adequacy of Jesus Christ to transform and fulfill all that preceded the incarnation. Two great axes of Judaism, the vertical and the horizontal, the priesthood and the Exodus to the Promised Land, are dramatically transformed. Preeminently, transformation is evident in the recognition of Jesus Christ as the great high priest whose sacrifice fulfills and completes all that had been foretold and previously achieved by the priestly tradition of the Jews, including Melchizedek, who was not a Jew. Transformation is further evident in the exodus motif, which supplies the immediate context of the passage. That is, Jesus represents the fulfillment and the completion of Moses' leadership, for in him the people are led all the way into the Promised Land, "the sabbath rest of God." The immediate background for the text is the claim that only through participation in the nature and work of Jesus Christ does one enter into the promises given long ago to the children of Israel. Only Jesus and the Word of God can and will determine the future of Israel with respect to their entering the sabbath rest of God.

If we turn now to this specific text, we can see immediately that it is neither explicitly focused on biblical anthropology nor on the soul/spirit distinction, but it does argue that such deep distinctions regarding the essence of human nature are not common knowledge; they must be disclosed through the Word of God. In effect, the text sets the decisive standpoint from which the definitive questions about the nature of human nature can be asked. More explicitly, the text is about the discerning power of the Word of God and the claim that this word alone can make the distinction between soul and spirit. Presumably this claim is not an apocalyptic foreclosure on further discussion. Rather, I assume that by faith

(Hebrews 11) one can gain insight into this distinction, but only as the Word of God may reveal it to the eyes of faith.

THE THEOLOGICAL MODEL

First, how might the Word of God be understood as a basis for interpretation here? Although there are many possibilities, the Word of God is revealed primarily and essentially in Jesus Christ. Following the classic Christian tradition, his inner nature is summarily and succinctly articulated in the Chalcedonian formula— one person, fully and truly God and fully and truly human. It is important to recognize that this formulation is not outdated dogma. Its apparent obscurity is also not the consequence of a conciliar compromise answer to questions we no longer ask. Rather, this classic formulation by the early church fathers is a theological version of the logic of complementarity, one of the most subtle and powerful forms of thought shaping contemporary science. We will say much more about the scientific context for this assertion in the following section on the model. At this point, note that the inner nature of Jesus as the Word of God can be conceived formally as a bipolar relational unity, expressing ultimate opposites in a unique relationality between God and humanity. The substance of the relationality *is* the unity, that is, the *hypostatic union*. Yet neither polarity is dissolved into the other. In this hypostatic union, Jesus' nature reveals in fully human form the very nature of God. Traditionally, this has focused on the *homousion*, the "linchpin of Christian theology," whereby it is possible for us to look at the humanity of Jesus and see God.

> The *homousion* . . . is of staggering significance. It crystallizes the conviction that while the incarnation falls within the structure of our spatio-temporal humanity in this world, it also falls within the Life and Being of God. Jesus Christ is thus not a mere symbol, some representation of God detached from God, but God in his own Being and Act come among us, expressing in our human form the Word which he is eternally in himself, so that in our relations with Jesus Christ we have to do directly with the ultimate reality of God. As the epitomized expression of that fact, the *homousion* is the ontological and epistemological linchpin of Christian theology. With it, everything hangs together; without it, everything ultimately falls apart.[1]

To put the description of Jesus' nature as the hypostatic union in the vivid metaphorical language of scripture, the Word is "living and active," a "two-edged sword." This suggests a vital and powerful unity that cuts both ways, combining the fullness and depth of humanity with the fullness and depth of God. By implication, this double-edged reality in its bipolar unity reveals both the truncated incompleteness of purely humanistic efforts to understand humanity, including its meager efforts at transcendence, and the vague, groundless insufficiency of contemporary theorists who seek to reenvision human nature through its spiritual aspect apart from the initiative of the origin of the spirit who has revealed this in a particular human being. Conceptualizing the metaphor of the two-edged sword in terms of Nicaea and Chalcedon avoids these reductionistic errors and suggests a logic that may work to unpack the remainder of the Hebrews text. Following the logic described below, we can see why the text makes the claim that only through the unique bipolar unity of the Word of God can such mysteries as the soul/spirit relationship be sufficiently disclosed.

Before proceeding further, I must pause here to lay out briefly the methodological pattern that underlies the development of the following discussion. Pascal once wrote:

> Faith embraces many truths which seem to contradict each other. *There is a time to laugh and a time to weep, etc., Responde, Ne respondeas,* etc.
>
> The Source of this [duality] is the union of the two natures in Jesus Christ; and also the two worlds (the creation of a new heaven and new earth; a new life and a new death; all things double, and the same names remaining); and finally the two natures that are in the righteous (for they are the two worlds, and a member and image of Jesus Christ. And thus all the names suit them; righteous, yet sinners; dead, yet living; living, yet dead; elect, yet outcast, etc.).

The analogical view he employs could be developed at much greater length for contemporary thought.[2] Suffice it to say here that the former mathematician, scientist, and theologian, Pascal, is working out some of the theological implications of a logic of complementarity as it appears most preeminently today at the core of quantum theory in postmodern physics.

The famous quantum physicist Niels Bohr once wrote: "[There are] two sorts of truth: triviality, where opposites are obviously absurd, and profound truths, recognized by the fact that the opposite is also a profound truth."[3] Behind this statement is Bohr's historic research into subatomic phenomena and his startling conclusion that the nature of light must be described as simultaneously both wave and particle. The generalization of his viewpoint yields the logic of complementarity or the complementarity of contradictions, which may be stated succinctly as follows:

> [Complementarity] is the logical relation between two descriptions or sets of concepts which, though mutually exclusive, are nevertheless both necessary for an exhaustive description of the situation.[4]

It has been argued elsewhere that a relational analogy may be constructed on that basis; it works across disciplinary lines but finds its ultimate theological expression in the bipolar relational unity of the hypostatic nature of Jesus Christ.[5] In the book alluded to above, *The Knight's Move*, this basic pattern of relationality, called the "strange loop model," is diagrammed as shown in figure 1.

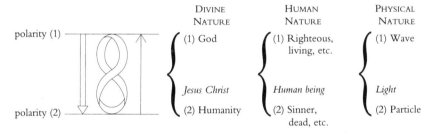

	DIVINE NATURE	HUMAN NATURE	PHYSICAL NATURE
polarity (1)	(1) God	(1) Righteous, living, etc.	(1) Wave
	Jesus Christ	*Human being*	*Light*
polarity (2)	(2) Humanity	(2) Sinner, dead, etc.	(2) Particle

FIGURE 1

The model describes an asymmetrical bipolar relationality in which there is reciprocity between polarity (1) and polarity (2). The double arrow at the left signifies that a kind of "marginal control" is exercised by polarity (1).[6] The Möbius band at the center illustrates the counterintuitive fact that, although it appears that two distinct polarities are being related, they are, in a more subtle and profound sense, a unity.[7]

For a discussion of theological anthropology, it is particularly notable that the Möbius band is a unique topological phenomenon discovered first by the grandfather of Paul J. Möbius, the latter being a psychoneurologist frequently cited by Freud and others in discussions of the mind-body relationship. This band was Paul Möbius's model of the interconnectedness of neurological and psychological realities—his solution to the mind-body problem. I am using it here in a much broader sense, but its specific anthropological implications are many and useful.

Finally, it should be quite clear that this formal model is only the basis for developing the disclosure analogies that follow. By using it to describe an aspect of the nature of Jesus Christ, I am in no way intending that it be a full or complete statement of his nature, though I believe no statement of his nature can be complete if it does not employ this form of relationality at its center. Christology is a far-reaching topic, but, for the sake of making interdisciplinary connections explicit, the model seems both accurate and workable without being reductionistic. With this model in mind, the connection between the nature of Christ and the scriptural metaphor of the two-edged sword will become generative of several implications.

TRANSITION INTO THE DISCUSSION

There are two major phases of the following argument that need to be discussed prior to any presentation of the several conclusions I want to draw at the end. The first phase consists of an effort to move into the text by natural reason, without the aid of the model; that is, without referring to the Word of God, which the text says is necessary for its being understood. Making this interpretation as plausible as possible will lay important groundwork; but as the text says of itself, the approach through natural reason will prove insufficient, and I will have to turn to the christological model. In the second phase of the argument, the deficiencies of the approach through natural reason will be analyzed, and alternatives will be constructed largely through the theology of the Spirit in Wolfhart Pannenberg's thought. The use of this source is also especially appropriate for this essay because Jim Lapsley and I worked through the Pannenberg text *Anthropology in Theological Perspective* together. Finally, we will draw certain conclusions for the theoretical foundations of pastoral care when the role of the Spirit is made definitive.

INTERPRETING THE TEXT

Apart from the christological model, let us begin to interpret the text, reflecting on the partially parallel notions: bone is to marrow, what heart is to intentions, what soul is to spirit. In a formal sense, this parallelism suggests that what is concealed from ordinary understanding is hidden because it is inside some container. Even the later reference to nakedness ("laying bare") suggests the same thing, for we hide our nakedness inside our clothing.

Further, as to substance, note how the container model works. One might simply say that marrow carries life to the bone, intentions and judgments animate the heart, and the spirit gives life to the soul. Thus the basic mystery here is the mystery of life hidden in the three "containers": bone, heart, and soul. One might see in this a tacit reference to the biblical theme that human nature is only inanimate dust until God breathes into it the breath of life and "the man became a living being" (Gen. 2:7). The bipolar unity of dust and God's breath is also exhibited in Ezekiel's experience in the valley of the dry bones. The creatures do not become living beings until God breathes into them the breath of life. Thus we seem to have a clear analogy between the dust/breath view of human nature and the death/life theme in the above three aspects of a person. Further, one might infer that the specific spirit/soul relationship is an expression of the more comprehensive breath/dust relationship and so arrive at the distinction that soul is bodily, earthly, and mortal, whereas spirit begins and ends in the very life of God.

Now we must ask what view of human nature does this imply, and does it square with human nature as revealed in Jesus Christ? Although this could entail a long discussion, it is apparent that this implies a psycho-spiritual dualism typical of agnosticism, and the conclusion is in no way reflective of Christ's nature. If the text is to be believed, then the relational nature of Jesus Christ as the Word of God must in some way be definitive for human nature and for the spirit/soul relationship in particular. Two key problems with the above interpretation will help focus an alternative. First, the container model of the relationship between soul and spirit is surely present in the text, but it is not sufficient or accurate when one views human nature through the relational nature of Christ. Second, the life/death theme is also present in the text, but a natural dualistic interpretation of this theme does not fit with the relationality inherent in Christ's nature.

Let us begin with the first problem and explore, in light of the christological model, forms of relationality and hiddenness that move beyond the container model. There are several other notions of hiddenness that point toward the sort of relationality that lies uniquely at the core of the incarnation. For instance, a thing may be hidden from sight and reason precisely because it is too large and too close for us to comprehend it. As someone said, the fish would be the last to discover water. That is, a thing may be hidden because it is the necessary condition for knowing anything; because it is the antecedent presupposition of all knowing, it can never become the object of it. Knowledge of such reality would have to come from beyond that knowing situation, that is, by revelation.

To explore the implications of this enlarged view of hiddenness, we will turn first to the writings of Wolfhart Pannenberg. Following the biblical vision of the Spirit and making surprising connections to postmodern science, Pannenberg gives an enlightening account of the Spirit as not hidden within the soul but hidden by its very transcendence with respect to it. His view envisions spirit, the ecstatic self-transcendence of life, not as something *in* the organism it animates; but rather, human spirit is a response of the organism to a power that seizes it and, by lifting it up beyond itself, the organism is inspired with creative life.[8] This squares well with persons who respond to questions about how they experience the Spirit by saying that the Spirit is both within and beyond them.[9]

An intriguing implication of Pannenberg's thesis is that it fits well with the concept of fields of force, which has been so influential in postmodern physics since Clerk-Maxwell and which underlies Einstein's theory of relativity. Pannenberg even notes that the field concept is historically rooted in the Stoic doctrine of *pneuma*. He goes on to argue that the biblical doctrine of spirit is closer to this notion than any other prevalent concept of spirit, such as those that relate to the mind (e.g., Hegelianism) or to an aspect of human existence (e.g., Gnosticism). Thus Pannenberg claims that God's Spirit can be described as a force field of infinite, creative, personal presence,[10] a mighty field of force that releases event after event into finite existence.[11] Note that this, more than the life/death parallel, is in keeping with the Genesis account; the Spirit is not only a bearer of life but the creator of man as a "living soul" (KJV) or "living being" (NRSV), as mentioned above.

Translating this model into experiential terms, it suggests that the reality of spirit is everywhere evident in the events of human life itself, but it is distinctively expressed at the human level where creative thoughts and innovative action transform intransigent or self-destructive forms of human and natural existence. Any conscious act of discovery, creation, or conscious participation in such an ecstasis or event, as well as every conversion, institutional transformation, and reformation, presupposes spirit. Yet one can only recognize spirit as such in retrospect. Spirit is the hidden presupposition of every genuine insight; thus, as an objective reality, it will always elude our objectivating consciousness. What has been revealed, however, is this: Spirit is the power of God to bring life out of inert matter or even out of nothing; and it is the power of human nature to create and compose worlds of intelligibility, meaning, purpose, and universality in the face of their opposites. Pannenberg, therefore, views spirit in human experience as expressive of the presence of God in history moving toward an ultimate and universal future that has been revealed proleptically in the resurrection of Jesus. This "exocentric centeredness" that human behavior uniquely presupposes, and by which it seeks to express the universality implicit in its acts of creation, implies that human nature is to be characterized as irreducibly spiritual.

Pannenberg's field theory view of the spirit and human nature points more adequately than does the container model to the quality of relationality that lies at the core of the incarnation. This is especially so because he views human nature as true to its spiritual nature when it intentionally creates culture and develops its own identity in accordance with and in the direction of God's nature and transformative work in history as revealed supremely in the resurrection.

There are certain major problems with Pannenberg's view. For our purposes, the primary problem is that he does not sufficiently distinguish the human spirit from the Holy Spirit. This distinction is essential for interpreting Heb. 4:12–13, for it is specifically the *human* spirit vis-à-vis the soul that is at issue there. In the Hebrews context, this distinction is to be understood in relation to, but not reduced to, the larger transformational work of the Holy Spirit described throughout the entire book, as discussed in the opening paragraphs of this essay. Moreover, it is not consistent with predominant New Testament usage to blur this distinction, as Paul Tillich, Karl Barth, Reinhold Niebuhr, and others have all recognized.

We must examine the relationship between human spirit and the

Holy Spirit further. From the standpoint of the Reformers Luther and Calvin, we are faced with the claim that the human spirit is either completely inert or is incorrigibly corrupt. Luther claims that the human spirit, unlike the soul, which is illuminated by the light of reason, has no light of its own. It is a dark room, like the holy of holies in the temple "where God dwells in the darkness of faith without light." Calvin saw the existence and persistence of idolatry as a proof that some sense of deity is inscribed on every human heart, but total perversity is inevitable in fallen human nature. Once redeemed, the human spirit plays no significant part in the human relation to God. Calvin rarely, if ever, speaks of the human spirit. The soul, not the human spirit, was the key to human nature because the power of the gospel, as he understood it, essentially obliterated the human spirit as it obliterated idolatry. Thus, for the Reformers, the human spirit was either passive or perverse, but in no case was it essential to faith or salvation.[12]

However, still within the Reformed tradition there exists an alternative view. In agreement with the long-time Princeton theologian George Hendry, I believe that human nature, deprived of an active spirit, of the power to transcend finite and mortal conditions, of the ability to act freely and to choose one's own destiny, is not truly human. Hendry argued that the incarnation has two aspects, *condescension* and *accommodation*, both of which are essential. However, the Reformers' position so overstressed condescension that it overlooked accommodation. The aim of the incarnation cannot be to obliterate what is essential to human nature, otherwise the end term of the incarnation (". . . was made man") would lack definition. Rather, the incarnation must accommodate to human nature, transform it, and restore it to its origin in God.

Assuming Hendry is correct, in what sense does the incarnation accommodate to the human spirit? Also, what does transformation and redirection of human spirit toward God—that is, restoration of human nature as spiritual—mean in the context of the incarnation?

This assumption can be squared with Pannenberg's view if we can take his own suggestion that human nature is endowed from birth with an "exocentric centeredness." For him, this tension between centeredness and exocentricity is the human spirit by which we create and compose our environment. However, the human spirit, thus understood, may turn on itself and/or become self-destructive, even through acts of creation if they are perversely conceived. In this respect, the human spirit is separable from the divine Spirit. Pannenberg wants to place the origins of such destructive separability not in the "original sin" buried in the past history of the human race, but in the unfinished history of the universe. The origin of sin is thus disembedded from the past and relocated in the future. Thus, as we have said, it would seem that constructive human action is a sound expression of the human spirit or truth-telling if it points toward or redirects history in some respect toward its fulfillment as revealed in the resurrection of Jesus Christ. Yet, even as we continue to act in accordance with our spiritual nature, the final assessment of such acts awaits the end of history. In these ways we can extract from Pannenberg's thought a distinction between human spirit and Holy Spirit without losing his subtle concept of hiddenness.

If this brief sketch of Pannenberg's view is at all correct, then the temporal origin of sin becomes an open question. However, the point for us is that the human spirit is subject to perversity and self-destruction as surely as it is capable of creative and redemptive acts. The question of the health or perversity of the human spirit depends, as we have said, on whether, in cooperation with the Holy Spirit, it is conformed to the nature of Christ. With this in mind, the above model of the relationality in Christ's nature becomes relevant. That is, the accommodation aspect of the incarnation, of which Hendry spoke, is accomplished spiritually as the relationality between Holy Spirit and human spirit recapitulates in human experience the relationality between the divine and the human in the nature of Christ. In other words, the relationality that pertains to the ultimate bipolar nature of Christ is experienced proximately in a bipolar relationship that pertains when our spirits testify with the Divine Spirit that we are the children of God (Rom. 8:16).

How can we be more concrete about this relationality and bring it into the matrix of human experience? The issue takes us into the second major problem with our initial interpretation of the Hebrews text; namely, the life/death theme. This theme must now be put in the context of Christ, the Word of God as a two-edged sword.

In light of a bipolar-relational understanding of the Word of God, it appears that the key issue in the test is not life vs. death, but relationality itself, which, if it is destroyed or distorted, leads to death. That is, in the relationality of the whole is life, and any of the parts, if separated from each other, yields death. Marrow and joints *together* give life, heart and intentions *together* are life, soul and spirit constitute a *totality* in which and only by which human life can be maintained. Moreover, it seems evident that these are not three aspects or subdivisions of the person, but three distinct ways of looking at the larger whole of the person and the relationships that constitute the whole of life.

This emphasis on interrelational wholeness can also be concretized by a critical appropriation of Pannenberg's theological anthropology. In the developmental history of the child, the "exocentric centeredness" with which we are endowed is characterized by universality. The holistic way in which the child enters the world, surrounded and nurtured by the maternal matrix, sets an enduring context within which all other developments take place. Pannenberg cites Piaget in saying that the sense of universality is never lost. Multiple differentiations and relationalities are constructed in this matrix over the course of a lifetime, but each subpart, however delineated, implies the whole.

Moreover, for Pannenberg, the implication of universality that runs in and through all the differentiations and developments of the personality is that the human spirit—in its creation of language, intelligence, culture, and social institutions—is always implicitly the bearer of a "religious thematic." That is, each differentiated achievement that issues from the human spirit implies a higher order of religious significance. Intelligence, for example, implies a higher order of intelligibility that gives it its ultimate meaning and purpose. Pannenberg is critical of Piaget for at first recognizing and asserting this fact, but then later losing sight of it in his preoccupation with the development of the part processes such as language and intelligence.[13]

If what we said before in relationship to Pannenberg's view of the Spirit/spirit relationality still pertains, then what we are seeing here is a further description of the human spirit as a relationality between the tacit sense of wholeness and the explicit differentiation of the parts within the whole from which the parts derive their meaning. In effect, the human spirit in relation to the Holy Spirit is itself a relationality (between tacit wholeness and explicit differentiated ego functions) that can only be fully itself as spirit when it is in a similar bipolar relationality with the Holy Spirit.

It will help our discussion if we refer here to a similar distinction concerning the human spirit made by Michael Polanyi in his post-critical philosophy entitled *Personal Knowledge*. Polanyi distinguishes between the tacit and the explicit dimensions of every knowing situation. This relational bipolarity can also be modeled by the strange loop pattern, and it is a helpful way to talk about the whole vis-à-vis the parts. The whole is always tacitly present and the parts explicit, but the whole exercises marginal control over the parts, as indicated by the strange loop model.

For our purposes of continuing to focus on the Hebrews text and to bring the discussion into the context of common human experience, we will first examine this relationality that characterizes the human spirit and then show how that relationality can be envisioned in the larger context of the Holy Spirit and its transformational work throughout the history of God's people. This will enable us to bring the incarnational model to bear upon the spiritual life in a graphic fashion.

Let us now turn to a fuller examination of the relationality that pertains to the inner nature of the human spirit. In his discussion of human intelligences, Howard Gardner mentions the remarkable capacity of a young male Puluwat native in the Caroline Islands to become a master navigator by combining knowledge of the stars, the topology of waves in the ocean, and geography with the knowledge of sailing.[14] By such an intuitive grasp of the whole, he can navigate efficiently through hundreds of islands. A documentary film shown on public television in 1990 showed a group of naval experts using modern technology following these Puluwat natives and marveling at how well these people could replicate the contributions of modern technology to navigation merely by their intuitive sense of the whole and where they were in it.

Although a careful study of the Puluwat techniques of navigation would reveal several distinct cause and effect connections that are turned to advantage for navigation, and a purely scientific explanation of modern navigation technology would involve links through mathematics and physics to a postmodern description of the entire known universe, the general contrast between these two approaches to navigation is striking. It illustrates quite dramatically the unexpected reliability of a sense of the whole, the power of the *tacit* dimension to yield up accurate and insightful knowledge that can then be reduced to the *explicit* level of techniques for solving problems as complex as those in navigation.

The documentary also illustrates a reverse emphasis. Seeing the efficiency of our technology, it is a great temptation to assume that it can become a thing unto itself, disconnected from its larger context. In an effort to eliminate the human error, we are tempted to eliminate the human being and the larger context of being itself. This account then has illustrative and parabolic value, because it describes the necessity for preserving on a large scale the bipolar relational unity between the whole and the parts. At the same time, it points out the hidden, powerful reliability of the tacit awareness of the whole, against which as background we can recognize that all proximate knowledge and awareness has an implicit, ultimate dimension from which it derives its meaning and purpose.

If we cast this Polanyi-like illustration back into the Pannenberg discussion, we can see that the primal sense of totality in the infant, as discussed by Piaget and Pannenberg, agrees from a developmental standpoint with a tacit sense of the whole that persists in all circumstances at all ages. Experientially, the newborn at first intuits the whole with uncanny accuracy, knowing far more for the first months of life than he or she can ever tell. Yet, even after the emergence of language and intelligence, and according to the cultural indices in which the child is raised, the tacit sense of the whole continues to function with remarkable generativity and gestaltlike accuracy, enabling the developing person to navigate often very complex and troubled relationships without losing a sense of where he or she is. This is an expression of "exocentric centeredness," provided this view of the human spirit can be construed as a reciprocal movement drawing from the tacit dimension to "make sense of" the exocentric world. It is this reciprocal relationality between the explicit and the tacit operating at all levels of complexity that I suggest constitutes the human spirit.

Note also that this is a spirit that can be broken or depersonalized if the dynamic interplay between the tacit and explicit dimensions breaks down. As such, this helps to explain the incipient spiritlessness of the most advanced technology as well as spiritlessness in a dysphoric personality: collapse of the relationality into either the exact and explicit or into the vague and diffuse can bury the spirit alive.

Ｔｈｅ Ｒｅｌａｔｉｏｎｓｈｉｐ ｏｆ ｔｈｅ Ｈｕｍａｎ Ｓｐｉｒｉｔ ｔｏ ｔｈｅ Ｈｏｌｙ Ｓｐｉｒｉｔ

Illuminating as this may be regarding the nature of the human spirit as inherently relational and implicitly religious, it does not yet describe either the relationship of the human spirit to the Holy Spirit, or answer the primary question of this essay concerning the distinction between soul and spirit. Nevertheless, this description of the human spirit is necessary background for dealing with both of these questions.

Before moving to the answers to these questions, let us focus this description of the human spirit in terms of the bipolar model. The basic unit being described is the human psyche, which has two polarities: (1) the *explicit*, which consists of the ego and the adaptational functions such as language and intelligence; and (2) the *tacit*, which consists of the various layers of unconscious life from the preconscious through personal and collective unconscious to one's organic connection to the physical universe (see figure 2).

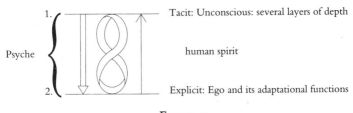

FIGURE 2

This differentiated unity, which characterizes the human psyche, is sustained as an ongoing relationality between these polarities, a relationality that we are calling the human spirit. Although much more needs to be said about this model of the psyche, this will serve as a useful summation of the discussion thus far.

The answers to the above two questions concerning the Holy Spirit and the soul are, as we will see, closely connected. In relation to the first question, recall that the overall context of the book of Hebrews describes a christological transformation of two main axes in Judaism: the vertical, or priesthood, and the horizontal, or the Exodus. This historic work of transformation can be attributed to the work of the Holy Spirit understood as *Spiritus Creator*. Transformation does not mean merely change. In Greek it is *metamorphe*, the alteration of the basic form (*morphe*) of something. It can be described by saying that within any frame of reference, when new previously hidden orders of meaning emerge to alter the basic axioms of that frame of reference, transformation has taken place. Thus, as we described it summarily, Christ transforms the priesthood by becoming himself both the priest and the sacrifice. In this, he fulfills and completes all that sacrifice was intended to accomplish as it was practiced for centuries in Judaism and so made its continuation as such unnecessary. Similarly, the Promised Land is not now Canaan, but as W. D. Davies once argued, Jesus himself. To enter into Christ is to enter into everything afforded by the Promised Land. In effect, to be in Christ is to have entered the promised "rest." All of this is accomplished by the transforming work of God's Spirit, whose principal task is to convict the world, call forth faith (Hebrews 12), and to transform all things in accordance with the nature of Christ.

Thus the relational nature of the human spirit participates in the larger, more sweeping work of the Holy Spirit when it can both sense at a tacit level and perceive at the explicit level what the transforming work of God is doing in the world and respond accordingly. To sense the presence of the Divine Spirit tacitly but to explicitly reject it, or to attempt to conform to the Divine Spirit by explicit efforts of intelligence, language, and moral judgment but to sense nothing or to have no recognition that the tacit dimension is feeding and directing explicit attention appropriately to the spiritual life in Christ, is a failure of the human spirit and a grievance to the Holy Spirit. To respond in accordance with the work of the Holy Spirit is to express explicitly and faithfully one's tacit awareness of the Divine Spirit while that *Creator Spirit* continually yields up new and often unexpected horizons of meaning: the capacity to care for the outcast and brokenhearted, the affirmation of life for oneself and for others in the face of despair and death, the joy of worship and the praise of God in times of defeat as well as in times of renewal, the capacity freely to return good for evil and to comprehend how it is that love can believe all things and never be deceived (Kierkegaard).[15] The extraordinary claims of faith and the extraordinary deeds of the faithful, catalogued in the famous twelfth chapter of Hebrews, and, indeed, the inspiration behind the writing of the text itself, are all the outcome of a dynamic relationality between the human spirit and the Holy Spirit, which replicates in its bipolar unity the very nature of Christ, the Word of God as a two-edged sword.

This is not to say that every prompting from the tacit dimension is from the Holy Spirit. That notion is the way to spiritual chaos and despair.[16] Rather, it is to say that the human spirit continually seeks an internal relational coherence as modeled by the strange loop that is in itself a small-scale version of the same relationality that pertains between the human spirit and the Holy Spirit. Spiritual integrity is the key to conscience; or, as Calvin put it, conscience is "inner integrity of heart," "heart" being often a biblical synonym for the human spirit. What I have added to Calvin on this point is the claim that such integrity is inherently relational, but always conformed to the fullest extent possible to the relational nature of Christ as the foregoing model, as previously described.

This leads into the second question and the major concern of this essay; that is, what is the distinction and connection between soul and spirit as interpreted in light of the relational nature of the Word of God?

In answer to this, were we to reflect for a moment on the model of the human spirit we have just laid out, we could scarcely avoid the conclusion that we had simply reinstated the container model with somewhat greater sophistication. This is to say, if we recognize that the *psyche* is the soul, then the human spirit is captive to it, giving it life and direction. The human spirit is unable to move beyond the adaptational concerns of the ego, which are, after all, guided more significantly by organic and unconscious concerns than by the spirit itself. In this model, the spirit simply assists the ego in satisfying the deeper needs of the psyche, maximizing satisfaction within the limits of securing survival. In fact, in psychological terms, the relationality that we have called the human spirit is less governed by any spiritual integrity of its own than by the so-called reality principle whose major tenets are survival and satisfaction.

If we are to justify our claim that this inner relationality is the human spirit and that it is not properly understood within the container model, we must turn back to Pannenberg's view of the Spirit and combine it with the transformational view of the Holy Spirit we see in the book of Hebrews. As we have said, Pannenberg views the tacit sense of wholeness and the religious thematic in psychological terms, vis-à-vis Piaget. Although he affirms that the exocentric centeredness of the psyche is spiritual, his view of the Divine Spirit far exceeds this effort to approach the nature of the spirit "from below." God's Spirit is a force field of immense power that manifests itself in both the infinitely large and the infinitely small dimension of the created order. As such, God's Spirit releases event after event into all aspects of creation, bringing forth persons who in turn manifest themselves as spiritual. How does the spiritual life become transcendent and at the same time preserve its imminent integrity in the context of human experience?

In basic agreement with the scope and magnitude of Pannenberg's position, and in keeping with the pervasive Christ-centered transformational view of the Divine Spirit in the book of Hebrews, we can conclude that the Divine Spirit calls forth the human spirit, disembedding it from its captivity to the psychic economy and making itself, the Divine Spirit, determinative of the spiritual life of the individual. No longer does the ego-centered psychic economy contain and govern the spirit in human life. Rather, the human spirit, although still in reciprocity with that psychic economy, is governed by the Spirit of God. This makes possible any number of behaviors that are not strictly consistent with the reality principle, such as returning good for evil, forgiving those who persecute, and rejoicing in suffering. Such behaviors, which must be ascribed to pathology of the ego in the psychological model, are the norm for those who "walk in the spirit." Indeed, without a spiritual transformation of the psychic economy, such behavior may well be expressive of masochistic or oppressed personality types. However, the *metamorphe* of the psychic life yields up a new being sustained by the birthing of the human spirit from within its containment in the psyche to communion with the Divine Spirit. Thus, "born of the Spirit," the person finds his or her soul at "rest" in the life of God. From within this spiritual context, one may come to recognize in this experience proximate forms of the Christomorphic life because it is the aim of the Divine Spirit to conform human nature individually and corporately to the nature of Christ. Thus his nature, not primarily the reality principle of the ego, becomes the new norm by which life is to be conducted.

This in no way eliminates the ego or the reality principle, but it makes the relationality between the ego and its tacit sense of wholeness much richer and less defensive. As this reciprocity increases in depth and intensity, the psyche becomes increasingly aware of itself as spiritual in the larger context of a Divine Spirit who is its origin and ultimate ground beyond any ultimacy or groundedness implicit in the psyche per se. On the other hand, the ego-centered psyche continues to bring language and intelligence to bear upon this intrinsically spiritual situation, but these now serve primarily as means of adaptation, not so much to the natural or social environment, but to the Divine Spirit. What the Divine Spirit is doing in the world to convict, to transform, and to conform the world to the nature of Christ becomes the new environment of the ego-centered soul.

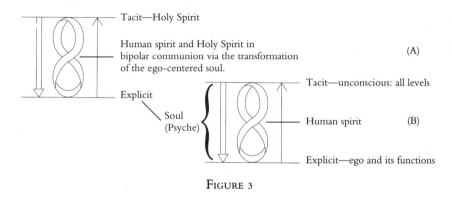

FIGURE 3

Figure 3 sets forth graphically the relationality between soul and spirit in terms of the bipolar model of the Word of God. Certain aspects are especially notable.

1. This describes the differentiated unity between the Holy Spirit and the human spirit that typifies New Testament usage.
2. The biblical view that the Divine Spirit creates and sustains the soul is preserved here without losing either the immanence or the transcendence of the human spirit in and beyond the soul.
3. The tacit sense of wholeness familiar to intrapsychic awareness is here given its ultimate ground in the Holy Spirit, who, beyond the created order, constitutes the relational unity within the Godhead.
4. The ego is preserved as the necessary focus of consciousness by which the Divine Spirit and the human spirit come into the arena of intentional human action.

5. This also makes the point that the two relationalities represented by the two strange loops are reciprocally related such that, if the loop at level B collapses, the significance of A will be greatly diminished. This is not to say that the Holy Spirit is contingent upon the condition of the human spirit in order to act in human life, but it is the case that the appropriation of the work of the Holy Spirit for faith and life is contingent upon the integrity of the human spirit.

CONCLUSIONS FOR PASTORAL THEOLOGY

It is in this last point that the specific pastoral concerns of practical theology come to focus. That is, pastoral care of souls would do well to refocus on the health and vitality of the human spirit in light of its ultimate ground in the divine life. This would shift emphasis away from ego and ego functions to the relational integrity of the "exocentric centeredness" by which we create and compose our worlds. I have made the argument elsewhere that this view of the human spirit can be understood as the stage transition dynamic that undergirds all the phases of ego development.[17] As such, it is "more powerful than the stages" (Piaget). To the extent that pastoral care, especially counseling, can be envisioned as redevelopment, it can be said that care of souls is more fundamentally and more profoundly understood as the care, nurture, and liberation of the human spirit.

Here we should be reminded that there is no responsible care for the human spirit, no recognition of its integrity, if such care is not grounded in the Holy Spirit. Only by the communion of the Holy Spirit with the human spirit will the human spirit avoid being absorbed into the ego and its efforts to maximize satisfaction and ensure survival. In contemplating a return to Judaism, the potentially apostate Hebrews were threatening to make precisely this move, and it is this move that the Word of God as a two-edged sword is designed to undercut.

NOTES

1. T. F. Torrance, *The Ground and Grammar of Theology* (Charlottesville: University Press of Virginia, 1980), 160–61.
2. The following model, building upon Pascal, is developed at con-

siderable length in James E. Loder and W. Jim Neidhardt, *The Knight's Move: The Relational Logic of the Spirit in Theology and Science* (Colorado Springs: Helmers & Howard, 1992), esp. chap. 3.

3. Commenting on a similar passage in Hegel, Kierkegaard's pseudonym, Johannes Climacus, makes a remark that suggests if Bohr's own statement is profound, it must also be false because the opposite of profound truths is also true. If this is not the case, then Bohr's statement is trivial. However, we will not labor this point, for Bohr's intention is clear.

4. Max Jammer, *The Conceptual Development of Quantum Mechanics* (New York: McGraw-Hill, 1966), 348.

5. To suggest an analogy of relationship centering on the nature of Jesus Christ is, of course, to suggest that Barth's anthropology lies behind the argument. To some extent this is the case, but I am using the model in a way not developed by Barth, and, by so doing, I intend to avoid some of the hierarchical and paternalistic problems in his position.

6. The phrase "marginal control" is taken from Michael Polanyi's thought, which stresses the relationship between tacit and explicit polarities of knowing. This model was developed in close connection with Polanyi's thought. See his major study *Personal Knowledge* (Chicago: University of Chicago Press, 1985).

7. It may be necessary for the reader to make a Möbius band if he or she is unfamiliar with this phenomenon. Take a strip of paper about 6 inches long and about one-half inch wide. Bend it into a circle, but before closing the circle, turn one end 180° to put a twist in the loop. Close the loop, and trace the edge of the surface of the loop. You will discover it has only one side and one surface. To appreciate the uniqueness of this topological phenomenon, try splitting it lengthwise.

8. Wolfhart Pannenberg, *An Introduction to Systematic Theology* (Grand Rapids: Wm. B. Eerdmans, 1991), 43ff.

9. Timothy Englemann, "Religious Experiences and Object Representation: An Alternative Model to the Object Relations School" (Ph.D. diss., Jeshiva University, 1993).

10. In Trinitarian terms, Pannenberg's reference to Spirit here is both to Divine life as Spirit and to the Holy Spirit, "who unites the three persons as proceeding from the Father, received by the Son, and common to both, so that precisely in this way he is the force field of the fellowship that is distinct from them both" (Pannenberg, *Systematic Theology*, 383).

11. The following statement, written largely by W. Jim Neidhardt, a physicist at New Jersey Institute of Technology, will make this connection more fully:

In physics, a classical field is a form of relationality representing the interaction (force) between elementary particles (the basic building blocks of matter). This field relationality is both (a) intrinsic to the elementary particle's very being, and (b) a continuum property of physical space which fills space and, under certain conditions, supports the propagation of continuous disturbances, i.e., wave patterns. In quantum field theory, the field relationality expressing the interaction between elementary particles is substantially modified: the addition of quantum properties to the field produces a discrete (quantized) countability in basic field properties which correspond to the behavior of new particles, i.e., field quanta (photons, . . .). These new particles associated with a quantum field mediate the interaction between elementary particles. Furthermore, under certain circumstances, quantum fields with their associated quanta take on a life of their own. Field quanta can interact with one another (and already present elementary particles) to create new events, including even the creation of other elementary particles. Thus the kind of creativity associated with quantum field theory is *heuristically analogous* to Pannenberg's assertion that God's Spirit in God's creation can be described as a field of creative presence that releases event after event into finite existence.

The above is a much simplified presentation of the subtle complexity of quantum field theory. A current understanding of physical reality incorporates both particle (discrete) and field (continuum) interpretations. The distinguished particle physicist Robert K. Adair summarizes current physical understanding as follows:

> There are two complementary faces to our description of the fundamental microscopic character of physical reality. Like Demokritos, we can consider that reality is constructed of sets of discrete source particles (such as electrons, protons, or quarks) with the modern addition that the forces between these particles take place through the exchange of field particles (such as photons, mesons, or gluons) created and absorbed by the source particles. Conversely, we can consider reality to be made up of sets of interacting fields (or better, one *united* field) in Farada's sense, ("I do not perceive in any part of space whether vacant or filled with matter, anything but forces and the lines in which they are exerted." M. Faraday) where the field is the ultimate reality and the particles are quantum condensates of the field. In such a description, source fields of electrons, protons and quarks interact with force fields of photons, mesons and gluons. Of course, there is but one reality, and the different aspects—particle or field—are different pictures of that reality. Indeed, the two views, particular as particles, and continuum as fields, are largely fused in modern theory. (See Robert K. Adair, *The Great Design—Parti-*

cles, Fields, and Creation (New York: Oxford University Press, 1989), 49.

Accordingly, quantum field theory represents a subtle holistic relationality where particles, considered to be quantum condensates of the field, are spontaneously created and destroyed through field interactions. However, quantum field theory is currently neither fully complete or consistent. This is why physicists are exploring other possibilities, such as the theory of superstrings.

For a more complete, introductory (but not superficial) discussion of the spontaneous character of particle generation (and annihilation) in quantum field theory, see: Robert H. March, *Physics for Poets*, 3rd ed. (New York: McGraw-Hill, 1992); Adair, *The Great Design—Particles, Fields, and Creation*; and Heinz R. Pagels, *The Cosmic Coke: Quantum Physics as the Language of Nature* (New York: Simon & Schuster, 1982).

12. This discussion is largely dependent upon George Hendry's study of *The Holy Spirit in Christian Theology* (Philadelphia: Westminster Press, 1961), chap. 5.

13. Wolfhart Pannenberg, *Anthropology in Theological Perspective*, trans. Matthew J. O'Connell (Philadelphia: Westminster Press, 1985), 341ff.

14. Howard Gardner, *Frames of Mind* (New York: Basic Books, 1983).

15. Søren Kierkegaard, *Works of Love*, trans. Edna Howard Hong (New York: Harper & Row, 1962), 213ff.

16. A major dimension of such a discussion as this is the nature and influence of the personal unconscious. If more space were available, the power and influence of a person's personal history should be taken up at this point. Surely that history has the capacity to free or to subvert the life and work of the human spirit.

17. James E. Loder, *The Transforming Moment* (San Francisco: Harper & Row, 1981), chap. 5.

11
Another Look at the Elderly

FREDA A. GARDNER

The church universal and its particular congregations live in the tension between ministry to all people and specific ministry to individuals and groups. Witnessing to Jesus Christ and trying to be Christ's body in the world are often shaped by conscious and unconscious decisions about which people are needful or deserving of ministry. Sometimes the church has taken the lead in calling attention to this or that group overlooked and neglected and now visible for, perhaps, the first time. Often, the culture provides the prick of conscience or the promise of possibility by focusing on those who have had little, if any, attention paid to them in the past.

A glance at what we once called mainline denominations in the past few decades will identify youth, single people, people with limiting conditions, unemployed people, people with AIDS or Alzheimer's disease and their caregivers as examples of emphases of particular forms of ministry. In many Roman Catholic parishes, attention to so-called lapsed Catholics and to divorced persons has shaped new ministry programs.

Elderly people qualify in these last decades of the century for the church's attention. One could spend a great amount of time and energy in asking, "Why now?" The church has always had old people in it. But their numbers are increasing. Research from a variety of perspectives gives us the statistics of an aging population and of the stresses on our society from the increased life expectancy and the corresponding needs of those who will probably live well beyond the biblical fourscore years and ten.[1]

174

The culture is moving, albeit slowly, toward the recognition that there are, on the one hand, a growing body of consumers in the postsixty crowd and, on the other hand, a growing body of those whose physical, mental, social, and emotional needs cannot be met by currently available goods and services. Presently available health care, education, transportation, housing and household goods, clothing, recreation, and entertainment are not, for the most part, appropriate for those in their seventies, eighties, and nineties.

Whether from a concern for the financial bottom line or a concern for the well-being of an increasingly high percentage of the nation's people, change is occurring and will continue to occur. As in all areas of change, we must expect that there will be false starts, manipulation, exploitation, and bias toward those with the most resources. However, there already exists authentic and caring experimentation to discover how to ensure, for those who live to an old age, the comfort, respect, and sense of self that the culture as a whole values.

Already the culture and the church are aware that there are as many differences among the old as we have come to recognize in the young. Awareness, however, does not always lead into embodiment when ministries are being shaped. Overworked pastors and busy laypeople hope for and often create programs that address the elderly as if they were merely clones of each other. A program has, more than a few times, been baptized as ministry by people who have a sense of what they are being called to do but have neither the will nor the time to do it and so settle, instead, for a programmatic illusion of ministry. To say it even more bluntly, we create the programs we know we can handle instead of some that might stretch us and address the realities of the people for whom they are designed—in this case, the elderly.

The particular characteristics of those in the later years of life— degrees of health, economic circumstances, location and dislocation, familial and social relationships, personality, continuity and discontinuity with earlier life, capacities for new experiences and growth, ethnic background values, gender and gender experiences—are extremely complex.

Feminist and liberation theologies have opened the eyes of many to a truth that our own experience might have taught us. Creation in God's image is as multifaceted as the God whom we come to know in Jesus Christ. Jesus' recognition of God in "the least of these" and his teaching in the parables have confronted us and called us from seeing everyone from only our own viewpoint to allowing the other to exist as one God loves and who might, indeed, be the neighbor or the stranger we are enjoined to welcome. We are born from particularity into particularity, and all our lives we are shaped and reshaped, inwardly and outwardly, by our legacy of particularity and our interaction with it and the life that embodies it. Particularity, which points to the differences among us, is something we have in common. The possibilities and limitations of our unique particularity are what make us different.

Attention to particularity often seems overwhelming to those who are trying to give shape to a church's ministry. These questions always come: How can we possibly take into account all the differences? Will we have to have a class, a group, a visitor, a supporter for each person? Good teachers and good parents know some of the answers to those questions. When planning for a group, whether it be a class or several children in a family, plan so that there is recognition and respect of differences, space for interests and abilities that vary, acknowledgment that not everyone can be accommodated all the time, commitment to making a place for everyone as often as is possible.

So far, attention has been focused on the uniqueness of the person. As important as that is, it is only a part of what might shape ministry. Equally important are the lenses through which we look to see the other or ourselves. We bring our own uniqueness formed by experiences, values, education, hopes, convictions, fears, to our observations which, as much as our ability to see, determine what we see.

What we have usually seen when we look at older people, including ourselves if we have reached old age, is embodied loss. They are not young, not attractive, not in control, not able to do what they once did, not as sharp as they once were, not living with families, and not long to live anyway. Older people are, in the eyes of many, what they have lost. One may protest rightly at this negative picture because, of course, many elderly people do not fit this picture, although most will bear some of these characteristics.

What ministry emerges if these negatives shape our concerns? Do we recognize that most of the negatives are the result of comparing older people with people at earlier stages of life? When we look at other age groups, we tend to focus on the restrictions of an earlier stage and, therefore, can celebrate feeding oneself or following directions or taking responsibility for one's actions or being able to make and keep friends or a budget. What we see is progress. What we see in the elderly is loss and deterioration. Recognizing our tendency to see the negative encourages some to overcorrection, to an avoidance of those painful realities at the heart of being old. Slogans, cute names like the Golden Years, and a "you can do anything you want to" optimism do not serve those in the later years of life any better than the recital of negatives. What seems called for is a realism about the possibilities and limitations of being old and a framework of interpretation that holds them in a healthy tension.

To find that realism, we turn to four areas from which we might draw positive or negative regard and a place to stand acknowledging both. They are the reality of death, the myth/sin of independence, body and gender perception of self and others, and discipleship and ministry.

The Reality of Death and the Myth/Sin of Independence

When an adolescent believes herself or himself to be invincible and, therefore, takes little or no account of potential danger, we may be concerned, but we expect and hope that the young person will move into a more mature understanding in due time. We know that as adults most of us become more realistic about both our vulnerability and our mortality, but there remains in many individuals, and in the society in which we live, a deep, pervasive, even primitive fear of death. Many in the church who are well intentioned, who recognize the realities of being old, and who would like to shape a ministry with older people are slowed down and diverted by such fear.

When one is a child, it seems good and exciting to anticipate being a teenager; and, in adolescence, to give voice to how one is going to be when adulthood is reached. But what comes next for the old is death. Even the realities we encounter in any group of the elderly are things we fear almost as much as we do death. We do not want to see ourselves alone or homebound, waiting for someone to take us to the store or to the doctor's, or to provide us with a social life. We do not want that, and we cannot face the milestone of death.

There should be no need to rehearse the lengths we go to in our culture to remove the specter of death from our daily lives. From cosmetic wizardry in the preparation of a dead body for viewing to the technological wonderland that surrounds the act of dying in a modern hospital, we hold death at arms' length. We may have read Jessica Mitford's *The American Way of Death* back in the 1960s or Ernest Becker's *The Denial of Death* in the 1970s.[2] We may have taken courses on death and dying where it seemed relatively easy to denounce the commercialism of death and to affirm the significance of dying in a familiar place. Even so, death is still the enemy to be avoided. As a recent cartoon depicted it, everyone wants to go to heaven but nobody wants to die in order to get there. We must deal, then, with faith questions: What is the nature of life after death? Can we trust God to continue with us in a life marked by growth and commitment and service and joy unmarked by the tears of the lives we now live? Is death a milestone to be celebrated?

If we live with a deep, pervasive, primitive fear of death, we also live with another message that we know at a deep level because it has been taught us in so many ways. Be independent. Independence is first a goal and then a plumb line by which we measure maturity. We are rewarded from our earliest years for what we accomplish on our own. The initiative and courage that created a new nation are still primary values in the institutions of that nation. "Self-made men" take on heroic proportions, and the echo of a three-year-old's cry "I can do it myself" can be heard from the lives of women and men decades older than that. Is it any wonder that we look at the later years of life and are afraid? We ask, "Who will I be when I can no longer be self-sufficient?" The only alternative to independence that most of us know is dependence.

Even long-time members of the church and students of the Bible and theology find it hard to counter the omnipotence of independence with anything but the culture's alternative. The message from the world is so loud that the message from scripture seems weak and ineffectual. Dependence on God who gives us to each other for mutual caring is a theme that runs through the Bible. God speaks to a people and promises to provide for them in measures adequate for their needs. God calls again and again for the people to care for the most vulnerable in their midst. Jesus responds over and over to the ones who least were attended to; he creates hospitality where none existed (see the feeding of the five thousand, John 6:1–15). He makes it clear that being God's child and Christ's disciple puts one into a trustworthy and supportive family that transcends one's own family. The early church seems to have caught Jesus' vision as people became "households of God" and cared for those who needed care of one kind or another.[3] Biblical as these notions may be, they fall hard on the ears of twentieth-century North Americans, especially if privilege is coupled with independence. The images from scripture are alien to the ideal life many of us strive to attain and maintain, a life built on the rights of ownership and unlimited consumption of the world's goods and privacy for me and mine at any cost.

What we deplore when we look at older people and what we fear as much as we anticipate the later years for ourselves may, in truth, be the entry point for a better way to be what God has intended for us from the beginning. God is the one who knows us in our mother's womb, who promises to be with us when we are old and gray (see Isa. 46:4), who knows that we must be carried.

BODY AND GENDER IN THE PERCEPTION OF SELF AND OTHERS

James Lapsley's latest book, *Renewal in Late Life through Pastoral Counseling*, gives us a richer way to look at the later years of life. Lapsley's spirit-self model encourages us to consider the older person as a complex being of body, mind, and spirit, forged earlier and now continuing with the possibilities and limitations of the later years of life. He defines human spirit as "the human form of life itself. It provides intensity of motion and direction toward other beings and toward a vision of the future."[4] Self "refers to the felt sense of ownness and sameness that a person perceives, together with the connections below the surface of awareness, and sometimes to disconnected fragments below the surface."[5]

Emphasizing the interaction of the spirit and the self, Lapsley brackets the mind-body problem while affirming the embodiment of both spirit and self. What he recognizes and cannot take up in the scope of his book does, nevertheless, beg for attention when one considers the elderly. Self-perception is in large part body-perception. As long as there are fears of Alzheimer's disease, changes in the body in both appearance and function, there will also be challenges to self-perception. Beneath the humor in jokes about old people's "organ recitals" is fear and despair over the failure of the body, the container of spirit and self. Clues from the body tell one what being old means.

Thrown back to the adolescent experience of having a body on one's hands, many older people cope daily with physical limitations, pain, and disfigurement that in turn give rise to frustration, depression, anxiety, and loss of self-esteem. The high impact of media images of bodily perfection, coupled with the not-so-subtle messages that one is never good enough as one is, affects the old as well as the young. The scarcity of older people in dramas, comedies, news broadcasts, and commercials teaches both the young and the old about who is valued and who is not. Mere awareness that the elderly are victims of ageism does not mean that they are no longer victims.

A look at the relational vectors identified by Lapsley may sharpen the point. By relational vectors he means "different objects or subjects of relationships (direction) and kinds and degrees of attachment (magnitude)."[6] Lapsley allows that there are undoubtedly others that might be mentioned, but he focuses on these: spousal relationships, one's own body, one's own children, friends, human community, nature and culture, God. Think, if you will, of the shaping and misshaping force on these relationships exerted by a functioning or barely functioning body. Consider also the operative norms by which we make judgments about the quality and value of the body-force effect.

The jokes about deterioration of the body seem to come at ever younger ages today. Birthday cards for thirty- and forty-year-olds make fun of the loss of strength or hair, increase of wrinkles and spots, inabilities to do or think as one once did. We laugh at stories of bodies that creak and are not as trustworthy as they used to be. But most of us over the age of fifty or sixty would probably confess that none of this is really funny. It appears to be a situation of "laugh so you won't cry," for crying would be as futile as a child's temper tantrum because he or she has blonde hair instead of black. Being old is bad enough for some of the elderly population, but to see it so blatantly displayed when one looks in a mirror or at one's peers is too heavy a reminder that, by all standards, we have failed and that the accompanying slowdown can only end in permanent stillness.

As a people, we are inundated with information about illness, disease, chronic disorders, and disabilities. Almost always the overt or not too subtle message is the advocacy of a remedy, be it drugs, surgery, preventive diets, or clear thinking. Rarely does anyone say that this condition is permanent or semipermanent and here is a way to live with it. "There's a solution to every problem" is our culture's motto, and the problem we are looking at here is a body that is not what we would like it to be; namely, a twenty-to-forty-year-old body.

The lack of prenatal care, little or no attention to nutrition and preventive measures in early childhood, the absence of corrective procedures for teeth, eyes, ears, and bones mean that many people never have a chance for a healthy body. For them the task is learning to do compensatory coping or simply to endure both the pain and stress of malfunction and its accompanying social stigma. Surely the "ideal body" is a harsh mockery to such as these.

Economics and values of particular ethnic, religious, or regional groups produce distinctive differences in the ways the body is involved in one's sense of self. Gender also must be included in such a list.

In identifying some of the characteristics of an ageist and sexist society, Christie Cozad Neuger points out that, until very recently, women were excluded from research in general.[7] Norms drawn from research were used to evaluate both men and women, even though women's experience was not a part of the data. Neuger continues by saying that even when women were included, older women were almost invisible and, in the proliferation of research on the elderly in the past two decades, gender differences are, to a great extent, ignored. To name just two such differences, Neuger quotes from Lois Grau and Ida Susser in recognizing that women live longer than men in our society and that they tend to be poorer and less healthy than men who survive into old age.[8]

Demographics and charts can tell us these things, but so can our daily contacts with parents, grandparents, elderly friends and neighbors. It does not take an expert to tell us what we can see for ourselves about the ways older men and women deal with loss, illness, challenges, and necessary adaptations. Even a cursory look at the images of women in our society should make us wonder what effect those images have on the way a woman views and values herself. Neuger refers to the double loss of self-worth when a woman can no longer bear children and can no longer hide the reality of an aging body. This observation is not a diatribe against a mysterious "they" who are out to get women. It is, rather, an appeal to women as well as men to recognize the windmills against which they tilt to little avail. Men and women are different, and women are different from each other. Neuger tells us, for example, of research that indicates that women leaving the labor force need to be actively involved in civic organizations and the church. Women who are retiring from homemaking need to have the opportunity for ongoing education. Yet when society dictates which differences to value and which to wish away, many women despair of fitting the norm.

Attitudes held by the pastor and people responsible for planning ministry with the elderly need to be named and addressed. We all, even the old themselves, have stereotypes about the old; and in order for those stereotypes not to dominate ministry, we must take responsibility for recognizing them. There are a variety of resources available for doing that work of recognition, but a good place to start is in looking, listening, and wondering about those we meet daily. The goal in all of this is freedom to live outside the prison of unreal and often impossible expectations.

DISCIPLESHIP AND MINISTRY

Have you ever heard:
I worked all my life; now life owes me. I took my turn; let the younger ones do it. Besides, no one wants to know what I think.

Our congregation is filled with old, white-haired people, some quite feeble; there's no one to do the work anymore.

Or can you picture someone:
Quietly listening to a turned-up-too-high television preacher decrying the erosion of long-standing values, proclaiming God's disgust with today's world, asking for financial contributions to fight the enemies so clearly and simply identified.

Clinging to visitors and helpers in an obvious effort to forestall emptiness and loneliness.

Dressing and grooming with what is available and meant for people 30–50 years younger, or making do with less and less in a world where clothing and its accoutrements do indeed "make the man" or the woman.

Withdrawing into the social isolation because the dark, the street, the steps, the noise of large groups of people, the rapid or mumbled speech of others, the busyness of everyone who pauses to make contact occasions outright fear or embarrassment, confusion, and sometimes despondence.

Could you not add to both lists if you took note of your congregation, family, older friends and acquaintances? Such words, images, and implications are a part of our lives. We either bury them in our unconscious or hold them at arms' length because they seem to ask for more of us than we can deliver.

The success of the Elderhostel Movement here and abroad is a mirror held before every congregation that seeks to minister to the elderly only by entertaining them. To be sure, the elderhostel movement must be seen for its elitist character. Its cost; its premise that all are capable of and interested in human interaction, attentiveness in lectures, and communal living; and its reliance on a fairly high degree of physical functioning make it a program for some but not all. Nevertheless, the response to it reminds us that many elderly people are eager to grow intellectually and are interested in more than the rocking chair of one stereotype or the endless golf game of another.

The number of elderly people serving as volunteers in hospitals, schools, day-care centers, nursing homes, soup kitchens, tutorial programs, and the like give the lie to the oft-repeated "the old ones can't do anything and don't want to anyway." It is true that some cannot or do not, and others think they cannot. Some preschoolers do not like to color, and some sixth-graders hate to do math or play sports, but that does not keep us from offering such options or from encouraging all children to try them. Of course, those children have a future, but . . .

What I am suggesting here is that the church, like the culture, thinks of the elderly as a different species of human being, maybe an obsolete human being. The church, with its own ageism that is frequently masked by a sweet piety and buttressed by biblical passages that suggest reverence for the old and wise, often takes one of two paths in its ministry to these "different" folk. As mentioned earlier, we entertain them and take somewhat superficial care of them, or we lump them all together and address whatever the majority tells us about themselves.

Until the church, each individual congregation, accords to the elderly the characteristics of all human beings and the particularities of individuals at every stage of life, its ministry will be merely programs and a soft benevolence that waits with them, somewhat remotely, to the end. This is a harsh judgment, perhaps, but it is more a cry to build a ministry on something other than stereotypes and fears.

What might that ministry be? Human beings are sometimes differentiated from other living creatures by their search for meaning. Most people want to live until they die. To be sure, some choose death as a way of life early on—victims of hopelessness, frustration, disappointment, loss, despair. But most look for meaning throughout the life span. As Christian people, we affirm that in Jesus Christ we have been given the meaning of life and the means to live it. It is in the church that the purpose of life is translated into daily living through the recognition of gifts and opportunities.

When we are called into relationship with God, we receive a vocation, a purpose, and a way to be.[9] That vocation has been described in various ways, but central to any definition is discipleship. To be sure, discipleship is frequently referred to as following Jesus Christ, but that may be too simple a description. A small child, speaking to a parent, said, "You remember I told you I was going to be a disciple? [The child's church school learning community was simulating life in Jesus' day.] Well, guess what, they didn't just follow him around; they had hard stuff to do." The "hard stuff" to the child's mind is the ministry of Jesus Christ into which God calls us. Maybe the hard part of discipleship is the discerning of what Christ is about because, in the last years of the twentieth century, we cannot pretend to do exactly what he did. What we are called to do is to care about what Jesus cared about and to find ways appropriate to our time and circumstances to act out that caring.

Discipleship, understood in these terms, is not only what one does in church—teach, organize, make decisions, preach, sing, visit. It is also what one does as parent, child, sibling, neighbor, volunteer, citizen, and employee. Our vocation claims our whole life for all of our life. The contexts and activities of discipleship may change over time and with circumstances, but the call to be about Christ's ministry is constant. To talk about a ministering Christian is like speaking of a jogging jogger.[10] If you don't do it, you can't claim to be it.

"I've retired, no thanks." "I can't sing, teach, go to meetings anymore, so count me out." Comments like these reflect an inadequate understanding of vocation and should make us wonder about what is being taught about vocation from the pulpit, in the classroom, at committee meetings—wherever the church gathers.

There is another theological pitfall in all of this. The culture values us for our productivity. We are what we can do. However, such activities and the products of them fall into a very narrow range. The church follows the culture when it bemoans the loss of many people who have become too old to do what they once did. Does that mean that we are gifted for ministry only when we are young or middle-aged? Surely not. God's invitation to the ministry of Jesus Christ is accompanied by gifts for the doing of particular ministries. The church, most often, plans programs and then searches for those with the gifts to make the programs go. Occasionally, the church might want to do it the opposite way. The church might inquire into the gifts given and wonder together about the ministries to which those gifts might point. If I cannot organize and cook a church supper, what can I do? If my life is a mixture of painful and pain-free days, what ministries can claim me, given the gifts I have?

The church frequently joins the world in seeing the elderly only in negative terms. If, as J. B. Phillips put it decades ago, our God is too small, then it is possible that our understanding of ministry is also too small. There are too many people who disavow the things they do, squirming if these things are labeled ministry. Are they poorly taught, perhaps? Does ministry include checking on a friend in the next room in a nursing home or down the street, praying for everyone's grandchildren living in a world never known, sending a card, listening with patience, showing a parent and a child what there is to love in the other? It would seem so.

What has been the point of looking at the reality of death and our fear of it, the myth/sin of independence, body and gender in the perception of self and others, and the meaning of discipleship and ministry? Must we settle for living the later years of our lives in fear of the next step, in shame of the bodies that are ours, with a sense of guilt because we are not self-reliant, without any sense that we still have purpose and place? The bodies, minds, and spirits of the elderly are generally found lacking, by the elderly themselves as well as others, because they are measured against a maturity that is assumed to peak between forty and fifty-five years of age. In our youth-conscious society, little value has been found in being old except, maybe, the freedom to be self-indulgent if one can afford it, or out of action, which looks good to the hassled middle-aged. To the extent that we settle for that, we must abandon the teachings of scripture and theology or, what is sadly, perhaps, more true, live out what the church in its conformity to culture has taught us so well. Maria Harris speaks of three curriculums: explicit, implicit, and null.[11] It is possible that what we would never set out to teach about being old has been taught as part of the life of the church, as implicit curriculum. If that is the case, we can begin to undo it—and to that we now turn.

MINISTRY WITH THE ELDERLY

A cursory reading of much of the literature on development leads one to draw one or two conclusions: development stops at age fifty-five or sixty, or the work of the later years of life is self-actualization. To view the later years of life as called, empowered, sustained, and shaped by God is to begin at a different place, to examine the later years with a different purpose, and to plan the church's ministry with the elderly in a different way.

Remedial Education

We who were lost have been found. We who have looked for life in all the wrong places have been shown the cruciform-shaped life that gives meaning to our existence. We who have borne the name and the power of Christ since our baptism are named and empowered for our whole lives. We who are wounded healers, to use Henri Nouwen's phrase, both need ministry and are ministers in the ordinary and crisis times of our lives.

Much of the educational ministry of the church might be seen as remedial. Because we live in many worlds, what we know and believe is a mixture of what has been taught and learned in families, schools, communities, and other institutions and settings. The church says to us, "You have heard it said, but we say to you." Then, drawing on scripture, tradition, and creeds, it tries to shape its best understanding of God's word for today.

Such remedial education might begin with attention to the curriculum, asking if what we have learned about being old and older people is, in fact, what the church has to teach. It is fairly easy to check the explicit curriculum, but more challenging to examine the implicit curriculum. To do the latter means listening to sermon illustrations, noting words and images on bulletin boards and pictures in classrooms, reading or listening to public announcements and invitations for what they imply about older people. It is to be ruthlessly honest about the size of print in church bulletins, hymn books, and prayer books; about lighting in hallways, meeting rooms, and sanctuaries, and about accessibility to those places; about enhanced hearing in places where the elderly would be; about safety and comfort measures taken for night meetings or away-from-home retreats. Does all that we do as a church say clearly to older people, "You are part of us, and we need you to be with us," or does it say the opposite?

Changing Perceptions

If that stance is to be more than a verbalization, we probably have to work at changing our perceptions of the elderly. Perceptions change when a new idea replaces an old one; new ideas that are experienced have greater power than abstractions. Firsthand experience is most effective. Getting to know older people can begin in the church nursery and in the early grades. Children and young people can meet, work, and play with older women and men in almost any of the church's activities if such is a goal. Preparation for encountering older people who may look or act differently can pave the way for more positive experiences of visiting old people in the hospital or caroling in a nursing home. The skin, voice, tremors, laugh, touch of an old person can be disconcerting or even frightening to children, teenagers, and some adults, and the contact can result in solidifying negative attitudes toward them.

Listening and talking to people with an awareness of the issues identified as significant for our understanding of how we perceive others and ourselves as elderly will produce significant knowledge for educational and pastoral ministries.

Stories, pictures, and films can provide exposure to older people who may not be represented in the congregation. As our stereotypes are confronted, we may be able to confess—in a context of trust—experience forgiveness, and move on. *The Shopping Bag Lady*, a film about a young girl's encounter with an older woman and the girl's eventual realization that the old woman was once her age, is especially good for adolescents, but worthwhile for all ages.

Confronting our stereotypes about ourselves is equally important, especially when we consider the impact of the media on self-perception. *Still Killing Us Softly* is a vivid recall of what is done to women's self-perception by the media and is important for both women and men to see.[12] It can be effective with teenagers also. Care needs to be taken to allow for our sense of being manipulated by society's values and the ease with which we are manipulated. Adequate time for discussing appropriate responses should be provided.

Terra Nova Films has many exceptionally well-done and moving films and videos that lift up the trials, thoughts, and triumphs of older men and women.[13] They are excellent for discussion in groups where people are free to respond to them in positive and negative ways.

A video produced by the National Film Board of Canada, *Strangers in Good Company*, is an absorbing story of a group of older women who are stranded when their bus breaks down. Real people whom you could expect to meet anywhere reveal some of themselves to each other, identifying what they share in common and how they differ.

A very useful listing of stories for children, books for caregivers, and general books on understanding older persons can be found in *Books and Periodicals on Aging for Church Libraries: A Selected Bibliography*.[14]

Study and Celebration of Ministry of the Laity

Ongoing study, begun probably with adolescents, on baptism, vocation, and gifts is essential to viewing older adults as continuing disciples of Jesus Christ. Classes or retreats that deal with these topics need frequent repetition as one's faith continues to seek understanding of what it means to be God's person today. Biblical study and theological interpretation of particular denominations can be followed by workshops focusing on the recognition and the naming of gifts. Affirmation of gifts already being used can be extended to exploration of other possibilities for ministry, employing the same or newly identified gifts. One helpful resource is *Monday's Ministries*.[15] A review of ten resource materials on identifying and using spiritual gifts, *Windows on Gifts*, was prepared in 1989 for the Episcopal Church.[16]

Interdependence and Living in Community

Because an understanding of the later years of life is shaped in the early years of life, it is in those years that we should begin to teach about aging. Through directed study and experience in the church community, we learn what it means to be and to do as children of God. What we come to know is a gift of God's revelation to us and, like all gifts, is given for the common good.

Public education, after decades of promoting individual achievement, is exploring new pedagogies that facilitate cooperative learning and produce communal ownership. Designed for the public sector, but adaptable for the church, *Circles of Learning: Cooperation in the Classroom* is a means for teachers in the church to become familiar with the concept.[17]

Similarly, adult study of books that struggle with an understanding of the nature of the church in our times as less hierarchical and more communal in its decision making and ministry can begin the exploration of what it means to be with and for each other in the body of Christ. Letty Russell's recent book, *Church in the Round: Feminist Interpretation of the Church*, is one such book.[18] Parker Palmer, quoted by Russell, holds before the reader an alternative vision of community from the one with which most of us live. His *The Company of Strangers: Christians and the Renewal of America's Public Life* not only challenges us to think differently about the ways we live, but provokes us to an exploration of how we might live.[19] Including the elderly in such exploration would provide opportunities for all ages to identify first, second, and third steps toward living more faithfully with the gifts God has given to each and to the church community.

Intergenerational activities in the church are limited only by our imaginations, stereotypes, and level of commitment regarding their value. Sharing meals and worship; extending family clusters so that families with single persons, both older and younger, feel included; adopting grandparents for families or classes or outings; engaging the elderly in dialogue with adolescents; arranging visits with the elderly by adults and children in short time frames; encouraging the elderly, with others, to sort and pack food or clothes for those in need; and having young members interview older members about the church and their lives are all examples of such inclusive activities. If older adults have purpose, if they have gifts, the church exercises poor stewardship in not finding ways appropriate to their capacities for them to be engaged in ministry.

Loss and Death

Pastors, counselors, and church visitors can probably testify to the willingness of many older people to talk about loss and death, and the simultaneous unwillingness of their children and younger friends to let them do it. Naturally, there are some older people who cannot and will not even use the word *death*, but their presence should not rule out interaction with the others. Talking about losses, survival of losses, and death should also begin in childhood, in a church where such talk can occur in the context of trust and convictions about the trustworthiness of God. Admitting to fears does not come easily to most people, and helpful discussions cannot go forward without an assurance that confessions will be held in confidence, that prayer for God's mercy and care will be forthcoming, and that the church believes, even when some individuals cannot, that the God who created and redeemed us will preserve us in this life and the next. In his book *Good Grief*, Granger Westberg stresses the importance of nurturing faith all along; otherwise we are unprepared to handle even the smaller losses that are a part of everyday living.[20]

Two other books are also helpful resources in dealing with these matters. *All Our Losses, All Our Griefs*, by Kenneth Mitchell and Herbert Anderson, is an excellent resource for pastoral care and can be used in educational settings as well. Likewise, Scott Sullender's *Losses in Later Life: A New Way of Walking with God* encourages older people to be free of the past and free for what is now possible at their stage in life.[21]

For people who are so inclined, literature is replete with reflections on death and our fear of it. At the close of his book *Another Country*, Karel Schoeman has the central character, dying of tuberculosis, reflect on his sojourn away from home in South Africa.

> Once, when he had just arrived here, . . . his walks in the evening had taken him to the edge of town and he had hesitated there, wavering before the landscape that had lain open before him, unknown and unknowable, and an inexplicable fear had filled him at the sight of that emptiness. But now there was no cause for fear . . . the emptiness absorbed you and silence embraced you, no longer as alien wastes to be regarded uncomprehendingly from a distance; the unknown land grew familiar and the person passing through could no longer even remember that he had once intended to travel further. Half-way along the route you discovered with some surprise that the journey has been completed, the destination already reached.[22]

Such readings may encourage people to talk about another's view until they are ready to talk about their own.

The Life of the Spirit

In some of the literature on the elderly there is a tendency to confine life in the later years to the realm of the spirit. For some, that realm seems detached from the rest of the person's life. Circumstances and the absence of much that demands attention in the earlier years do seem to make many older adults more ready and able to attend to their inward selves, to become reflective and philosophical, to find greater satisfaction in prayer and silence. Quietness and centeredness are unknown to many younger people and are viewed with suspicion because of the inactivity they exhibit. That these capacities need not be escapes or unrelated to the rest of life is something for pastors, children, and friends to learn if they are to provide ministries for older people and appreciate the ministries offered by older people. A resource for considering this is Parker Palmer's *The Active Life: A Spirituality of Work, Creativity and Caring*.[23] Prayer and contemplation may be gifts of the elderly to the rest of us as we discover in such ministries a peace and purpose that the world cannot give.

The whole life of the church—worship, education, fellowship, service in the larger communities of neighborhood, nation, and world—stands to be enlivened and enriched by the recognition that the oldest among us are, with us, seekers, believers, and ministers. Trust in God for this life and the next is the context for our continuing search for what it is to be faithful and for our continuing life for others who are empowered by God's gifts and the church's recognition of them as the means for ministry.

NOTES

1. See Ken Dychtwald and Joe Fowler, *Age Wave: The Challenges and Opportunities of an Aging America* (New York: St. Martin's Press, 1989).

2. Jessica Mitford, *The American Way of Death* (New York: Simon & Schuster, 1963); Ernest Becker, *The Denial of Death* (New York: Free Press, 1973).

3. Letty Russell, *Household of Freedom: Authority in Feminist Perspective* (Philadelphia: Westminster Press, 1987). This concept is developed further in her most recent book, *Church in the Round: Feminist Interpretation of the Church* (Louisville, Ky.: Westminster/John Knox Press, 1993).

4. James N. Lapsley, *Renewal in Late Life through Pastoral Counseling* (New York: Paulist Press, 1992), 32.

5. Ibid., 33.

6. Ibid., 35ff.

7. Christie Cozad Neuger noted this lack in an unpublished lecture given at United Theological Seminary of the Twin Cities in Minneapolis.

8. Lois Grau and Ida Susser, eds., *Women in the Later Years*, Women and Health Series, vol. 14, nos. 3–4 (New York: Haworth Press, 1989).

9. Interpreted from Karl Barth, *Church Dogmatics*, vol. 4, pt. 3 (Edinburgh: T. & T. Clark, 1962).

10. Nelvin Vos, *Monday's Ministries* (Philadelphia: Parish Life Press, 1979).

11. Maria Harris, *Fashion Me a People: Curriculum in the Church* (Louisville, Ky.: Westminster/John Knox Press, 1989), 68–69.

12. *Still Killing Us Softly*, Cambridge Documentary Films, P.O. Box 385, Cambridge, MA 02139 (617/345–3677).

13. Terra Nova Films, 988 S. Winchester Avenue, Chicago, IL 60643 (312/881–8491).

14. This listing can be secured from the Center on Aging, Presbyterian School of Christian Education, 105 Palmyra Avenue, Richmond, VA 23227.

15. See Vos, *Monday's Ministries*.

16. *Windows on Gifts*, Episcopal Church Center, Office of Ministry Development, 815 Second Avenue, New York, NY 10017.

17. David W. Johnson et al., *Circles of Learning: Cooperation in the Classroom* (Alexandria, Va.: Association for Supervision and Development, 1984).

18. Russell, *Church in the Round.*

19. Parker Palmer, *The Company of Strangers: Christians and the Renewal of America's Public Life* (New York: Crossroad, 1983).

20. Granger Westberg, *Good Grief* (Philadelphia: Fortress Press, 1963), 6.

21. Kenneth Mitchell and Herbert Anderson, *All Our Losses, All Our Griefs* (Philadelphia: Westminster Press, 1983); Scott Sullender, *Losses in Later Life: A New Way of Walking with God* (Mahwah, N.J.: Paulist Press, 1989).

22. Karel Schoeman, *Another Country* (Trafalgar: Sinclar-Stevenson, 1992), 9.

23. Parker Palmer, *The Active Life: A Spirituality of Work, Creativity and Caring* (San Francisco: Harper & Row, 1992).

ADDITIONAL BIBLIOGRAPHY

AARP Publications. American Association of Retired Persons, 601 E Street, N.W., Washington, D.C. 20049.

Aleshire, Daniel. *Faithcare: Ministering to God's People through All the States of Life.* Philadelphia: Westminster Press, 1988.

Bonhoeffer, Dietrich, *Life Together.* New York: Harper & Row, 1954.

Maitland, David. *Aging as Counterculture: A Vocation for the Later Years.* New York: Pilgrim Press, 1991.

Vogel, Linda. *The Religious Education of Older Adults.* Birmingham: Religious Education Press, 1984.

12
Forgiveness, Lost Contracts, and Pastoral Theology

JOHN H. PATTON

James Lapsley's article "Reconciliation, Forgiveness, Lost Contracts" is a methodological prototype for the pastoral theological method developed by Seward Hiltner.[1] It underscores a characteristic element in pastoral theology, recovering a dimension of an important human problem that has been lost or insufficiently emphasized in contemporary theology. This essay uses some of Lapsley's contributions to pastoral theology as a dynamic for rethinking, both theologically and psychologically, important issues concerning human forgiveness.

At the time he wrote the article, in the midsixties, Lapsley was concerned that in theology and ministry's haste to emphasize reconciliation there was a danger that reconciliation's predecessor—forgiveness—would be overlooked.

> I am contending in this article, that it is not true that the law is dead or dying. Rather it has gone "underground" in the experience of most, if not all persons, and forgiveness is yet a vital necessity in the life of the Christian in the literal sense of release from debt.[2]

The function of pastoral theology, as he illustrated it in the article, was to use pastoral experience, informed by psychological theory and theology, to address a human problem and move toward a theological correction.

Over the years, when students have asked, "What is pastoral theology?" (if they did not ask, I found a way to tell them anyway), I have given them copies of the "Lost Contracts" article and asked them to become familiar with the steps in Lapsley's method. I examined the method again as I began to work on this essay, and I found myself reflecting upon the word *lost* and Lapsley's explanation of "lost contracts" as those that have "gone underground." What became clear in that reflection was that the pivotal point of pastoral theology's method, as exemplified in Hiltner and Lapsley, was discovering in one's pastoral experience an aspect of theology that has been "lost" and explicating that experience in a way that attempted to deal with that loss. Because in working with students I had always been more concerned with focusing upon pastoral theological method than with specific content, it was only later that I realized the contribution of the article to the concern with human forgiveness that developed in my pastoral counseling practice.

My own work on forgiveness grew out of the repeated experience in pastoral counseling of my counselees' explicit use of forgiveness as an interpretive concept for their experience. Although thinking and talking about forgiveness seemed important to them, some of those same persons insisted that they could never forgive the person who had injured them for what he or she had done. Others seemed to claim that they had forgiven so easily that I had difficulty in believing them. Thus my clinical experience led me to conclude that something had been lost in the way that human forgiveness was being understood, both by those who expressed its importance in their experience and by those who interpreted it in ministry and theology.

The search for what seems to have been lost theologically or psychologically can take a number of forms. The one that seemed most relevant to me both from clinical experience and from the study of family therapy literature was the concept of "reframing." When something cannot be seen clearly in a photograph, an enlargement can be made so that a particular feature can be seen more clearly and, perhaps of more importance, the obscured feature can be seen in its relation to other elements in the picture. When the frame is enlarged, there is no change in the basic elements included in the picture, but new insight into the relationship of the various features becomes possible.

I examined my relationship to pastoral counseling clients who seemed to have been struggling with forgiveness to see what features in their stories might become clearer if I looked at them through a larger frame. The two things that became most quickly evident were (1) the shame these persons had experienced in whatever injury they had received; and (2) that, for those few who appeared to be forgiving toward those who had hurt them, forgiveness seemed to have occurred when they stopped trying to forgive—when forgiveness moved out of the center of the frame and became more peripheral. I put these observations together in a paper entitled "Reframing Forgiveness" and continued my study of the literature on shame and human forgiveness.[3]

Several years after "Lost Contracts," James Lapsley wrote another article that also influenced my clinical practice and teaching, "A Psychotheological Appraisal of the New Left." What was most important in the article was Lapsley's assertion that young people "no longer experience guilt and shame the way we did and still do. They don't need alcohol or the gospel to release them from guilt." Their concern is not with guilt, he continued, but with shame, shame understood "as an apprehension of failure, of not measuring up" in which "the core feeling is weakness."[4]

As I recall it now, my primary response to the article at that time was, "How am I going to get along without guilt?" I was aware that much of my parish ministry, my chaplaincy in a general hospital, and my pastoral counseling had focused upon guilt and grace. I had attempted to help persons find release from guilt and discover grace in their lives. As a result of the reflections stirred by the Lapsley article, I intensified my study of the phenomenon of shame and the literature interpreting it.

Up to that time, my primary understanding of shame had come from Erik H. Erikson's discussion of it in *Childhood and Society*.[5] As my exploration of the shame literature proceeded, I remember developing a lecture and discussing with students in pastoral counseling how the counseling process might involve a developmental move from shame to guilt based on Erikson's view of guilt as occurring at a later developmental stage than shame. I was concerned to maintain the importance of guilt in the midst of an increasingly "guiltless" and shame-oriented culture.

Although in 1969 Lapsley had called my attention to shame and its increasing cultural and psychological importance, particularly among young adults, what I found fifteen years later was that the literature on shame was still quite minimal. In the pastoral theological arena, Carl Schneider's *Shame, Exposure, and Privacy*, the

Lapsley article, and a chapter in Donald Capps' *Life Cycle Theory and Pastoral Care* were the primary things available.[6] In psychology, the major resource was Heinz Kohut's self psychology supplemented by the work of Gerhart Piers and Milton B. Singer, Helen B. Lewis, Helen Merrell Lynd, and Gershen Kaufman.[7] Perhaps the most striking thing, particularly in the light of the large amount of shame literature that has emerged in the last few years, was that in order to do a library computer search on shame ten years ago it was necessary for me to search for articles on guilt in order to find anything on shame.[8]

Certainly, shame and guilt continue to be closely related. They often "feed on" or intensify each other in what has been called a "shame-guilt" cycle. From a pastoral theological perspective, however, what seems most important to recognize is how dependent the church and ministry have been upon guilt and the ability of the two to orchestrate or, at the least, to respond to it as the primary pain in persons' lives.

In spite of its affirmation of the importance of relationality and community, Western Christianity has been heavily dependent in its ministry upon guilt and the behavioral-type psychology associated with its management. The rediscovery of the importance of shame in both psychology and religion reaffirms the importance of relationality and community in overcoming shame as prior to dealing effectively with one's guilt.

Parenthetically, another pastoral issue involving shame that has been insufficiently emphasized in the literature is the potential for shame and abuse in the pastoral relationship itself because of the power differential between the participants in that relationship. This is the type of shame inherent in the process of asking for help and thus in becoming dependent upon the helping person. Carl Schneider has spoken of this vulnerability in terms of the psychotherapeutic relationship involving asymmetrical disclosure and, consequently, asymmetrical power. The patient or parishioner is seen when he is not himself and when he is vulnerable to intrusion. In pastoral care and counseling, it is important that the pastor be able to respect the parishioner or counselee at a time when she may be unable to experience, maintain, or claim such self-respect.[9]

I have been struck in my own experience as a hospital chaplain and clinical pastoral education supervisor by what sometimes happens after a patient "opens up" to a visitor about some of his worries and concerns. The pastoral carer goes away feeling as if she has done well, established trust with the patient, and is on the way toward a significant relationship. On the next visit, however, the carer is surprised to find that the patient acts as if he hardly knows the visitor. In radical contrast to the visit the previous day, he seems closed and distant. The pastoral visitor goes away feeling confused and, perhaps, wondering how she has failed.

Probably, the only failure is the failure to be aware of the function of shame in relationships where people "open up." Without being aware of it, the visitor may have encouraged the patient to share more of himself than he was ready to share. One hopes that the next time she may be more aware of the patient's need to protect himself from the shame of too much openness and sharing. Moreover, the patient may be seeking help from the pastoral carer because of some abuse in the past. One of the pastor's major responsibilities is seeing to it that no further abuse takes place in the pastoral situation that reinforces what happened earlier.[10]

What I found in my study of the literature on human forgiveness was integrally related to the literature on shame and guilt. Most of it was behavioristically oriented. Forgiveness was conceived of as doing something, and although it was generally acknowledged to be difficult to do, a person was expected to try as hard as possible to do it anyway. In some of the popular literature, forgiveness was touted like oat bran, just naturally good for you. Much of the explicitly Christian literature centered around interpretations of the fifth petition of the Lord's Prayer as a conditional and behavioral transaction: "You forgive and God will forgive." Other interpretations, like William Barclay's often used commentary on the Matthean version of the prayer, were more like a threat, "No one is fit to pray the Lord's prayer so long as the unforgiving spirit holds sway within his heart."[11]

Most of my pastoral counseling clients were aware of forgiveness as an issue for them, but they could not respond either to the threats or to the affirmations of how "good for you" it was to forgive. Thus, on the basis of my clinical experience, I became convinced that forgiving was not primarily an action or a decision. Or perhaps, following Lapsley, something important in the understanding of forgiveness had been lost or gone underground. Perhaps human forgiveness was not, as so much of the literature had insisted, a behavior—something done or not done. As I reflected upon what had happened with some of my "forgiveness" clients who had overcome the initial hurt and shame of their injury and developed a significant relationship with me, it appeared that they became able to talk about the person or persons who had injured them without focusing upon the injury alone. They could see something other than what had been done to hurt them. It was as if the frame had been enlarged, and they began to see other things in the picture. What follows is my response to one of them when this had happened:

PASTOR: Elmer sounds almost human!

EMMIE: What?

PASTOR: I had never thought of him as an ordinary human being before, but listening to you then, the thought did occur to me. You sounded as if you were concerned about his predicament.

EMMIE: Well, he got himself into it.

PASTOR: I know. I was just noticing how you sounded. For the first time I can remember, he didn't seem like the enemy—just an ordinary human being.[12]

In reflecting upon this interaction and others like it, I was perhaps overly influenced by my dissertation study of Harry Stack Sullivan's interpersonal psychology and his affirmation that even included those persons who seem most different from us: "We are all more alike than otherwise." What seemed to be happening with Emmie and others was that they were making a discovery that they were not so different from those who had injured them. The injury had moved from the center of their lives to the periphery, and they were moving on. On occasion, there was discovery of their having let go or forgiven as a type of religious experience.[13] More often, as with Emmie, it was just a going on, with some awareness that keeping the injury focal was no longer particularly important.

My exploration of shame and forgiveness had grown out of a clinical experience that dealt primarily with relationships within the family. I was questioned about the narrowness of my focus when I was in the process of publishing an article on human forgiveness in The Christian Century.[14] The copy editor, apparently caught up in both the substance of the article and concern about the correctness of the copy, wrote in the margin, "What do you do with the Holocaust?" I became aware that I had not dealt in any way with how human forgiveness relates to the massive issues of human evil and destructiveness.

Later, my daughter, who had been a rape victim, let me know that seeing herself as "like" the person who had threatened her life and victimized her did not seem very realistic, but just made her more angry. Moreover, even though by the circumstances of my clinical practice and my own choice I had been concerned in my book about forgiveness in the family, I had not dealt at all with the physical, psychological, and sexual abuse that occurs in the family. I had drawn attention to an important issue that had been lost or gone underground, but there were other lost issues with respect to forgiveness that also needed attention.

In *Is Human Forgiveness Possible?* I dealt with what seemed to me to be the church and religious literature's behavioristic dispensing of forgiveness and encouraging persons to dispense it in a similar way. I had seen and interpreted this in terms of works righteousness, not abuse. My daughter's comments, my more recent clinical experience, and the literature produced by women pastoral counselors and theologians have made me aware not only of the *works righteous* way in which forgiveness has been interpreted, but also of the *abusive* way it has been used.[15]

One of the most striking recent examples in the literature on human forgiveness deals with the question of forgiveness after criminal violence perpetrated by strangers. The author of one article, Richard P. Lord, deals with the situation of a woman whose sons were killed and who herself was shot and left for dead by an unknown group of men who broke into her house. One of the men later wrote her from prison saying that he had "found Christ" and asked her to forgive him. She asked her pastor, "Am I obligated as a Christian to forgive in this situation? Just what does the church mean by 'forgiveness'? He did not say, 'I'm sorry' . . . just forgive me."[16]

In this fascinating clinical situation, the pastor responds by telling his parishioner that if she will give him six months, he will try to give her an answer. (How many pastors and clinical pastoral education students have wished for that kind of time lag between question and answer?) The merit of the pastor's response, however, is that it takes very seriously the difficulty of the question and, in effect, underscores how something important about forgiveness has been "lost" or "gone underground" in the search for quick answers.

Some of what may have gone underground is revealed in the pastor's analysis. He identifies two problems in forgiving: forgiveness as forgetting and forgiveness as excusing. With respect to forgetting, he comments:

> When we forgive someone, it usually implies that we will try to act as though nothing has happened. Can we do this without showing massive disrespect for the victim of violence when those close to him or her are deeply concerned that their loved one not be forgotten?

With respect to excusing, he asks the question, If an abuser has a religious experience after the abuse has taken place, does this mean that "now we should act as though a crime wasn't committed"? And, in reflecting on his proclamation in worship, "Your sins are forgiven," Pastor Lord imagines a battered wife thinking, "Who gave you the right to forgive the one who beats me?" As a consequence of this reflection, he argues that forgiveness cannot be "a commodity that can be handed out" by the church or anyone else, and he concludes that pastors and other well-intentioned Christians "have no right to insist that the victim establish a relationship with his or her victimizer to effect a reconciliation."[17]

The issue for ministry that Lord's article raises is not a simple one. It may involve another contract that church and ministry have lost or let go underground, and it may take more than six months to find the answer. Lord's move toward an answer was focused in an understanding of repentance as involving three conditions: remorse, restitution, and regeneration. None of the three was evidenced in the prisoner who has "found Christ." Thus the pastor concluded that to "offer forgiveness when these conditions are not met is not gracious. It is sacrilegious." The pastor's answer to the victim was "No." She did not have to forgive.

Almost more striking than the original article was the negative response it stirred up among the *Century*'s readers. For example:

> How can I be a Christian and refuse to forgive? . . . If you do not forgive others their trespasses, neither will your Father forgive you. I cannot call myself a Christian and refuse to forgive others or hope to have my sins forgiven.

Or consider this response:

> Lord's comments highlight for me a major problem with Christian
> ministry—the appeal to human experience as the plumbline for
> moral decisions. . . . Lord sought answers from other victims of vi-
> olent crimes. He would be far better served by going to the Bible to
> see what Jesus says about this subject. As a victim of violent crime
> myself, I want Lord to know that not only did I forgive the perpe-
> trator, but I have never had a resurgence of feeling unforgiving
> toward him since then.[18]

The intense resistance to Richard Lord's answer to the "Do I
have to forgive?" question suggests that there is still a good deal
about human forgiveness that has gone underground and that
needs further exploration by pastoral theology.

An answer not unlike Richard Lord's is found in a secular publication, *Voices*, published by the American Academy of Psychothera-
pists, in which Karen Olio responds not to a parishioner or client
but to a statement in a children's book. The book *I Can't Talk about
It: A Child's Book about Sexual Abuse* insists that the abused child
must forgive her father. In response, Olio argues that such insistence on forgiveness

> contributes to the revictimization of survivors, who for so long
> were forced to conform to an external version of reality, by insisting
> the path to wholeness and freedom can only be found by adopting
> one particular way of thinking and feeling toward the abuser.[19]

She challenges this "one way" forgiveness by noting its presumption that the victim's judgment must be suspended. She argues to the contrary that, in fact, judgments offer a significant
contribution to the healing process for survivors of sexual abuse.
She comments that the

> defense mechanisms, denial and dissociation, which are developed
> to cope with the emotionally overwhelming and physically over-
> stimulating abuse experiences, render survivors particularly suscepti-
> ble to the suggestion that forgiveness is a necessary step toward
> resolution of the abuse trauma.[20]

It is "no doubt crucial for resolution of the trauma that survivors
be able to view the abuser as a human being, and that they not
depersonalize him/her in the same manner that they themselves
were depersonalized." But, she insists, compassion and forgiveness

"are optional." Olio denies the argument of the recovery movement and twelve-step programs that taking responsibility for forgiveness is an important part of an abused person's empowerment. Instead, she argues that survivors, "who already must struggle with the feelings of self-blame caused by the abuse," should not have to take on the further blame of not being able to forgive.

In another secular treatment of human forgiveness, psychologist Sidney Simon and his wife Suzanne, who work with incest survivors groups, insist, like Richard Lord, that forgiveness is not forgetting and that victims of abuse should not forget.[21] Their experiences and the pain caused by those experiences have a great deal to teach them about living. What is more, forgiving is not excusing or condoning. It is important that the victim not say that what was done to him or her was acceptable or "not so bad." Forgiveness is not absolving the abuser of all responsibility for what he has done. He is still responsible for what he did and must deal with it himself. Most important, forgiveness is not a clear-cut, one-time decision. A person cannot simply decide that on today he or she is going to forgive. If it happens, it happens as a result of confronting painful past experiences and of the healing of old wounds.

Forgiveness, these authors argue as I did in *Is Human Forgiveness Possible?*, is a discovery. It is the by-product of an ongoing healing process. Failure to forgive is not a failure of will but happens because wounds have not yet healed. Forgiveness is not something done, a behavior. It is something that happens as a sign of positive self-esteem, when the victim is no longer building his or her identity around something that happened in the past. The injury is not all of who one is but just a part, a part of life that has at least started to move out of the center of the frame.

When forgiveness is discovered, the injured person no longer needs the hatred and resentments that have been so important and no longer needs to punish the people who hurt her or him, wanting them to suffer as much as the victim did. Realizing that punishing does not heal, forgiveness is putting to better use the energy once consumed by rage and resentment and moving on with life. It is, as I put it earlier, "a reframing."

A final, recent contribution to those "lost" issues regarding human forgiveness that can be noted here comes from Roberta Nobleman, an actress and victim of child sexual abuse. In a play in

which she acts in a one-woman performance, Nobleman has created a drama to express the pain of abuse and the attempt to get on
with life. The play, *Masks and Mirrors*, presents various dimensions
of child abuse from the perspective of both the abuser and the
abused. Nobleman was sexually abused by her father when she was
a child; and at age forty, when the repressed memories of the abuse
reemerged, she created her drama as a way of dealing with her own
abuse and as a way to help others address theirs. In a workshop that
she conducted after the drama was performed in our seminary
chapel, I heard a number of persons affirm the value of Nobleman's
work in helping them deal with abuse they had experienced.

Nobleman understands her work as affirming "the goodness of
life even in the midst of pain." A person can do this, she says,
"only after progressing through survival to reconciliation and forgiveness." "For me," she states, "the only way beyond survival was
forgiveness. People have to forgive themselves, and they have to
make peace with a world that allows child abuse to happen." Nobleman says in a recent article about her work:

> When I speak of forgiveness, immediately people jump down my
> throat and say, "You want me to forgive that bastard after what he
> did to me?" But I'm not saying that. Forgiveness is a gift. It's not
> something we can will to happen.

She believes that by requiring forgiveness from the injured person,
the church has sometimes reinforced victimization by shifting the
blame back to the victim again. As Payne has pointed out,

> in the past, victims have been urged to forgive much too quickly.
> Forgiveness is possible only late in the healing process. . . . Forgiving
> the abuser is possible only when you understand that within yourself
> lies the same potential for abuse. . . . Usually those who cannot for-
> give are people who recycle the pain, get stuck in the anger. Then it
> is almost impossible to see anything beyond the abuse, so that the
> abusive person is no longer anything but the abuser.[22]

Although she acknowledges that this is not possible for every
abused person, recognizing the common humanity between herself
and her father enabled Nobleman to recover positive memories
about him as well as the memories about him as abuser. This is
exemplified in the climax of her play when she takes off the mask
of the abuser, exposing underneath the mask of the innocent child,

one who was in all likelihood abused himself as a child and for whom violence became a way of life.

One of the strengths of Nobleman's play, as I experienced it and discussed it with others, is its chaos and confusion. The power of its symbols—most often the masks, one coming in rapid fire after the other—creates a sense of ambiguity as well as a sense of deception and denial. The violent abuser, who is also a child, points to the character of the human situation and the ambiguity both of forgiving and of not forgiving. Victimization and violence are not denied, but there is the suggestion that something other than vengeance sometimes can follow them.

Nobleman's work and much that I have observed and experienced in pastoral counseling suggests that human forgiveness itself is ambiguous and imperfect. If, however, the demand that forgiveness is something that every injured person must *do* can be surrendered, forgiveness can sometimes be *discovered*. What has been lost in much theological writing about forgiveness and reconciliation and what can be clarified by actual human experience is that neither forgiveness nor reconciliation is perfect. Scars remain. Those involved do not "live happily every after." Reconciliation—in this world at least—means living with and going on. Nobleman and many others may be able to remember and possibly even reexperience positive things with the abuser, but something has been irretrievably lost and broken. Much in the relationship with the person or the memory cannot be reclaimed. Nevertheless, for some, life can go on reframed and refocused in a different direction.

What I have done in this essay is to interpret the method of pastoral theology, as exemplified in some of the work of James Lapsley, as growing dynamically from something important that has been lost or gone underground in contemporary theological understanding. I have suggested that the dynamic of pastoral theological method is the uncovering of some of what has been lost or gone underground in the human being's relationship to God and to other human beings. I have examined a number of "losts" with respect to human forgiveness, particularly those having to do with issues of abuse and shame. The human condition is such that we will continue to lose touch with important issues in life, theology, and ministry. I believe, therefore, that pastoral theology will always have lost contracts to uncover and explicate.

NOTES

1. James N. Lapsley, "Reconciliation, Forgiveness, Lost Contracts," *Theology Today* 23, no. 1 (April 1966): 44–69.

2. Ibid., 45–46.

3. John H. Patton, "Reframing Forgiveness," *Cura Animarum* 36, no. 1 (May 1984): 40–48.

4. James N. Lapsley, "A Psychotheological Appraisal of the New Left," *Theology Today* 25, no. 4 (January 1969): 446–61.

5. Erik H. Erikson, *Childhood and Society* (New York: W. W. Norton), 251–54.

6. Carl D. Schneider, *Shame, Exposure, and Privacy* (Boston: Beacon Press, 1977); and Donald Capps, *Life Cycle Theory and Pastoral Care* (Philadelphia: Fortress Press, 1983).

7. Gerhart Piers and Milton B. Singer, *Shame and Guilt: A Psychoanalytic and Cultural Study* (New York: W. W. Norton, 1971); Helen B. Lewis, *Shame and Guilt in Neurosis* (New York: International Universities Press, 1971); Helen Merrell Lynd, *On Shame and the Search for Identity* (New York: Science Editions, 1961); and Gershen Kaufman, *Shame: The Power of Caring* (Cambridge, Mass.: Shenkman Publishing Co., 1980).

8. Of the "recovery literature," which has brought shame into the public's consciousness, the most useful book to me has been Merle A. Fossum and Marilyn J. Mason's *Facing Shame: Families in Recovery* (New York: W. W. Norton, 1986). Other valuable recent literature on shame includes Michael P. Nichols' popular *No Place to Hide: Facing Shame So We Can Find Self-Respect* (New York: Simon & Schuster, 1991); Gershen Kaufman's expansion of his earlier work on shame, titled this time *The Psychology of Shame* (New York: Springer Publishing Co., 1989); Francis J. Broucek's *Shame and Self* (New York: Guilford Press, 1991); Carl Goldberg's *Understanding Shame* (Northvale, N.J.: Jason Aronson, 1991); and a valuable collection of essays by a number of authors associated with the literature on shame that is edited by Donald L. Nathanson, *The Many Faces of Shame* (New York: Guilford Press, 1987).

9. Carl D. Schneider, "Shame," in *Dictionary of Pastoral Care and Counseling*, gen. ed. Rodney J. Hunter (Nashville: Abingdon Press, 1990), 1162–63.

10. John Patton, *Is Human Forgiveness Possible?* (Nashville: Abingdon Press, 1985), 19.

11. William Barclay, *The Gospel of Matthew* (Philadelphia: Westminster Press, 1969), 130.

12. Patton, *Is Human Forgiveness Possible?*, 19.

13. Cf. ibid., 138–39.

14. John Patton, "Human Forgiveness as Problem and Discovery," *The Christian Century* 102, no. 27 (September 11–18, 1985): 795–97.

15. See, for example, Maxine Glaz and Jeanne Stevenson-Moessner, eds., *Women in Travail and Transition: A New Pastoral Care* (Minneapolis: Fortress Press, 1991); and "Forgiveness: The Last Step," in Marie M. Fortune, *Violence in the Family* (Cleveland: Pilgrim Press, 1991).

16. Richard P. Lord, "Personal Perspective," *The Christian Century* 108, no. 28 (Oct. 9, 1991): 902–3.

17. Ibid., 902.

18. "Readers' Response," *The Christian Century* 108, no. 34, (November 20–27, 1991).

19. Karen Olio, "Recovery from Sexual Abuse: Is Forgiveness Mandatory?" *Voices* 28, no. 3 (Fall 1992): 73.

20. Ibid., 74.

21. Sidney B. Simon and Suzanne Simon, *Forgiveness: How to Make Peace with Your Past and Get on with Your Life* (New York: Warner Books, 1990), 15–20.

22. Pamela Payne, "A Liturgy for Survivors," *The Christian Century*, 109, no. 8 (March 18–25, 1992): 303–4.

13
The Recovery of Soul

HERBERT ANDERSON

Thomas Moore begins his book on *Care of the Soul* with an analysis of our present plight. The primary cause for the maladies of our time, he argues, is that we have neglected the soul. When we are inattentive to the needs of the soul, we are likely to become personally bereft and flounder without meaning.

> The great malady of the twentieth century, implicated in all of our troubles and affecting us individually and socially, is "loss of soul." When soul is neglected, it doesn't just go away; it appears symptomatically in obsessions, addictions, violence, and loss of meaning. Our temptation is to isolate these symptoms or to try to eradicate them one by one; but the root problem is that we have lost our wisdom about the soul, even our interest in it.[1]

When the soul is damaged, there is a deficit of human spirit. Without soul, we are easily distracted and susceptible to seduction. A lost soul, in common parlance, is someone who is without purpose or community. Many of the human struggles to which we give psychological labels in therapeutic settings may also be understood as maladies of the modern soul.

What I mean by soul is something like the vitalizing center of life. It is the quality or dimension of living with ourselves and others. Soul is not something one can take out and look at. Soul is everywhere but nowhere. It is, therefore, more accurate to say "I am a soul" than "I have a soul." Soul is the source of human genuineness and depth and mystery. The care of soul begins,

Moore observes, with "an appreciation of the paradoxical mysteries that blend light and darkness into the grandeur of what human life and culture can be."[2]

This understanding of soul has much in common with Old Testament understandings of the person. The Hebrew word frequently translated *soul* means something like a life principle. We cannot limit soul, however, to the intellectual or rational function of the individual. As a life principle, soul does not exist apart from that which gives it form. It is not an extension of either mind or body. Soul reflects the totality of the person that may express itself in the body as a whole or may constitute itself in some part of the body, like the kidney or liver.

We are both embodied souls and soul-filled bodies. The soul thirsts and hungers (Ps. 42:2), even though it also becomes the seat of ethical wisdom (Wisd. Sol. 1:4). Because the human being is a unity, soul or liver or kidney or spirit may refer to the individual as a whole. So, for example, the literal translation of Proverbs 23:16 is that "my kidneys will rejoice when your lips speak what is right." Souls yearn and flesh cries out. "It takes a broad vision to know that a piece of the sky and a chunk of the earth lie lodged in the heart of every human being, and that if we are going to care for that heart we will have to know the sky and earth as well as human behavior."[3] This double orientation makes soul an effective metaphor for thinking paradoxically about being human.

RECOVERING SOUL

This essay is about the recovery of soul. My aim is threefold: (1) to recover the meaning and use of soul for our time; (2) to examine how the recovery of soul might enhance our theological anthropology; and (3) to explore some of the implications of a recovery of soul for pastoral care. If Moore's analysis of the modern plight is accurate, and I believe that it is, we need first to renew our interest in soul. If we become studious observers of the soul, the primary metaphor by means of which we think about people will change. The *self* has been and still is a very useful image for thinking about the human dimension of becoming a person, but the self is more readily understood as a social construction than it is as a gift from God. Images of the person linked with *spirit*, *ego*, or *psyche* identify specific dimensions of the human person, but none has the capacity of soul to hold "earth and sky" in paradox.

Our anthropology is theological when the images of the human person link us to God as well as to the earth. Soul makes these links. Therefore, the recovery of soul is at the same time a retrieval of the transcendent in human life. The human person is a bio-social-spiritual unity. No word reflects that unity more profoundly than soul. The language of soul adds a transcendent reality to our emphasis on the unity of the person. We have our life from God. The ultimate aim is to put "soul at the center of our lives" in order to understand more clearly people who are trapped in a soul-less existence. Soul-less existence is *the* malady of the modern soul.[4]

My interest in rethinking soul has been precipitated in part by the growing frequency with which students refer to the recipients of care as clients. "Client" is an improvement over sheep as a metaphor for people seeking help, but it implies a kind of relationship that does not fit easily with either theological anthropology or the historical tradition of *seelsorge* (care or cure of souls). Simply at the level of language, the recovery of soul provides an alternative metaphor to personality or psyche or self for thinking about what is the core of an individual. As long as the troubles of the soul have been understood in the language of psychology, it is not surprising that the cure of souls has been linked to the methods and diagnostic categories of psychotherapy. This volume is a needed addition to the development of a theological anthropology for pastoral care.[5]

There are several implications of this perspective for pastoral care: the recovery of soul connects pastoral care with its roots; it changes our thinking about the diagnostic categories; it avoids the technologies of care; because the soul lives in paradox, insisting on the other or rejected side is part of care; we listen to the anguish of the earth and sky because the soul is linked to the world's soul. The sacred work of soul care is more art than science because it is the application of poetics to everyday life. We will return to some of these themes later. First, we must determine more fully what a soul is by observing what soul does.

Soul Is What Soul Does

Soul is mysterious. We can only know in part, see in part the human soul. We cannot penetrate its essence. We may observe its struggle to survive or thrive, but we cannot capture the mystery of soul. We may watch a soul struggle to hold earth and sky together, but only God knows the soul. We bring this exploration into the recovery of soul with the assumption that God understands human experience better than we do. For mortals, the soul is ineffable. The recovery of soul, as Moore observes, begins with an acknowledgment of mystery.

Nonetheless, we must speak and write about soul. Because soul is more process than substance, we can say what the soul does more than what it is. However, even those images are tentative. What we see is the soul's "backside," the residue of human essence as it passes by. The language of soul is therefore not technical or scientific. It is embodied in poetry and song. Imagination is the expression of soul. What we can say about soul in its essence is drawn from what a soul does in its existence.

1. *Soul is the making of meaningful memory.* It is soul, James Ashbrook has observed, that expresses meaning and making meaning depends on memory.[6] It is memory that makes our lives personally meaningful by linking the past and the present. Without memory, we have neither history nor identity. We are "soul-less" without the sense of continuity that memory makes. When we do not take the time to remember the many facets of our lives or when we have lost our memory, we have also lost our soul. Restoration has its beginning in telling the deep myths of the soul. "Like all narratives, the story of the self or deep myth of the soul has a plot that embodies a sense of beginnings, a continuing story line, and a more or less problematic ending."[7] The sacred work of care restores the soul when we listen to the story to make a meaningful memory. Even when we cannot remember, we are held in the memory of the community. And if the community forgets, we are still held in the memory of God.

Making meaningful memory is essential for the soul because of its liminal character: it is simultaneously of the earth and of the sky. As part of the earth, the soul has its own time and its own rhythm. The soul does not run as fast as our bodies, and it certainly does not calculate as quickly as computers. For that reason, both rest and activity are necessary for soul making. That is one significance of "remember the Sabbath." We remember so that we do not outrun the soul. When we lose ourselves in a multiplicity of activities and concerns, we endanger the soul. We need to remember the Sabbath in order to have time for making memory.[8]

2. *Soul is being vulnerable.* The great enemy of soul is pretense and deception. We endanger the soul when we obscure human vulnerability with glittering images or glamorous powers. What I mean by vulnerability as a description of the human is that we are susceptible to being wounded. The nakedness of soul should not cover over our vulnerability. The way of being soul is like a trapeze artist swinging above the earth with her feet planted firmly in midair. What is certain in being soul is uncertainty. What is sure about the soul is susceptibility. The posture of soul is to be rested in neediness.

Being soul is living with our nakedness. When we are free from hiding or pretense, we are able to move toward all things without comparison and with compassion. When we can be naked, we know that God's graciousness touches everything we have hated in ourselves with mercy for ourselves and mercy for the world. As a friend of mine once observed, "I do not go lightly from someone who has held my soul." It does not work to use soul to cover our nakedness. We nourish the soul instead when we live without pretense of self-knowledge or protection. And we are free to live without pretense because we believe soul is ultimately hidden in God. The way of the soul is the way of the fool.

3. *The soul waits actively.* Since Aristotle, the metaphor of soul has been used to describe that which animates our being. The images in Hebrew scriptures are particularly graphic in ascribing significant activity to soul. "My soul longs, indeed it faints for the courts of the LORD," says the psalmist (Ps. 84:2a). And yet the soul is not simply action or participation. It *is* that, but more. The way of the soul is passivity. In *The Stature of Waiting*, W. H. Vanstone has observed that both activity and passivity belong to the being of God and therefore to the human way of being.[9] We are human when we wait as well as when we act.

Again, we encounter another paradoxical mystery of soul. It is active passivity. The soul acts and is acted upon. For that reason, what is happening is getting done. It is not just that God does it, or that I do it, but that the action of soul flows from a different place. In one sense, the soul is a symbol of individuality and personal uniqueness. Soul is what we call our own and what distinguishes us from all others. Yet we do not possess our life, nor do we possess our soul. Soul is who I am, but it is from God. When we say "what is happening is getting done," we mean that our action is beyond us. The soul is not simply autonomous agency. It is from God and for God. It is soul that takes the adventures that God sends.

Each of these images drawn from the soul's activity points to the complexity of the soul. In order to be a lover of souls, our own included, we need to have some appreciation for complexity. What troubled souls often bring to a situation of care is a longing for simplicity. Could it be this or that? they will ask, in the hope that some one thing will erase their disease. The task of *seelsorge* is to empower people to embrace paradox, glimpse the contingency of life, acknowledge vulnerability, and learn to live as a trapeze artist with both feet planted firmly in midair. In order that this might happen, those who engage in *seelsorge* must appreciate the paradoxical mysteries that shape the grandeur of human life.

PARADOXICAL MYSTERIES OF THE SOUL

The recovery of soul is an invitation to rediscover the paradoxical mysteries of human nature. Focus on the soul is a reminder that humankind is always both/and: *both* a creature who is finite like all other creatures *and* someone just a little lower than the angels; *both* trapped by the collective and individual sins of the past *and* free to move beyond one's limitations to become a fulfilled human being; *both* an individual with particularity and autonomy *and* a member of a community whose identity cannot be separated from that community. It is the soul that has the potential to hold these paradoxical mysteries in a balanced tension for the sake of human life and culture.

The paradox of *self-transcending finitude* has been described effectively by Ernest Becker as *the* existential dilemma. Humankind is split in two. On the one hand, we claim a special uniqueness because we stick out of nature with "towering majesty." Yet, in the end, we return to the ground in order "blindly to rot and disappear forever."[10] Human beings, according to Becker, are gods who shit. That is our plight. We are out of nature and hopelessly in it. The ultimate dilemma of humankind is that we are aware of our creatureliness.

Any dualism ignores this paradox. It is an effort to settle a necessary contradiction by insisting that human beings are mostly this way or that way, mostly spirit or mostly body. Some denial in human life is necessary. We cannot live with the full truth of human contingency. Yet, as Becker aptly describes it, we may spend an inordinate amount of time and energy developing and maintaining the "character armor" that is a shield against the reality of human finitude. "The irony of man's condition is that the deepest need is to be free of the anxiety of death and annihilation; but it is life itself which awakens it, and so we must shrink from being fully alive."[11] In order to flee from the anxiety of death, we hide from life itself.

Keeping a paradoxical view of human nature is a complicated task. Dualisms die hard. We are reluctant to celebrate being a body because such an affirmation links us more with the other creatures in creation than with the angels. At one level, sexism is a continuance of old dualisms as long as women are linked primarily with body and men with spirit or intellect. Passivity, dependence, irrationality, and sensuality are all characteristics of repressed bodiliness that are ascribed to the feminine or to childhood. The alienation of the mind from the body cannot be separated from the alienation of the masculine from the feminine or childhood from adulthood.

What is at stake in maintaining the paradox of *self-transcending finitude* is the freedom to live without pretense and anxiety. When we attempt to establish emotional well-being by denying finitude, we are trapped in anxiety-producing character armor. Reality is remorseless, as Becker reminds us. The denial of the reality of finitude leads to a life of pretense and the loss of soul. We are more likely to recover soul if we can be naked in the world, without pretense or bravado. That takes courage because seeing more clearly will only bring into play new and sharper paradoxes, new tensions, and more painful disharmonies.

The second paradox about the nature of human nature is most aptly characterized by the juxtaposition of *no longer and not yet*. We are no longer what God intended humankind to be, *and* we are not yet what we might become. There is nothing more complicated in presenting an anthropology that is biblically grounded than to insist on this paradox. Because human beings are inextricably linked to creation, we are also part of the fallenness of that creation. So the apostle Paul wonders, "Who will rescue me from this body of death?" (Rom. 7:24). Yet that same apostle Paul describes his own efforts: "Forgetting what lies behind and straining forward to what lies ahead, I press on toward the goal for the prize of the heavenly call of God in Christ Jesus" (Phil. 3:13–14).

This paradox has been understood through the history of the Christian church as a tension between the restitutionary view of Augustine and the consummation view of Irenaeus. John Hick described it this way:

> The ideal state, representing the fulfillment of God's intention for man, is not a lost reality, forfeited long ago in "the vast backward and abysm of time," but something lying before us as a state to be attained in the distant future.[12]

In psychological terms, this view of human nature as not yet finished is replicated in humanistic psychology and its conviction that human beings (individually and collectively) have not yet achieved all of their potential. The more conservative notion is reflected in the Freudian notion of repetition compulsion and the inclination to keep repeating the past. It is as necessary as it is difficult to hold in balance the psychological and theological truth of both views. Humankind is no longer *and* not yet.

There is a variant of this paradox that has particular consequences for the work of care. It is generally easier for us to be supportive of those people whose plight is outside their control. They are victims, whether of abuse and dysfunctionality in the family or violence and discrimination in the wider society. The dilemma they bring to a pastoral conversation, they want us to believe, is not of their own doing. They believe they are victims of outside forces and, therefore, are not responsible for their plight. Others will take blame that is not theirs.

One of the most delicate pastoral tasks is to sort out responsibility and accountability. We are often victims. At the same time, we continue to be responsible actors. Sometimes, however, we contribute to our plight. This tension is another variation of the misplaced debate between free will and determinism.[13] The answer is another paradox. Both are true. In most instances, when we have trouble of some kind, we are *responsible victims*. Because we live in a society in which people are violated daily in a variety of ways, it is easy to think of oneself as victim without responsibility. It is important to keep the paradox in order to keep alive the reality of human agency and accountability.

The third paradoxical mystery of humankind is conveyed by the phrase *communal autonomy*. In most Western societies, the human person is understood as a particular and uniquely bounded creature with an identity, a name, and a history. It is a vision of being human that presumes the independent functioning of ego or spirit distinct from soul or body in the development of self. This highly privatized, highly individualized concept of human autonomy is not universal, however. Most societies of the world begin their consideration of the person with the community. The African theologian John Mbiti has described this sociocentric view of the world with the dictum "I am because we are."[14] Personal identity is derivative of the community. Egocentric perspectives on the person cannot be separated from sociocentric realities.

The identification of soul with "making meaningful memory" reflects this paradox of communal autonomy. It is a very particular identity that is shaped by remembering and sabbathing. Making a memory, however, is a communal activity. We remember with someone. Some years ago, Krister Stendahl offered a provocative critique of the immortality of the soul.[15] It was, he said, both too much and too little. It was too much because it promised more about God's future for us than we can possibly know. It was too little because it was too narrowly individualistic. The preservation of my own particular soul or identity presumed that our individualistic notions of personhood accurately reflect God's intentions for humankind. Soul that is formed by waiting and remembering and walking naked in the world is simultaneously individual and communal.

SALVATORY PARTICIPATION AND
THE PARADOX OF SOUL

There are indeed other variations of the paradoxical mystery of being human. I mention these three because they can be so closely linked with understandings of soul, and because they point to the strengths and limitations of the anthropology implicit in James Lapsley's scheme on salvation and health as interlocking processes. His emphasis on participation in his landmark book *Salvation and Health* linked two elements of personhood often overlooked.[16] Participation implies community; and the end of health is discipleship.

Lapsley is correct when he insists that there is, in fact, no individual gospel—"only a salvation by participation in which the identity of the individual is lost."[17] There is, for Lapsley, an inescapable communal dimension to being human that corrects the individualistic anthropology of pastoral theology.

Lapsley's emphasis on salvatory participation also lifts up the meaning or vocational aspect of human life. In an assessment of Lapsley's legacy, Rodney Hunter observes that discipleship is the ultimate question that confronts every form and occasion of human participation.[18] Neither salvation nor health are ends in themselves. The aim of becoming more healthy is to enhance our participation in God's work in behalf of the world. The question of meaning can never be excluded from our anthropology, and the possibility of vocation is the end of the healing work of pastoral care. Two decades after Lapsley's book was published, Regis A. Duffy, O.F.M., developed a similar perspective: we are healed for the sake of others.[19] Pastoral care cannot achieve its real purpose if it does not renew a sense of mission and enhance participation in building and rebuilding the kingdom of God.

The recovery of soul, as a bridging metaphor between health and salvation, also deepens the sense of paradox in Lapsley's anthropology. There is a danger in his theory that Lapsley does not intend. As Hunter pointed out, the stress on salvation conceived of largely in terms of levels of participation could be interpreted to exclude children and the aging. Moreover, the emphasis on activity or participation is not balanced by the other half of a soul's life— passivity and rest.

James Lapsley's recent work on *Renewal in Late Life through Pastoral Counseling* continues the emphasis on participation. The interaction of spirit and self is at the core of the person.[20] Spirit is on "loan from God" to provide motion and direction in life. Soul, according to Lapsley, is the "resulting structure of human existence which belongs to human beings in a sense which spirit does not."[21] That is true enough, but it is not the whole story. Because soul is from God, it links us to sky *and* to earth. What seems to be missing in Lapsley's use of spirit in particular, and his understanding of human nature more generally, is the possibility of paradox that is central both for the life of the soul and for theological anthropology.

Implications for Pastoral Care

Several of the implications of the recovery of soul are of particular significance for the practice of pastoral care today.

1. *The recovery of soul connects the pastoral care movement with its roots.* The principal importance of John T. McNeil's *A History of the Cure of Souls* was that it traced the history of *seelsorge* according to the practice of reconciliation. His was one of the last books to use the image of soul to refer to the recipient of pastoral care. McNeil defined soul as the essence of human personality. It is related to the body, but it is not a mere expression or function of bodily life. The soul is capable of vast ranges of experience and is susceptible to disorder and anguish.[22] The welfare of the soul is the welfare of the person. For most of the history of the church's ministry of care, the aim has been the restoration of the soul.

In a recent volume on spirituality and spiritual direction entitled *Soul Friend*, Kenneth Leech links the rapid development of spiritual direction in our time with the climate of contemporary culture.[23] We are searching for soul, as Leech describes it—that is, soul without the definite article. Not "a soul," as in the manner of the old dualism, but soul as a metaphor for meaning and memory in our time. Although the image of "soul friend" is common to both pastoral care and spiritual direction, we have been more inclined to link soul searching with spiritual direction than with pastoral counseling. Being a "soul friend" is not a professional activity.

The recovery of the language of soul as a metaphor for the human person is one way to reconnect present modes of pastoral caretaking with its tradition of *seelsorge*. Soul care is the common agenda for everyone who is in this tradition. In our counseling ministries and in hospital or parish visitation, or in conversations over coffee after morning worship, our aim is the same—to attend the souls struggling to survive or to thrive. Listening to souls unravel their stories one by one, hour by hour, is an extravagant act of grace. As a caregiver friend of mine once put it, a lost soul is worthy of our full attention and our steadfast care.[24] The language of soul in the work of counseling and psychotherapy is a reminder both of the origins and aim of our work—to attend to the human soul for the sake of restoration.

2. *The recovery of soul is a challenge to dualisms that linger.* Despite the fact that the unity of the individual is a generally accepted

belief, there are still residues of the ancient spiritualistic dualism in which the body was regularly regarded as inferior to the soul. Belief in the immortality of the soul after death persists in the operational theology of many people who would otherwise reject any notions that the body is evil and the soul is good. As we have already noted, the ancient body-soul dualism exists in the present in the form of sexism against women or in the contempt of children.

The more pervasive dualism in modern American culture is what one labels physicalistic dualism in which the body is everything and the soul is incidental. We spend much more time and money attending to our bodies than our souls. For some, health club membership, aerobics, weight machines, racquetball, or jogging are appropriate ways of exercising the body for the sake of health. For others, however, preoccupation with muscle tone and flat tummies becomes an end in itself. The body is primary. The spiritual dimension of the person is treated with benign neglect.

The glorification of the body is a new kind of alienation that ignores human holism by absolutizing the body instead of the spirit. In one sense, the preoccupation with the body is motivated by the same fear of death that prompted spiritualistic dualism. If we do not believe that our souls are immortal, we are determined to make our bodies last forever. Bodies without blemish are promoted as the goal. If daily workouts at the health club do not build the body desired, a surgeon can with the help of a little silicone. The recovery of soul is a countercultural word in response to people who believe that "being a body" is everything.

The deepest paradox of Christianity is the incarnational one: the finite can contain the infinite, and the infinite can be in the finite without either losing uniqueness. The incarnation of God in Christ is a declaration that spirit and matter, soul and body are not permanently irreconcilable. Further, the maintenance of human wholeness requires that neither spirituality nor physicality is alienated from the other. The well-being of the person as a whole is threatened if we ignore or exaggerate either soul or body. The recovery of an anthropology faithful to the whole Christian tradition requires that we keep alive the paradox of the incarnation. To be somebody is to be a soulbody. That is another way of continuing to locate the soul in both the earth and the sky.

3. *The recovery of soul changes our diagnostic categories.* A lost or

struggling soul is not a category of psychopathology. It is rather a way of thinking about the individual's life before God. To be healthy and whole, it has been said, is no substitute for being penitent, forgiven, and holy.[25] Using the language of soul is a way of returning to the view that character matters. To be a troubled soul deepens diagnostic categories like borderline or narcissistic disorders. The "dark night of the soul" is not simply a psychological malady but part of the journey to God. There is the darkness of privation (when the soul is deprived of the delight of all worldly things), there is the darkness of faith (when understanding is hidden from believing), and there is the darkness of God. One of the tasks of soul care is to distinguish between darkness in general and the dark night of the soul, to discern the darkness.[26]

The soul is a metaphor that reminds us that the human creature comes from God and is destined for God. We need to recover the use of soul in order to be reminded of our relationship to God. There is much we have to do to care for our bodies and to keep our thinking clear. But the cure of souls touches yet another dimension of being human that longs for relationship with God. Despite the importance of human agency, the soul is not an autonomous agent. To tend to a soul is to lead it in the ways of God, who is the source and end of our journey. The recovery of soul reminds us that all of life and health depends on God, whose Life is perfect freedom.

The language of soul is also a reminder that human beings are always more than they appear to be. In the course of a day, we move in and out of many roles. Sometimes the roles we live are so inextricably linked with our identity that we cannot distinguish our soul from our roles. We are trapped by them. People will describe situations in which their repertoire of roles is restricted by a time in which one's soul is in danger. Even the role of client is restricting. The experience of transcendence in human life is a reminder that we cannot be confined by our roles. The remarkable mystery of the human soul is that we are always more than the present situation. The experience of soul happens at the moment we transcend the preoccupation with roles and other confinements of being.

4. *If paradox is central to our understanding of human life and faith, then saying the other side becomes an essential dimension of the church's ministry of care.* We are not likely to choose paradox. One might trace the whole of human history as an ongoing effort to avoid the

inevitable paradoxes of life. We would rather things be this way or that way rather than this way *and* that way. We are uncomfortable with freedom that is finite and with grace that is unmerited. Often, Thomas Moore has observed, "When spirituality loses its soul it takes on the shadow-form of fundamentalism."[27] It is precisely because of our inclination to absolutize alternatives or polarize options in ways that ignore the essential ambiguity of life that we must develop a ministry that carefully keeps "saying the other side."

It is the restoration of soul, I believe, that will enhance the recovery of paradox in human life. The soul is from God and in time. It is in every cell of the body and capable of self-transcendence. The soul participates fully in its salvation even while it waits for the Lord. Insisting on the soul's paradox will not eliminate dualistic impulses or modify absolutizing tendencies. It will, however, articulate an anthropological vision that is deep enough and broad enough to encompass the diversity of human life today. The recovery of soul will also provide a basis for reconnecting the work of pastoral care with the ancient tradition of *seelsorge* for the sake of communities of faith.

NOTES

1. Thomas Moore, *Care of the Soul: A Guide for Cultivating Depth and Sacredness in Everyday Life* (New York: Harper Collins Publishers, 1992), xi.

2. Ibid., xix.

3. Ibid., 20.

4. In John S. Dunne's book *The Reasons of the Heart* (New York: Macmillan Publishing Company, 1978) there is a chapter on "Recovery of Soul." For Dunne, the recovery of soul is solitude and back again into the human circle. "Only by laying down my soul, it seems, by willingly losing the person I have lost, by willingly losing even the new and unknown life I have lost, do I actually recover my soul." (p. 114) We are, in effect, soul-less until that recovery occurs.

5. Don S. Browning's *Religious Thought and the Modern Psychologies* (Philadelphia: Fortress Press, 1987) is a penetrating and comprehensive analysis of the anthropological assumptions in modern psychological theories.

6. James P. Ashbrook, "Soul: Its Meaning and Its Making," *Journal of Pastoral Care* 45, no. 2 (Summer 1991): 159–68.

7. Charles V. Gerkin, *The Living Human Document: Revisioning Pastoral Counseling in a Hermeneutical Mode* (Nashville: Abingdon Press, 1984), 114.

8. Ashbrook, "Soul: Its Meaning and Its Making." "Abraham Heschel told of a medieval sage who declared, 'The world which was created in six days was a world without a soul. It was on the seventh day that the world was given a soul. This is why it is said: "and on the seventh day God rested' " (quoted in Ashbrook, p. 168).

9. W. H. Vanstone, *The Stature of Waiting* (London: Darton, Longman & Todd, 1982).

10. Ernest Becker, *The Denial of Death* (New York: Free Press, 1973), 26.

11. Ibid., 66.

12. John Hick, "Toward a Christian Theology of Death," in *Dying, Death, and Disposal*, ed. Gilbert Cope (London: SPCK, 1970), 19.

13. Frederic G. Reamer, "The Free Will—Determinism Debate and Social Work," *Social Service Review* (December 1983): 626–84.

14. John S. Mbiti, *African Religions and Philosophy* (Garden City, N.Y.: Anchor Books, 1970), 141.

15. Krister Stendahl, "Immortality Is Too Much and Too Little," in *Meanings: The Bible as Document and as Guide* (Philadelphia: Fortress Press, 1984), 73–83.

16. James N. Lapsley, *Salvation and Health: The Interlocking Processes of Life* (Philadelphia: Westminster Press, 1972).

17. Ibid., 131.

18. Rodney J. Hunter, "The Lapsley Legacy," *The Princeton Theological Bulletin*, n.s., 13, no. 2 (1992): 176–86.

19. Regis A. Duffy, O.F.M., *A Roman Catholic Theology of Pastoral Care* (Philadelphia: Fortress Press, 1983). "Throughout this book I have suggested that pastoral care cannot achieve its real purpose if it does not renew a sense of mission in all whom it touches. Pastoral care allows Christians to hear once more Christ's challenge: Rebuild my house. . . . Pastoral care retools Christians so that they can *participate* [emphasis mine] in this rebuilding with a new sense of purpose" (p. 85).

20. James N. Lapsley, *Renewal in Later Life through Pastoral Counseling* (New York: Paulist Press, 1992), 33.

21. Ibid., 31.

22. John T. McNeil, *A History of the Cure of Souls* (New York: Harper & Row, 1951).

23. Kenneth Leech, *Soul Friend: A Study of Spirituality* (London: Sheldon Press, 1977).

24. This sentence was included in the presidential address of William M. North, Jr., to the Annual Convention of the American Association of

Pastoral Counselors in May 1990. The care of individual souls, he said, is an "extravagant act of empathic attention."

25. Michael Ramsey, *The Charismatic Christ* (New York: Morehouse Barlow Co., 1973), 45. Soul is a way back to thinking that character matters without, at the same time, returning to old forms of asceticism. The recovery of soul, as I understand it, presumes a rather earthy view of holiness.

26. The emergence of a growing body of literature on spiritual assessment is another dimension of the recovery of soul. See George Fitchett, *Assessing Spiritual Needs: A Guide for Caregivers* (Minneapolis: Augsburg Fortress, 1993).

27. Moore, *Care of the Soul*, 234.

14
Gender: Women and Identity

CHRISTIE COZAD NEUGER

The question of women and identity is surrounded by theological, psychological, and cultural paradox. In fact it is, I believe, the attempt to develop identity and meaning in the midst of irresolvable paradox that is the most damaging aspect to living as a woman in a patriarchal context. Some of those paradoxical realities include:

You are valuable as a woman because of your nurturing and relational capacities. As a culture, we value independence and autonomy.

You are created in the image and likeness of God. God is male.

You are small, weak, dependent, and in need of male protection. You have the power to destroy the lives of men and children.

You represent moral and spiritual purity. You are the sexual object to more than fourteen million readers of pornography.[1]

You represent moral and spiritual purity in your endurance, steadfastness, and lack of self-interest as woman and mother. You are responsible for sin (especially sexual sin) in the world.

You need to be submissive, patient, and supportive in your family life. Why didn't you leave your battering husband? You must, at some level, like the violence.

You must keep your body pure and sexuality contained. You must use your body and keep it accessible to sell products and to make men feel good.

You are a welcome, valuable, and full member of the church. Your vocation is to support the work of the church from behind the scenes—not from the pulpit.

224

You need to be protected by an intimate male partner. One-third of all female homicides are killed by their husband or "lover," and 50 percent of women are beaten by their significant male other at some point in their lives.[2]

You, as a woman, are to be respected, cared for, and protected. A woman is raped in the United States every 1.3 minutes.[3]

You can be anything you want to be. Sixty percent of all women workers are in either clerical, retail sales, or service jobs, and most women work in jobs in which at least 75 percent of the workers are female.[4]

You are weak and vulnerable. You are so dangerous as tempter that you must be dominated and controlled.[5]

The church supports and empowers justice. The church says for women to be silent and submissive.[6]

These are just a few of the many paradoxical messages of the culture in which girls and women develop. Paradoxes, especially paradoxes that go unnamed, create double-binding situations. Much of women's distress can be traced to living with these confusing imperatives about gender. As Ellyn Kaschak says, "Women's development and identity are characterized by no one trait more than paradox."[7]

The purpose of this essay is to explore the question of women's identity in the midst of the cultural paradoxes that make up patriarchy. I am in fundamental agreement with Jim Lapsley's position in his important text *Salvation and Health* that the main purpose of the human being is full participation in the divine intent; that in the midst of God's presence within the human community, we are to be engaged in the ongoing work of creation. In this essay, psychology, social analysis, and theological critique will be used for the purpose of trying to understand better the ways women have been kept from a full participation in that work.

It is important to be aware of the dangers of generalization. At many points, I will be making sweeping statements about women's lives in this culture. I am aware that the tension between the general and the particular must be carefully held. Each woman has her own story, with all of its particularities due to personal life history, her own talents and training, her experiences of harm and of healing, her support communities or lack of them, her physical abilities, and, especially, her race, her class, her sexual orientation, and her ethnic heritage. These particularities are foundational to her developmental process of identity formation. Yet I share the opinion of many feminist theorists that gender is the most primary organizing human category. Because of that, each woman's identity is formed in response to her gender training in a sexist and patriarchal culture, and each woman's story is linked by that reality. The differences among women are significant, but every woman is deeply affected by the systematic devaluation and double-binding of the culture. Racism, classism, and heterosexism are not additive oppressions to sexism but form their own matrices of oppressions in combination with sexism. Each requires its own analysis. My purpose is to focus on the issue of gender and identity more than on any particular or generalized woman's story.

The issue of particularity and generalization is at stake in theological anthropology, too. John Patton, in his recent book on pastoral counseling, reminds us that classical anthropology has identified three dimensions of describing human life. They are (1) the universal; (2) the cultural; and (3) the individual.[8] There are two important concerns in recognizing these three dimensions. First, both theology and psychology have paid the most attention to the universal and individual dimensions of being human. We have not paid enough attention to how the culture shapes people in ways that are most useful to the culture's power and work arrangements. I will focus on the way meaning and identity are shaped by the cultural rules and how women's identity, in particular, causes in women a kind of "harmful adaptation" that works against their wholeness and their full participation in the culture. The second important point about cultural identity is that women have not been given the right, the access, or the credibility to help create the important symbols and meanings of this culture that in turn form human identity. Thus women are left out of the meaning-making process on all fronts—the cultural and the personal. And, as many feminists have pointed out, this sets the stage for seeing women as objects in the culture, not women as subjects. The work of helping women move from being objects in their own eyes and in the eyes of the culture to a place of subjective voice is the primary work of a feminist pastoral theology. It challenges the assumptions and meanings of a patriarchal culture, and of all of us who have been formed in that culture, in such fundamental ways that we have only begun to understand what that challenge will mean. As this essay reflects, we are still very much at the stage in theology building where we are attempting to expose the damaging theological, psychological, and social assumptions of patriarchy, and are only just beginning to hear and build from women's own subjective experiences.

The question of theological anthropology is, What does it mean to be human, understood in a theological frame? When looking at a feminist theological anthropology, the task is to understand how gender arrangements function in the culture to further and/or to hamper God's intent for humanity. There have been a variety of ways that feminist anthropologists have attempted to understand gender arrangements in our culture.

Prior to a feminist analysis, there was a general belief in biologically based complementarity between the sexes that was at the heart of gender difference. This assumption was supported by work from various fields of inquiry from social psychology, to medical physiology, to developmental theory, to theology and the orders of creation. This approach supported and explained the status quo and was accepted by most as factual rather than political.

However, there have always been women who knew that fact and truth are created by those who have the most invested in the explanations. So various feminist approaches have emerged over the years that attempted to understand and explain distorted gender arrangements. First, there was a minimalist and androgynist approach to this problem that focused on the problems that gender distinctions had caused. The conclusion was to eliminate gender by creating a single androgynous category. In that process, we also ended up with an androgynous God. Unfortunately, two problems arose. First, androgyny tends to reinforce rather than eliminate gender difficulties because it relies on stereotyped notions of feminine and masculine. People are said to embody both masculine and feminine traits as if there are fixed traits that can be defined by that terminology. It also tends to maintain masculinist norms because the dominant cultural norms have been derived out of male experience. We also end up with a male God, albeit one who has a more whole personality, because this new image of God contains some of the so-called feminine traits of relationality, nurture, and empathy.

Another approach to feminist anthropology has been to locate the political problems within women's biology. In other words, it is because of women's ties to pregnancy, birth, and lactation that the divisions of labor have occurred as they have. In order to solve the problems of gender arrangements, then, new ways of addressing these reproductive tasks must be arranged. This analysis of the problem located the problem in women and restricted political analysis.

The third feminist approach to anthropology was again through biology and had to do with identifying women's biology as determinative and positive instead of negative. This is still a popular approach to feminist anthropology. Women are described as inherently more relational and inherently more at one with nature. Both of these biological consequences of being female are defined as a means by which the human race can be improved. In other words, women can teach their innate relational capacities to men, and their ties to nature may very well produce a more ecologically responsible way of being. There are, of course, benefits to this analysis, but in my mind the liabilities outweigh the rewards. It is a return to biology as destiny and only reverses the interpretation of that. Is it not more accurate to note that both women and men are tied to nature through their very real and similarly finite bodies and that women and men are both fundamentally relational, even if that relationality is expressed in different ways? I will return to this discussion later as we look at some of the developmental issues of identity formation.

The fourth approach to feminist anthropology is the conviction that women and men are made rather than born. Many feminists have made this point. Alison Jaggar states, "Feminists for more than two hundred years have recognized a sense in which women are made rather than born, but radical feminists have driven this insight deeper than before and used it as their main tool in constructing a comprehensive critique of women's oppression."[9] If we agree that women are made and not born, that gender (socially constructed) is a more powerful category than biological sex in terms of identity building, then this approach has powerful political implications and requires an in-depth analysis of cultural power dynamics and relations. Let us turn, then, to an analysis of the kind of culture into which women and men are born and in which matrix they develop identity.

Henrietta Moore states, "Probably the most outstanding contribution feminist anthropology has made . . . has been the development of theories relating to gender identity and the cultural construction of gender."[10]

Although there is no one single theory of feminist anthropology, there is a common conviction that the cultural construction of gender is a reality and that it has been, for the most part, a harmful process for women.

It is not my purpose to trace the roots of patriarchy in detail, but suffice it to say that patriarchy has been a part of Western culture from the beginning. Some authors have located the source of patriarchy in a warrior paradigm, with women serving as more controllable prisoners who, because they were held captive, demoralized but also integrated elements of the opposition. Others have seen the roots of patriarchy in the need men had to assure paternity. Others have focused more on the nature of industrialization and the split of domestic and public work spheres as foundational to patriarchal power arrangements. Some have made more psychological arguments around womb envy and other bio-psycho sources. Whatever the cause, patriarchy with its attendant need to keep women in a lowered position has been the Western cultural context. As Dale Spencer says:

> The "proof" has changed over the centuries but the necessity for establishing the inferiority of women has remained much the same. . . . Women's understandings, however, have not been incorporated into our cultural heritage, with the result that men have continued to explain the absence of women from the record in terms of women, not in terms of men. While the subject of male control has for centuries been a problem for women, it has never presented a serious problem for men, with the result that they have not addressed the topic and have often dismissed the whole area as unimportant and insignificant.[11]

Several feminist theorists have proposed paradigms within which to understand the cultural realities that serve as the source of women's distorted gender identity. Mary Ballou and Nancy Gabalac have put together a paradigm they call harmful adaptation. This is a developmental and repetitive spiral process that happens for girls and women from birth onward. It is a five-stage paradigm that describes a process that begins with humiliation. This, they say, is the experience of being devalued in one's own and others' eyes. It is both a chronic process and, frequently, an acute experience. It would include things like being exposed to negative images of women on television, reading stories where boys achieve and women are passive, being given inadequate attention for academic achievement in school, being told about your physical inadequacy when wanting to play baseball with boys, and so on. Of course, the acute experiences would include things like child sexual abuse or seeing one's mother beaten by one's father.

The second stage of this paradigm is inculcation, which is where the rules of correct gender behavior are taught to girls who are predisposed to learn because of the humiliation process. Those rules include things like being valued for being sweet, quiet, attractive, thoughtful, giving, and generally "feminine." They also include the prohibitions, such as: don't go out alone at night; don't do things better than any boy you want to attract; and don't tempt men to engage in violent or sexually aggressive behavior with you. These rules are learned "by heart."

The third stage is retribution. This is the experience of punishment for breaking the rules of correct gender behavior and might include name calling, abuse, being labeled by any one of a number of systems (including legal, welfare, and psychiatric), and isolation. Mary Ballou and Nancy Gabalac say that this stage generally extinguishes any desire to continue to break the rules.

The way one deals with having to follow rules that do not arise out of, or fit with, one's own needs and primary identity is what Ballou and Gabalac call conversion, the fourth stage. In this stage, women learn to believe that what they are called to do and, of more importance, who they are named to be is really what is true and natural for them. For example, it is woman's nature to serve others, to be relational, and to operate in the domestic rather than the public realm. She may even learn to call it salvific to be this self-sacrificing person.

However, a fifth stage is needed in this paradigm, because converted women hear the voices of other women who are still protesting this distorting identity formation process. That fifth stage is called conscription. This is where women persuade other women that the definitions and identities of patriarchy are really the true and best ones. Conscription is the betrayal of women by women.[12] This paradigm of harmful adaptation is, I believe, a powerful descriptive model of what happens in the process of women's identity formation.

Another explanation of identity formation in a more psychological rather than sociocultural mode is provided by Ellyn Kaschak in her work entitled *Engendered Lives*. She suggests that the Oedipal paradigm proposed by Freud about boys' and girls' development is not accurate for girls being raised in a sexist culture. She proposes the Antigone paradigm, in which there are two primary phases, although she also talks about the resolution of this complex, which I will describe later. About this paradigm, Kaschak remarks: "Becoming a woman involves learning a part, complete with costumes, make-up and lines. Learning to behave like a woman involves learning to sit, stand, and talk in the appropriate ways and to make them appear natural, to have them become natural, or more aptly, second nature.[13] Women are taught to create a false identity and then to forget that it is false.

In the early Antigone phase, which is in early childhood, there is a real and valid attachment to the mother, Kaschak explains. In the midst of that attachment, through the incomplete gratification of her needs, the girl learns that she must limit her needs accordingly. During this phase, the father (and all men) is seen to be central in importance, and the mother (and all women) is identified as secondary. And, through her teachers, the media, and other adults, the girl learns to limit herself and her explorations for the sake of safety. (As studies show, girl children are restricted in the amount of space they are given for exploration compared with what is permitted for boys. This continues through life, with women being restricted in the amount of space they are to take or explore and men given almost unlimited range.) The other thing that often happens during this early Antigone phase is that girls are sexually abused. Abuse is a strong teacher of a girl's "place." Kaschak calls it an "initiation rite."[14]

The Antigone phase itself stretches from midchildhood through adulthood. Kaschak describes its ingredients as a denial of birth and origins, danger embedded in pleasure, denial of authentic physicality (which results in both invisibility and hypervisibility), permeable boundaries, physically based self-hatred with a focused concern on appearance as central to value, self-esteem based on self-denial, compulsively relational orientation with one's own identity as secondary, fragmented physical and psychological safety, and an identification with the "indeterminate observer," which means that she uses her eyes to see from a male's perspective.[15] These, again, are powerful descriptors of women's identity/ loss of identity through the cultural rules of patriarchy.

There are two issues within this description of the Antigone paradigm that I believe to be central in looking at a feminist anthropology. The first is the issue of embodiment. It is well documented that women are identified with their bodies, and this forms a primary source of identity that is different for them than it is for men. Women's bodies are seen as existing for men. Whether we look at the statistics of incest (approximately 40 percent of all girls are sexually molested/abused by the age of eighteen either inside or outside of their families[16]); through the realities of advertising (women and parts of women being used to sell products; girls ten years old and younger being dressed and made up to look seductive for the sake of selling a product); through the realities of our entertainment industry (more than one half of the music videos on MTV feature or suggest violence, present hostile sexual situations as acceptable, and/or show male heroes abusing women for fun);[17] or through the cosmetic industry (more money is spent on women's looks each year in the United States than on social service programs[18]), we can see that women are alienated from their bodies at the same time that they are identified with them.

This identification of women and body is extremely negative for women's lives. As Kaschak says:

> In losing control of the meanings of their own bodies, of the bodies themselves, women lose even more—the opportunity to develop a well-integrated sense of self that is more internally than externally defined, that is relatively stable rather than subject to redefinition based on changes in appearance or evaluation thereof, and that is grounded in an accurate testing of abilities and skills rather than passive evaluation.[19]

She goes on to say, "Women, as a result, have a strong tendency to a particular sort of disconnection from their own bodies and their own cognitive/affective/physical experience—that is a tendency to watch themselves through male eyes."[20]

These are serious identity issues. It is, I believe, problematic that many feminists have attempted to reframe this identification of women with body, although putting it in a positive context. The identification has such a long and negative theological and psychological history that I do not believe it is reclaimable. From the various church fathers like Origen—who said that God did not deign to glance at female embodiedness, and identified anything female with weakness and impurity—to Aquinas, who found that women's bodies were "misbegotten" and of inferior worth and provided sinful temptation to men, the church's identification of women with body has been persistently negative and destructive. Psychologically, women's bodies (as with Freud and others) were deficient, mutilated, and limited. For these and other theological and psychological reasons, we need to reject women's primary identification with body and rebuild the larger connection between humanity, embodiment, and earth. As Kaschak says:

> Women are identified with their bodies in a more material and inseparable way than are men, but not because women, as many male philosophers have argued, are more tied to nature. After all, men have bodies and hormones, too. . . . Virtually every aspect of it is interpreted to have meaning about her—who she is, how she is to be viewed and treated. This association has been shown to begin as early as among preschoolers, who show no deferential treatment to boys related to attractiveness but a clear difference in the treatment of girls.[21]

The second important point implied in both the harmful adaptation and Antigone paradigms is that of the nature of women's relatedness. Kaschak suggests that women become "compulsively related" in this developmental process. She suggests that women in this society are "driven to relatedness" by the process of alienation from themselves.[22] Carol Gilligan's recent work about adolescents, published in a book entitled *Meeting at the Crossroads*, draws a similar conclusion about women's relatedness. Gilligan and Lyn Brown did a longitudinal study of girls moving from age eight into their early teen years. They found that younger girls were in significant relationships with their peers and would speak directly and clearly about violations and injustices done to themselves or to their friends. By the age of eleven, these same girls were moving away from their own knowledge, using the phrase "I don't know" much more frequently and expressing implicit and explicit knowledge of the rules they were to follow in order to be acceptable and "in relationship." Gilligan and Brown summarize their findings by saying:

> At the crossroads of adolescence, the girls in our study describe a relational impasse that is familiar to many women: a paradoxical or dizzying sense of having to give up relationship for the sake of "relationships." Because this taking of oneself out of relationship in

order to protect oneself and have relationships forces an inner division or chasm, it makes a profound psychological shift. . . . Women's psychological development within patriarchal societies and male-voiced cultures is inherently traumatic.[23]

Many feminist scholars in women's development agree that adolescence is a crucial and generally closing down/traumatic life stage for women. They suggest that adolescence is a shaky time for males, too. The difference is that men seem to emerge from their traumatic adolescence with an intact and generally positive identity, but women do not. However, even more than adolescent issues are involved; the issue of women's "natural" relatedness is at stake here. It is a human issue to be related and in community, not a woman's issue. Yet some feminist psychologists and theologians have taken a reactionary stand to the traditional and negative use of women's relatedness and reframed it positively as being particularly a woman's trait. Nancy Chodorow, an object relations psychologist, has been particularly influential on this topic as she has described parenting traditions in patriarchy as creating women who are relational and men who are separate. She suggests that because women primarily parent and male parents are generally more absent, girl children define themselves in continuity (relationally) with their mothers, and boys must define themselves separately in order to become men. Her suggestion is that if men parented in equal proportion to women, then we would have men and women who were equally relational, and sexism would be, in large part, defeated.[24] The problem is that studies show that male parenting of girls tends to recreate the dynamics of patriarchy as the male parent reinforces traditionally "feminine" traits in girls. It has been demonstrated that men are rougher, show more favor to, and value more their boy children, and that they comfort daughters more than sons and reinforce pleasing behavior in daughters.[25] In addition, in the studies where fathers had been the primary parent, there was no evidence of gender identity or behavior change from more traditional parenting arrangements.

Again, it seems to me that refocusing relationality on the human condition rather than on the female reality would be the more useful approach. Men are as relational as women if we define relationality more broadly. Even competition and men's experience of having the right of access to women, to children, and to space show a relational nature, even if it is not the preferred nature of relationship.[26] Defining relationality and empowering it in ways that benefit women, men, and creation have more positive potential than reframing it as being the positive domain of women.

These two issues of embodiment and relationality are central identity concerns for women. I have spent considerable time in this essay talking about the constraining and destructive contexts in which these and other identity elements are formed in women. There are two other dimensions that have been implied but about which we need to speak more directly. The first is the resolution or correction of these negative identity formations. The second, a more distant possibility, is the creation of a cultural milieu where women's identity is formed with integrity out of their own authentic experience.

Ballou and Gabalac propose a second and parallel counterpart to harmful adaptation, which they name corrective action. Corrective action is a therapeutic paradigm designed for psychological counseling, but its elements can be applied to a way of being for women outside of the professional context. The first phase of corrective action is separation, where a woman is helped to reclaim herself as existing outside of the demands of those around her. She is helped, using Gilligan's conclusions, to regain the capacity for authentic relationship without fearing isolation. In so doing, she begins to see her real identity as having been distorted by the gender rules of patriarchy. The second phase, which overlaps with separation, is that of validation. The woman's experiences are validated as real and meaningful. She is, often for the first time, given the chance to name, define, and value her life experience for herself. The paradoxes of her identity formation are explored and resolved by naming the false sides of those double binds. In the third phase, called association, women come together mutually to validate one another and to help reality test each other's and their own perceptions from which they have become alienated. The fourth phase is called authorization, in which women make choices for themselves for which they hold themselves accountable. These are choices in which they take action that is congruent with their newly forming identity. The fifth phase is called negotiation, in which women work to maintain their more authentic identity in the face of a culture that still seeks to distort it. They rely on support communities and on their own strengthened sense of self-knowledge. This paradigm is directed toward deconstructing an identity that has been perverted by patriarchy and reconstructing a more authentic and whole self-understanding.[27]

Kaschak also proposed a resolution to her notion of the Antigone paradigm. This resolution also begins with a psychic/spiritual separation from the father(s) in order to return to herself in an authentic way. In that, she is also able to return to the ability to be in real relationship with women. She works, during this resolution process, to claim her own vulnerability and her interdependence with others. She develops the eyes to see herself for herself instead of having to see herself through the indeterminate male eyes. She becomes able to deal creatively with male relationships after she is able to claim an identity for herself as woman and as human being—an integrated whole. She is also able to be interdependent upon the resolution of this process and to have flexible but not permeable boundaries.[28]

These two paradigms have a number of similarities, and they also echo the most recent work of Gilligan and Brown as they attempt to help women regain authentic identity and relationships of integrity.

All of these studies and conclusions have significant theological implications that find their most telling example, I believe, in our image and understanding of the Divine. The three issues that I would identify from this cultural feminist investigation are (1) the nature of women's embodiment; (2) the nature of women's relationality; and (3) the nature of identity distortion through the culture's false mirroring of who women are. I have spoken explicitly about embodiment and relationality and implicitly about the issue of mirroring. Let me say a few more words about that.

The paradoxes of women's lives mean that women look in a distorted mirror as they seek to discover who they are. They look in the mirror assuming they will see one thing, but they see something else. They look in the mirror expecting to see their own eyes, but they see those of the "indeterminate male." They look in the mirror expecting to see their own strength, but they see their reflected weakness and inferiority. They look in the mirror expecting to see their own familiar body, but they see a mannequin and a mask. After a while, women do not know what they expect to see, and they disguise what they do see to make the difference/deviance invisible. They lose even the knowledge about the distortion. This is the tragedy of women's gender identity formation in patriarchy.

The theological implications of embodiment and relationality are profound in terms of God's availability and accessibility. They are also included when we examine the implications of God's mirroring/reflecting qualities. What does it mean for women to have a primary god image that can reflect back to women only the way a father or man or the indeterminate male can mirror? What does it do to women's identity to be seen only through a male God's eyes?

One of the questions I routinely ask in pastoral counseling with both women and men is, "How do you think that God perceives you at this point in time?" That question has become more revealing than another one I have frequently asked in the counseling relationship, which is, "How do you perceive God?" What is striking to me is how much more dramatic a question it is to women than to men. Both women and men are able to answer the "How do you perceive God?" question without much creativity, novelty, or involvement. They generally "know" the answer to the question, and only if they are in a faith crisis do they really struggle with it. The question of God's perception of them tends to create more thoughtfulness in both men and women, but men are generally not thrown off balance by it. Women, though, engage this question of God's looking at them with a great deal of energy and anxiety. And they *know* how God looks at them, especially if God is male. Generally, it is in a negative way. God reflects them to themselves generally in ways similar to those of the male culture.

When, in the course of pastoral counseling, women have developed new images of God that reflect authentic female experience and identity, then there is a strengthening of self. The process, in my experience and research, has been a spiral. Women who gain in self-image and self-esteem are more likely to find it possible to find a positive female god image, and positive female god images are more likely to strengthen positive female self-images.[29]

If we are to continue to struggle to create a culture in which women can find themselves in authentic and nondistorted, nonexploited ways, it will be important that we in the church also struggle to find god images that reflect the divine intention of women's wholeness and power. A God who can reflect only maleness (and maleness as understood in a patriarchal culture is always distorted through that cultural interpretation) will not be the faith resource to enhance authentic integrity for women. And, ultimately, the good of all creation depends upon the full participation of women and men in their wholeness and integrity.

NOTES

1. Nikole V. Benokraitis and Joe R. Feagin, *Modern Sexism: Blatant, Subtle, and Covert Discrimination* (Englewood Cliffs, N.J.: Prentice-Hall, 1986), 10.

2. Rachel Hare-Mustin, "The Problem of Gender in Family Therapy Theory," in *Women in Families: A Framework for Family Therapy*, ed. Monica McGuldrick, Carol Anderson, and Proma Walsh (New York: W. W. Norton, 1989), 63.

3. *Statistical Abstract of the United States of 1989* (Washington, D.C.: U.S. Department of Commerce, Bureau of the Census, 1989).

4. Benokraitis and Feagin, *Modern Sexism*, 52.

5. Grace Jantzen, "Who Needs Feminism?" *Theology* 93 (September-October 1990), 341.

6. Margaret Anderson, *Thinking about Women: Sociological Perspectives on Sex and Gender*, 2d ed. (New York: Macmillan Co., 1988), 248.

7. Ellyn Kaschak, *Engendered Lives: A New Psychology of Women's Experience* (New York: Basic Books, 1992), 157.

8. John Patton, *Pastoral Care in Context* (Louisville: Westminster/ John Knox Press, 1993), 42.

9. Alison M. Jaggar, *Feminist Politics and Human Nature* (Totowa, N.J.: Rowman and Littlefield Publishers, 1988), 85.

10. Henrietta Moore, *Feminism and Anthropology* (Minneapolis: University of Minnesota Press, 1988), 187.

11. Dale Spencer, *Invisible Women: The Schooling Scandal* (London: Women's Press, 1982/89), 15.

12. Mary Ballou and Nancy Gabalac, *A Feminist Position on Mental Health* (Springfield, Ill.: Charles C. Thomas, 1985), chap. 4.

13. Kaschak, *Engendered Lives*, 89.

14. Ibid., 83.

15. Ibid., 84.

16. Catherine MacKinnon, *Feminism Unmodified: Discourses on Life and Law* (Cambridge: Harvard University Press, 1987), 51.

17. Benokraitis and Feagin, *Modern Sexism*, 10.

18. Ibid., 18.

19. Kaschak, *Engendered Lives*, 97.

20. Ibid., 112.

21. Ibid., 95.

22. Ibid., 124.

23. Lyn Mikel Brown and Carol Gilligan, *Meeting at the Crossroads: Women's Psychology and Girls' Development* (Cambridge: Harvard University Press, 1992), 216.

24. Nancy Chodorow, *The Reproduction of Mothering* (Berkeley: University of California Press, 1978).

25. Kaschak, *Engendered Lives*, 118.

26. Ibid., 127.

27. Ballou and Gabalac, *A Feminist Position on Mental Health*, chap. 5.

28. Kaschak, *Engendered Lives*, 84.

29. Christie Cozad Neuger, *A Study in Women's Spiritual Growth Using Psycho-Imagery Techniques* (Ann Arbor, Mich.: University Microfilms, 1987).

15
Responses, Arguments, Musings, and Further Directions

JAMES N. LAPSLEY

When I was asked by the editors of this volume to respond to the contributions of my colleagues and former students, I looked forward to the prospect with great interest—mixed with some trepidation. If it were not for the honor of the thing . . . After all, the contributors have done me the honor of taking the trouble to write these essays, when, likely as not, they would rather have been otherwise occupied. So it seemed at first rather ungracious of me to set out on a project of responding in an academic and personal manner bound to sound like less than fulsome praise, even though there would be plenty to commend. At length, however, I realized that for their efforts I owed them as serious an analytical comment as I could muster, and that to offer less was truly ungracious.

Thus, what follows is a *seriatim* commentary on the contributions by essay, omitting the personal comments of my longtime friend and colleague Liston Mills, and the introductory essay by David Waanders, neither of which I saw prior to publication. After completing the commentary on the individual essays, I will try to offer some additional words intended to fulfill the "musings and further directions" part of the chapter title.

I count almost all of the contributors as my personal friends. Some have been students, others colleagues, and still others fellow laborers in the same or adjacent vineyards. So I will not make personal remarks in my comments, except to record a few matters of fact about my relationships with them that may be of interest to the reader.

RESPONSES AND ARGUMENTS

RODNEY J. HUNTER's "Participation in the Life of God: Revisioning Lapsley's Salvation-Health Model" gave me the impression, at once gratifying and a bit intimidating, that Hunter knows more about this model than I do—especially after the twenty-three years since it was put in the form in which it appeared in *Salvation and Health*. I appreciate the careful and rather detailed and accurate understanding of this model and his lucid exposition of it. He got all the main points right and saw correctly that the principal focus of the model is upon the lives of the ordinary people who are most often met in ministry as elsewhere, even though the extraordinary also get some attention, as do those in extremis, and that the intention was to provide both overall vision and detail enough to be useful in ministry.

Especially do I appreciate his defense of the notion of hierarchy, and, indeed, of its inevitability in any serious effort to understand the world and those in it, and of the concomitant distinctions among persons that must be made in any attempt at responsible ministry, as unpopular as these may be with seminarians and some ministers. His discussion of these points was the best that I recall ever seeing.

Now I will turn to his constructive proposals for the further development of the salvation and health model. These are in three areas: participation motifs and concepts, the inclusion of systemic modes of agency, and radical evil as an active force.

Hunter is right that the concept of *participation* is at the heart of this model. He is also right that it needs further work. His principal point is that too much stress is placed upon participation as contribution and not enough on participation as receptivity. This point is well taken, in that receptivity is not sufficiently developed in *Salvation and Health*, although it is present. Hunter sometimes puts this point in terms of the activity/passivity polarity, and with this I have more trouble.

Absolute passivity rarely characterizes human beings, even from a commonsense point of view; and from the point of view of process metaphysics, it never does, unless the person is dead. He seems to be concerned more with relative passivity than absolute passivity, and I must point out that relative passivity, especially receptivity, is also relative activity, as his "accepting form of participation" implies. John Milton, dictating reflections on his blindness, is actively creating great poetry advocating active acceptance of limitation. The contemplative life and the life of prayer are far from passive, moreover, if these are considered examples of passivity.

With meaningless suffering I have even more trouble. First, I must point out that Hunter sometimes seems to mean apparently meaningless suffering that turns out to be meaningful after all—in which instances, of course, it is not meaningless. The suffering of Jesus, viewed by his followers, seems to have been of this kind. I think we have to face the tragedy of truly meaningless suffering as just that, a tragedy that cannot be redeemed by calling it participation. He has the right answer, insofar as we have an answer, in stressing finally God's empathy for tragic suffering.

I note that he has a further implied category of active meaningless suffering in his discussion of the married couple in a crisis of conflict. As he suggests, such conflict sometimes leads to reconciliation and new learning and development, in which cases the suffering is not meaningless. Sometimes the suffering is truly tragic in that no positive turning occurs. The notion of suffering glorified, and hence often sought, has been a blight on some representations of the Christian tradition, as processions of flagellants on Good Friday remind us. Although suffering is a notion at the heart of the Christian faith, it must be approached with great care to avoid costly abuses.

From my point of view, the key to understanding salvation as participation lies in a theological vantage point where Reformed and process theology intersect. From there persons are not valued by God according to their contributions, but according to the mysterious interactions of law, by which participation is judged by responsiveness in accordance with capacity ("From everyone to whom much has been given, much will be required . . . ," Luke 12:48), and grace through Jesus Christ, by which all, or at least all responders, are valued alike in a pilgrimage in which some walk better than others. Whether in responding in trust to the providence of God or to a lure toward participation in God's life, both theologies echo the experience of Moses at the burning bush, where he found that he must trust, without being able to control, either the pilgrimage upon which he was setting out or the God of the pilgrimage, whose name was wrapped in the mystery of being (Exod. 3:1–15).

Systems modes of agency is the concept that Hunter has chosen with which to discuss the corporate dimensions of salvation. First, let me say that the corporate dimension of salvation is by no means absent from the salvation and health model. The point in the book about continuity with the work of Walter Rauschenbusch, who stressed individuals as well as the social gospel, was not an idle one.[1] Corporate life is present in more than just in principle. There is a discussion, for instance, of institutions, the concept by means of which I chose to approach corporate life. The main point that I will cite here is that institutions are maintenance oriented, unless some individual or individuals move them toward development.[2] Although I concur with Hunter that systems approaches to various forms of helping have often been fruitful, I think they share the above-mentioned characteristic with what I earlier termed institutions. They are maintenance oriented, resisting change, and moreover exemplify, as Hunter suggested at least indirectly in his comments about "transindividual systemic" ways, our continuing confusion about agency.

Recently, Elizabeth Wolgast has highlighted this confusion in her study of agency and ethics, *Ethics of an Artificial Person*.[3] She found that the concept of agency in law goes back to Hobbes's *Leviathan*, where he developed the notion of the artificial person as a way of explaining how the state can represent individuals as their agent. After a penetrating discussion, she recommended that the concept of agency be discarded altogether—perhaps too radical a remedy, but one suggesting the depth of the problem, which, I believe, also exists in systems theory. Does the concept of the artificial person also underlie it?

Having offered these words of caution, I welcome any effort Hunter or others may make to develop the salvation and health model in its corporate dimension. I agree that it was only sketched in the book.

Evil as an active force is a notion much discussed at the present time, and the ideas of René Girard about sacrifice seem to me to make a contribution to this discussion. However, I see no reason at this time to change my basic position about evil as it was stated in *Salvation and Health,* even though it can be developed and elaborated. Indeed, it contains a rather radical view of evil, far deeper and more pervasive than "bad choosing" attributed to it by Hunter, although that is certainly included.

I have learned that the notion of evil, and its human manifestation as sin, is rather inconspicuous in the book. It is a bass note, not the melody, but as such apparently has not been heard. Hunter is not the first to have missed it. So I must take responsibility for not blowing on the horn about evil loudly enough.

The most systematic statement is in note 1 on page 137 in *Salvation and Health*: "Yet, both clinically and politically, man's destructiveness is so massive in its manifestation that it cannot all be ascribed to the frustration of constructive aims." Underlying human evil is the mutual destructiveness characteristic of all nature, an implicate of process thought explicitly stated by Whitehead.[4] Salvation is from evil in this sense and from perpetual perishing.

David Griffin's idea of the demonic as accumulated, semiautonomous effects of human evil, cited by Hunter, has merit. For a long time I have had an interest in psychological and theological perspectives on evil, and once taught a course on that topic. Many perspectives shed light on evil, but none exhausts it. Currently, I am still working in this area, broadly conceived.

JOHN B. COBB, JR., has urged us to take a more flexible position regarding the salvation/health question in his "Salvation and Health: A Pluralistic Perspective" than he perceives me to have taken, even though he has indicated his basic agreement with much of what he found in *Salvation and Health*. Before offering some analytical comments about Cobb's proposal, I want to acknowledge here my indebtedness to him. It was through reading his *A Christian Natural Theology* that I first grasped the possibility of making use of a perspective in process theology in a theoretical text in pastoral theology.[5] Before that time I had become familiar with process thinking, particularly with Whitehead, but it took Cobb's work to make it plain enough and cogent for me to be comfortable in working with the material.

Cobb urges us to adopt a "stipulative" position about the meaning of salvation and health and their relationship. That is, within some broad parameters of meaning of which they have been a part, we can stipulate what these terms are to mean for our own purposes. He apparently thought that my own proposal contains a more fixed position than I intended. *Salvation and Health* contains a specific disclaimer about the temporal limitations of its model (p. 25), although none about spacial ones, that is, cultural limitations. I can say here that it certainly had cultural limitations, even though I believe its basic principles have wide cultural usefulness. It was intended primarily for the use of parish ministers in North America at the time of publication (1972) and somewhat beyond.

Cobb sees many issues with penetration and clarity. His proposal makes a contribution toward our understanding of questions involved in the salvation/health relationship, especially in interpreting shades of meaning and the history with which meanings are laden. He was particularly helpful in his discussion of the possibilities and limits of global pluralism. His point that asking Buddhists to consider salvation is to ask the wrong question altogether is something many global frontierspersons need to hear. We can ask Buddhists about enlightenment and perhaps can find some parallel strands with some of our notions of salvation, but that is as far as we can go.

He offers us a selection of three ideas of health and six of salvation that we are invited to combine in various ways to suit our contexts, needs, and traditions. That is, we are invited to stipulate which ones we will use. He himself does not clearly favor one set of definitions and combinations, though I got the impression he favored the unitary model of meaning in which salvation and health mean about the same thing.

Cobb is clear that we cannot just choose any ideas to represent salvation and health. Rather, "It is better that new formulations of the end or goal of life emerge organically out of individual traditions as they experience one another in new ways." I believe that he would agree with Max Stackhouse in his reflections on the recently held World Conference on Human Rights, that, when the rights of individuals are considered, pluralism in the name of sanctity of social location and particular tradition, urged by some nations, has definite limits. Torture as a means of obtaining human goals is not permitted as a part of any ethical (or salvation/health) scheme, to state the most prominent point.[6]

Although I think that at least a semicafeteria of ideas about salvation and health are inevitable, and that there are problems, at least in theory, with uniformity, at the present time our greater problem is to find some common ideas we can use for communication and as a basis of action. Practical theology is finally not focused on discussion but upon ministry, which can then serve to correct and amplify theory, thus providing for an ongoing dialogue that should prevent the ossification of rigid theory. I agree that it also needs contributions from other cultural points of view.

CHARLES V. GERKIN has offered us an insightful, provocative, and potentially fruitful idea about the origins of the God image in his "Projective Identification and the Image of God: Reflections on Object Relations Theory and the Psychology of Religion." I first met Gerkin in 1965, when we were both members of a committee to make proposals regarding one of the several reorganizations of *The Journal of Pastoral Care.* Since that time we have enjoyed a relationship that can be characterized as always lively and sometimes combative about the means of thinking about pastoral care and pastoral theology, but, so it seems to me, based upon shared assumptions and ideas about the ends.

In the spirit of our relationship, I will pause to question Gerkin's statement about the disciplinary status of his essay before going on to comment on its substance. Although I agree that the essay can be understood as a contribution to the psychology of religion, I do not concur with Gerkin that the issues he is discussing cannot be brought directly into theological discourse. Indeed, early on, Gerkin himself indicates that he wants to "appropriate a contemporary form of psychotherapeutic psychology for theological purposes." If this is to be done, some kind of connection between psychological discourse and theological discourse must surely be possible, even though such a connection might seem strange to some theologians. I believe it is possible and that, indeed, virtually all theologies make some use of other disciplines, consciously or unconsciously. As a pastoral and practical theologian who has consciously done it for years, I think Gerkin's ideas about the projective identification and introjective identification of the God image are, in principle, directly appropriable by practical theologians as correctives and amplifications of theological anthropology employed by them. Ministers need a univocal theory upon which to base their actions, like all other professionals, not two (or more) separate disciplines with which they must constantly contend.

Now, as to these ideas themselves, I confess to a certain degree of ambivalence. The Scharffs basically propose that W. R. D. Fairbairn's idea of the three projective identifications of the infant in the first year of life—the need-exciting, the rejecting, and the ideal of the mother, and their subsequent introjective identification—are useful in understanding the interaction of married couples. Gerkin takes these dynamics and proposes that they may also represent the basis of the images of God in the developing personality. These dynamics might account for some of the varied modes of relating to God found in the lives of persons, so Gerkin avers, somewhat tentatively, or as he puts it, "playfully." So they might, and they offer a tempting hypothesis. However, they are based more directly upon the dark vision of the first year of life proposed by the brilliant but exotic founder of the object relations school, Melanie Klein, than are many of their other well-known contributions, such as Winnicott's transitional object and Bowlby's work on attachment and loss. Klein held that in the first six months of life, the infant comes to view the frequently absent breast with rage and frustration—which she termed the paranoid/schizoid position. In the second six months, resignation and guilt (over the rage of the first six months) set in—the depressive position. Along with these, the infant splits off the good mother from these unconscious fantasies and idealizes her consciously.

I have always found this scheme to attribute too much organization to the infant personality to be plausible as it has been presented, but it probably does contain a kernel of truth. The splitting off of the good mother from the bad mother seems the most likely candidate for the kernel and may offer us a clue to the absolute goodness/badness of the God image, although it cannot be denied that infants have negative emotions and that these are experienced primarily in relation to the mothering figure.

I may add that Klein also thought that the infant came soon to attribute a penis to the mother, for which it also longed, having conflated images of father with mother from the primal scene.[7] I find this point rather dubious and cite it as an instance of the basis of my reservations about Klein.

Gerkin is right that we could have a good conversation about this matter. He is imaginative and knowledgeable, but also a sophisticated clinician who searches the boundaries of plausibility and practicality.

JAMES G. EMERSON, JR., has contributed an essay designed to broaden my and all our perspectives on theological anthropology in his "K'ung Fu-tze, Meet Jim Lapsley." It is indeed an unexpected honor to be in the same title as the illustrious Chinese sage, whom we usually refer to as Confucius.

Jim Emerson is something of a sage himself. He is a writing

pastoral theologian who spent his entire career, except for one five-year stint as the administrator of a social service agency, in the parish ministry. That is, he did so until he retired, and the world became his parish, to paraphrase the words of John Wesley. Currently, he has a special interest in the churches of the Pacific rim and was on a teaching tour of Southeast Asia when he wrote this essay. Since meeting in the early 1960s, we have collaborated on projects and were colleagues at Princeton Seminary for a time, where he held an adjunct post while serving in parishes in the New York City area. I have been particularly indebted to him for his early volume *The Dynamics of Forgiveness*.[8]

I will focus on only one broad issue presented by Emerson—the nature of the self, East and West, and its shame/guilt corollary—for it is an issue with many practical ramifications in ministry and one that I have long puzzled about, especially when teaching students with non-Western backgrounds.

This last phrase leads me to one modification in the discussion presented by Emerson. The sense of self as primarily individual seems to be native only to Europe, and particularly northwestern Europe, and its North American offspring in the entire world. Though there are many differences, for instance, between North American Native Americans and Koreans or sub-Saharan Africans, they all share the characteristic of a communally based sense of self. Thus, numerically speaking, it is we who are the queer ones and not they. Some of my comments will be addressed to this grand division of the world's selves and some to particular manifestations, especially to the mainland East Asian self, the one in focus in Emerson's essay.

To state it flatly, there is nothing in the human personality that makes it inherently communal or individual. All human selves contain both aspects, but culture and the individual determine which aspects will be developed more. In other words, I am agreeing with Emerson's East Asian colleagues (and himself) when they say that the distinction between individual and community selves is overdone, while recognizing, as Emerson also insists, that the distinction is real. I further agree that certain advantages inhere in the more communal self—a strong sense of belonging both to present and past generations, particularly to one's extended family, a sense of obligation to support the community, particularly the family, and respect for the elderly. (I note here that Eastern Orthodox

Christians, as well as East Asian Christians, observe periodic mourning rituals.)

I must also assert that the individual self must have its due; without it we would not be here, so to speak. Even Robert Bellah, the archfoe of what he has taken to be the overindividualized self, recently and, I think somewhat reluctantly, agreed that individualism has some value: "Individualism has a positive side, however. It emphasizes our responsibility to be true to ourselves, to find a way of life that is authentic and valuable."[9]

What we need is the best of both selves while finding ways not to have to put up with the worst. Speaking of the worst, I note here that some of the least endearing characteristics associated with individualism, such as greed, hedonism, and power needs, also may characterize communal selves, where these same character traits are sometimes put to use in the service of the family.

It is true, as Emerson suggests, that we have only relatively recently discovered shame as a potent factor in the lives of our own people as well as of those of far-off communities. I apparently gave the impression to Emerson that I regarded shame as only a result of personal failure. This is a false impression, for I have always thought it due to failure to live up to community expectations, represented first and foremost by the mothering figure. These expectations get incorporated into the self and thus become personal, but the community is never far away, psychologically speaking.[10] Shame is a sense of threat of abandonment, accompanied by a gesture of covering or hiding from the community in the hope of averting it.

Like Emerson, I believe that we have much to learn about the mature self from the heirs of Confucius. They may well represent at their best, for instance, an ideal of the mature self set forth by self-development scholar Robert Kegan; this ideal mature self is clearly connected to the family but not embedded in it. Their principal danger is that they will be embedded in it, contrasted with the danger of isolation and estrangement more typical of Westerners, males in particular.

Guilt and shame are pervasive of human cultures and frequently intermingle as painful sanctions, as well as serving as boundaries of the way through which lives are to be steered. But ours is the one where guilt has predominated. We are the heirs of Cain and the House of Atrius. So, I believe, we will remain, even while we acknowledge anew the force of shame.

DONALD CAPPS, my colleague for eleven years at Princeton Seminary, in his "The Soul as the 'Coreness' of the Self" has offered what, at first reading, seems to be an amplification of the model of human being that I developed beginning in 1985, based upon the relation between self and spirit. Noting that I commented once that some writers have used the term *self* to refer to the "core" of the person, he proposes to reclaim the term *soul* to refer to the "coreness of the self" that lies beneath the surface, and to explain the existence of "disconnected fragments below the surface," to which I alluded. He goes on to connect the soul firmly to the body, suggesting that the ancient tradition of it being closely associated with the liver ought to be honored, at least metaphorically.

So far, I can see that retaining the concept of soul as a link between self and body might have some advantages. It was the ancient principle of animation in nature and might serve to anchor more firmly the self/spirit to the gut level.

However, I wonder if he has the best Greek (*psyche*) and English translation (*soul*) for his purpose. I might suggest to him at this point that he have a look at the New Testament term *splangchna*, which referred primarily to the digestive tract and was translated "bowels of mercies" (Col. 3:12), or bowels of compassion (1 John 3:17) in the King James Version, reflecting the Hebrew belief that the bowels were the seat of the positive emotions of love and compassion. According to Thayer (a Greek-English Lexicon of the *New Testament*), it also meant heart, lungs, or even soul in other contexts, and might serve him better to make his point about the soul than psyche, especially in view of his interest in Luther's famous concern with his digestive tract. Bettelheim, whom Capps also cites, notes that psyche, depicted as a young woman with gossamer wings (once the symbol of White Rock beverages) is "invested with connotations of beauty, fragility, and insubstantiality."[11] This point clearly indicates that the ancients did not have a unitary notion of psyche as an earthy, bodily phenomenon.

The ambiguity of psyche leads me to ask the question whether Capps really is trying to correct or amplify a model that I used or whether, as I think more likely, he wants to take it as a starting point toward a much more Platonic-like model in which soul (read body) and spirit (read mind) are in intense conflict. "The aspirations of the spirit and the core of the self (or soul) are fundamentally at odds with one another." He repeats this emphasis on soul/ spirit conflict and toward the end of his essay equates the soul with the unconscious and the self with the conscious mind.

Although I can welcome the notion of soul as core of the self as an amplification of the self/spirit model, I cannot accept Capps's emphasis on soul/spirit conflict as apparently at the heart of the person, tending as it does toward the dualisms of the past that have caused so much trouble. Nor do I find the scholarship of James Hillman, upon which it is partly based, to be convincing. Peaks and valleys are ambiguous symbols. Dale, a virtual synonym for valley, is at the top of the list of names for real estate developments. I live in an area that our Chamber of Commerce calls the Valley of the Sun, by which it hopes to attract winter visitors. Capps lives in what many call "the happy valley," even though it is not even literally a valley at all. Mountains can be remote, forbidding, and fraught with danger. Thus, although recognizing the power of geographical/topographical imagery, I also find it to be a wobbly base upon which to erect an argument for the association of soul with depression.

BRIAN H. CHILDS, the indefatigable coeditor of this volume, in his "Whose Participation and Whose Humanity? Medicine's Challenge to Theological Anthropology" has offered us a stimulating essay that focuses on the putative boundary between medicine and theological anthropology in relation to some aspects of my work.

Childs is correct, of course, in his first proposal to amplify the salvation/health model. In the more than twenty years since the publication of *Salvation and Health*, developments have taken place, particularly in the area of bioethics concerned with the ever more complex means for prolonging life (though along with Childs, I acknowledge the role of other factors such as public policy), which render any purely psychological approach less than adequate. I readily concede that psychology needs supplementing with biology and bioethics, and, in fact, I presented a discussion of biological factors in aging with a focus upon the immune system in *Renewal in Late Life through Pastoral Counseling* (pp. 18–29).

His second proposal requires more comment. As I understand it, he is proposing a more explicit role for the human community in all its dimensions in understanding its effects on individual actors "who may act only minimally, if at all." This proposal seems to be similar to Hunter's call for more emphasis on receptivity and on the corporate dimension of participation, but is more focused upon the specific effects of community on the salvatory participation of individuals, especially on the participation of individuals whose responsiveness may be weak or nil. I will not repeat here points made in response to Hunter, but rather will confine my comments to the specifics of Childs's proposal.

It was my intention when I developed the salvation/health model originally that it be inclusive of the very weak and dying, the newborn, the comatose, the severely retarded and handicapped, and the catatonic, because most theological anthropologies with which I was familiar did not include them. I did include them in Level One, but not sufficiently to please some of those clinicians who regularly ministered to them, as soon became apparent. These chaplains to the mentally retarded and severely handicapped, in particular, thought that their charges, and hence their ministries to them, were slighted in the model, even though they may have been also gratified to have them included at all. In time I came to agree with them.

Childs proposes a narrative theology approach to an important aspect of this problem—that of the fragmented and sometimes absent consciousness of these persons. Although I have reservations about the overall adequacy of narrative theology, I believe that he has made a creative move in this use of it. We can indeed see by means of the narrative lens that the "narrative" personal consciousness is impaired, fragmented, or absent in these persons and that, yes, parts of the "narrative" may be supplied by members of the community, both family and helpers, to provide meaning for themselves in the often painful decision making in which they must engage and, I would say, in enhancing their helping relationships with these persons—both aspects of their own salvatory participation.

I must say, however, that this approach does not fundamentally answer the question of the *worth* of those whom we think of as near the boundary of human existence any better than I tried to answer it in *Salvation and Health*, even though Childs's story of the twenty-one-year-old severely retarded man who was deemed worthy of palliative but not life-saving care, partially through narrative attribution of projected worth, adds poignancy to this picture. Narrative is, after all, a verbal model borrowed from the study of literature and has limitations when applied to the depths of human existence that lie beneath the surface of consciousness or, as the case may be, nonconsciousness. We still must rely on God's valuation for our valuation of and our ministries to such persons. Their participation is often beyond our ken, but not, we believe, beyond God's.

DON BROWNING's essay "Immanence and Transcendence in Pastoral Care and Preaching," despite its rather lofty and austere-sounding title, is a rather conversational piece arguing that both pastoral care and preaching are forms of conversation, hermeneutically understood. His approach to this question through reminiscence about our student days in the Divinity School at the University of Chicago brought back many memories, although I did not share the acutely felt sharpness of the Rogers/Barth split that he so vividly describes. But I can appreciate it. Neither Barth nor Rogers had any tolerance for ambiguity. Positive regard had to be unconditional. The gospel had to be thrown like a stone with no human contaminants sticking to it.

I was aware of Hiltner's differences with Marcus Barth, of course, but I had learned theology principally from John Newton Thomas at Union Seminary in Virginia; Thomas was too much of a rationalist to be very enthusiastic about Barth, an attitude that probably reinforced one I had already and retain to the present day.

Browning's argument is forceful and persuasive, as usual. We can see that from the point of view of hermeneuts Gadamer and Ricoeur, both pastoral care and preaching are conversation. Both can alter assumptions and understandings and bring new doubts and questions. Browning does acknowledge some differences in the kinds of conversations that pastoral care and preaching represent, with the depth of the person's question and the role of the person of the caregiver more emphasized in pastoral care.

It seems to me that Browning has indeed highlighted the similarities between preaching and pastoral care through the idea of conversation. But it also seems to be only an analogy (as he indicates Gadamer himself thought) in which differences as well as similarities must be identified. A chief difference between a conversation in which there is mutuality of status between the conversants and both preaching and pastoral care is what I sometimes call "the Saturday night question." In a once celebrated public conversation between Carl Rogers and Martin Buber, Rogers was urging with considerable passion that psychotherapy, the way he conceived it, was just like Buber's I-Thou relationship, to which Buber replied that it was not, for he, Buber, if he were Rogers's client, could not ask him what he was doing last Saturday night. There are limits and parameters surrounding all conversations, but those obtaining in pastoral care and preaching are too narrow to allow for more than very partial mutuality of inquiry and response. Too much is out of bounds—less in pastoral care than preaching, although preaching feedback groups in some churches provide a venue for a partial corrective.

A few minor points in Browning's piece prompt a response. The first is that the preacher cannot stand aside and let the text speak, as Browning urges. The text can speak only through the personality of the preacher. Browning seems to make a Barthian assumption that the preacher can get out of the way, so to speak. I do not believe this to be possible, and I think it much better for the preacher to acknowledge this and try consciously to use his or her personality to the best advantage, lest it inadvertently get in the way. The second point is that Seward Hiltner was careful not to identify himself as a Whiteheadian or member of any other theological "school," even though he made similar kinds of assumptions about the nature of reality and sources of the knowledge of God, and spoke favorably of process modes of thought, if a bit cryptically.[12] I think he can best be characterized as an empirical theologian trained in the old Chicago School. Toward the end of his active career he became more conservative and less inclined toward process theology.

EMMA J. JUSTES, in her essay "We Belong Together: Toward an Inclusive Anthropology," continues a conversation she and I have been having off and on for the past twenty-five years. Justes believes that those of us, mostly Caucasian males, who have been engaged in producing theological anthropologies for the past nearly two thousand years have distorted the picture of "women, people of color, and people of varied languages and cultures," in two ways. On the one hand, we have written as though we have included such persons, whereas in actuality we have not recognized their differences with us; and on the other hand, we have misidentified differences that do not exist, such as Barth's claim that women cannot be leaders. The remedy for this state of affairs is that "different voices must be heard and incorporated into our understanding of theological anthropology."

I cannot really quarrel with this position as a general description containing more than a grain of truth. There undoubtedly have been distortions, and different voices can help correct them—indeed, are correcting them.[13] Further, I can only applaud Justes's insistence that analysis and synthesis belong together. Her lifting up of the question of self-esteem of girls and women as being especially vexing and debilitating seems to be increasingly supported by research, even though this does not seem to be true of all girls and women, and the causes are far from clear. Her emphasizing of the need to perceive difference as a means of shoring up identity I give a hearty amen to.

There are, of course, aspects of Justes's position that I cannot support. In light of my use of, and defense of, the notion of hierarchy in anthropology in discussing Rodney J. Hunter's contribution, I cannot agree with her attack on this idea. Hierarchy of one sort or another is found everywhere in nature, and Justes herself seems to employ the notion implicitly in her valuing of community effort over individual effort—a hierarchy of values, suggesting an underlying structural hierarchy. I think that she wants to reject the specific hierarchies associated with monarchy and patriarchy in our society, and with that I can agree.

At one point she seems to endorse ambiguity, tension, and contradiction (paradox?) as a basic principle of theological anthropology, or "our anthropology becomes distorted." She also wants to get more clarity about true differences and likenesses between women and men. This is a seeming contradiction in method and approach, but perhaps she means to say that we must seek clarity about the actual paradoxes and seek to clear up the seeming ones. Endorsement of ambiguity, however, as distinguished from acknowledging it, always raises the suspicion in me that there is something the researcher does not want to know.

One last point about which I have questions is her valuing of community endeavor over individual endeavor, apparently without any qualification. I had my say about individual/corporate tensions earlier in commenting on the work of James Emerson. I will not elaborate here, except to say that I do not think the tension is so easily resolved as Justes seems to suggest in her comments on her illustrative story of two classrooms. Although context seemed to her to argue for the corporate approach to reporting, we do not know what values may have been lost that way.

JAMES E. LODER, my longtime colleague and teaching collaborator, in his "Incisions from a Two-Edged Sword: The Incarnation and the Soul/Spirit Relationship," has offered a major constructive statement of his views about the relationship of spirit and soul, at least in outline, and much else besides. His is a complex, intricately worked out statement, and I can only applaud its principal points: the relational character of spirit; the close connection between the human spirit and the Holy Spirit; the spirit as closely related to the soul, connecting tacit or unconscious elements to explicit, or conscious, elements (as I understand his use of soul here, it is close to, but not identical with, my use of the term *self* as including both ego and unconscious aspects of the person), but also transcending the soul in its analogy to a field of force, and expressive of exocentric, creative advance, following Pannenberg, whose work I have also employed.

This is not to say that our views are identical. I am not sure that I understand fully the diagram of his model, especially the relationship of level A to level B in figure 3. The diagram seems to indicate that the connection is through psyche or soul, but much of his text seems rather to indicate that it would be through spirit. The human spirit appears in both levels, but the connection between these two representations is unclear to me.

He has far more confidence in the principle of complementarity than do I. At best it seems to me that the Chalcedonian christological formula is an analogy, and a rather partial one at that, to the wave/particle complementarity that Niels Bohr had in mind, because the former is about relationship of entities (two natures), and the latter is about behaviors of one entity (see Loder's note 11 citing Robert K. Adair, ". . . one reality . . . different aspects"). I think that another one of Loder's favorite categories, paradox, is a better way to characterize Chalcedon.

Although I can agree that a christological interpretation of Hebrews 4:12–13 is a possible one, it is not the only one, or even the most likely, according to Westcott, for pertinent instance, who opts for Word of God as revelation, while noting that the two-edged sword is issuing from Christ's mouth in Revelation 1:16.[14] Although the connection to Christ is clearly present in Hebrews, the context does not require Christocentric identity with the Word of God. I can agree that unaided "natural reason" is not likely to find its way here, or even be looking, but theologians who believe themselves to be guided by the initiative of the Holy Spirit are not all necessarily Christocentric in the sense that Loder is urging it.

Another long-standing difference that we have, which shows up in this essay, is Loder's position that transformation, a key idea for him, is more or less all or nothing change in the direction of "proximate forms of the Christomorphic life." I hold that partial "transformations" are more usual and may be unstable (here siding with Loder's Methodist ancestors), although the proximate forms of the Christomorphic life do occur.

These comments, although intended to clarify certain differences with Loder, should not be construed as detracting from his achievement, which I regard as being of potentially great importance for pastoral care and other forms of ministry. He spells out convincingly a plausible matrix of relationships involving human spirit, psyche, and Holy Spirit.

FREDA A. GARDNER, who began and ended work at Princeton Seminary on the same days that I did, has provided the only essay in this volume focused mainly on ministry, thereby placing me particularly in her debt. In her "Another Look at the Elderly" she has made insightful comments on several current themes: the reality of death, the myth/sin of independence, body and gender in perception of self and others, and discipleship and ministry. Rather than comment on each of these, however, I have chosen to discuss some points that I believe are particularly characteristic of Gardner's outlook and ministry, which, although not absolutely unique to her, nevertheless represent a quite distinctive contribution, especially to the life of the church. These are the culture's message to the elderly, the need for gender specificity in considering the elderly (especially to highlight the strengths and needs of women), and highlighting the often overlooked details of ministry to the elderly.

Although many have pointed out the culture's negative messages to the elderly, Gardner has been insistent on the idea that, loud though the messages be—whether about the ugliness of aged bodies, the inadequacies of aged memories, or the uselessness of aged lives (which, some would say, should at least function independently, so as not to drain the resources of the truly living younger generations)—the church has messages of hospitality in the family of God adequate to counter these, if we attend carefully enough to the many possibilities for teaching them in classes, retreats, and workshops.

To this point I will add a note of urgency and warning. We cannot expect the culture to change its tune, no matter how many voices join the chorus defending the elderly. This is because it is not, strictly speaking, in the survival interests of the culture to do so. The elderly in our culture are expendable. They have no function in the survival of the culture, in which their role as potential consumers is only marginal. Wisdom was provided by the elderly in former times when they were in much shorter supply. Now they are too numerous, and wisdom is supplied, so it is thought, by computers. Their only function—those who are able, save for some limited grandparenting—is to supply money and other resources to those coming after them, and the means are at hand to obtain these by force, if necessary, through taxation and similar measures.

Citing some work done by former colleague Christie Cozad Neuger, Gardner cogently makes the case for gender specific research regarding the elderly, so that we may know better how women fare at that stage of life. It is true that not enough research has been done on older women, or specifically on older men, either, though sometimes findings on studies of men, or mainly men, have been wrongfully generalized to include women.

It is also true that we do not always know enough to know when it is appropriate to do gender specific research and when the genders should be treated together. An approach that assumes that women are in every respect different from men is as wrong as one that assumes that there are no differences. Proceeding with caution is advised.

One of Gardner's special gifts is a knack of lifting up the obscure but important details in a phenomenal matrix, as well as following through with details of ministry that make a difference. Both of these are manifested in this essay. As an instance of the first, she proposes that the church find out what the gifts of members are and shape ministries around them, a rather revolutionary suggestion. She also sees that the church may have an "implicit" curriculum that denigrates the aging (following a clue from Maria Harris). She proposes a remedial ministry guided by the concept of vocation, rather than self-actualization, and carried out by attention to myriad details, such as size of print in church materials, the reaction of youngsters to wrinkles, and individual needs within groups. I note that repeated details are especially important in the ministry to older persons, who are reassured by the familiarity and support conveyed through them.

All these add up to a contribution to practical theology that Gardner herself has been too reluctant to define as such. Hence, I take the liberty of stating on her behalf that discerning the negative messages of the culture and deciphering them, identifying the needs and aspirations of older women (and men) as such, and pointing up the need to attend to all the fine points of ministry in order to have a valid relational influence are grist for the mills of practical theologians who have eyes to see.

JOHN H. PATTON, who has been on the trail of forgiveness for more than twenty years and who has contributed a major work on the subject,[15] has now offered us his latest reflections on this focal, but illusive, topic in "Forgiveness, Lost Contracts, and Pastoral Theology." I will pause here to say that forgiveness has received more attention from modern pastoral theologians in the Chicago-Princeton axis than any other theological idea with doctrinal status. As noted earlier, James Emerson led off with *The Dynamics of Forgiveness* in 1964, followed by my "Lost Contracts" article in 1966, to which Patton has alluded. In 1971, Donald P. McNeill, a priest of the Order of the Holy Cross, completed a prize-winning Ph.D. dissertation at Princeton Seminary entitled "The Dynamics of Forgiveness in Community," which unfortunately has not been published. Brian H. Childs shifted the focus to early childhood in his Ph.D. dissertation at Princeton, "Forgiveness in Community in Light of Pauline Literature and the Experience Among Pre-School Children" and later wrote the article "Forgiveness" in the *Dictionary of Pastoral Care and Counseling*. Doris Donnelly, then teaching at Princeton Seminary, though not in pastoral theology, treated the thorny issue of repeated offenses in her article "Forgiveness and Recidivism."[16]

I mention these earlier contributions to say that, although it is true, as Patton says, that we have not found or discovered all about forgiveness, we have made considerable progress, in my estimation, with Patton in this essay, drawing on earlier work, bringing us the furthest yet down the trail.

Overall, Patton's work reflects both his professional dogged determination to track down the meaning of forgiveness and his personal anguish as the father of a raped daughter, which makes him very sympathetic to the anguish of other wronged persons. I believe his essay to be on the cutting edge of the current discussion about the best attitude for victims to take toward their victimizers.

Specifically, I think that Patton is correct in his central contention that forgiveness comes about as a by-product of a healing process through enlarging the frame of healing and is not a conscious act that stands in isolation in the experience of victims. In this connection, however, I do not agree with him that forgiveness does not have the quality of an act. Rather, persons do perceive themselves *retrospectively* to have let go of, or released, the putative offender from the relationship of bondage in which they were holding him or her. Indeed, Patton says as much: "On occasion, there was discovery of their having let go or forgiven as a type of religious experience." Such releasing does have the quality of an initiated act, even though the forgiver was not conscious of it at the time.

I further agree with him that forgiveness is not an all or nothing phenomenon, humanly speaking; it may be partial, ambiguous, and in need of repeating for those deeply hurt who may have permanent scar tissue. It may be likened to a chronic disease such as diabetes or, speaking from experience, periodontal disease, which requires active treatment and attention to control, but which does not go away.

Recently, I myself have returned to the trail of forgiveness, as a part of a concern to investigate human vindictiveness, vengefulness, and the violence generated in that cauldron. To be sure, vengefulness is not the only factor in the production of violence, but it is essential for the perpetuation of cycles of violence that are the plague of humankind. I have some questions about the realistic possibilities of forgiveness where the psychic wounds have produced deep shame and the threat of more shame. Patton shed considerable light on these questions in his book, especially in relation to family-centered betrayal. Other questions are about the realistic possibilities of nondestructive alternatives to forgiveness, where forgiveness seems impossible. Maintaining a relationship of bondage in which the victim futilely seeks redress or harm to the perpetrator damages both victim and perpetrator. Still others are about the appropriateness of forgiveness in different kinds of situations.

We do not, and should not, forgive swindlers, for instance, without restitution.

Behind all these questions is the bottom line question of human nature—must it ever seek to balance the scales of justice, no matter the cost? Can a God of justice and mercy still be expected to relieve some of this personal burden? Hence, the issues regarding forgiveness are very much alive for me, and I think for everyone. Patton has again placed me in his debt (thus tilting the justice scale) with this essay.

HERBERT ANDERSON, who was once my colleague at Princeton Seminary, has offered us an essay at once thoughtful and passionately emphatic in his "The Recovery of Soul." Anderson's work is above all a reminder that, unlike most of its predecessors (Justes's essay is a partial exception), which were devoted mainly to the attempt to clear up matters—ideas, concepts, attitudes—pastoral theology has to do also with mystery, transcendence, and the limits of knowledge. He conducts no systematic historical survey of how the term *soul* has been used in different cultures over the centuries, nor presents any examination of what precisely it means now in the hands of different contemporary scholars, although he does allude to some of these. He is primarily interested in the connotations of the term, not in its denotations. Above all, he is interested in what he believes to be its paradoxical character.

Paradox is the central idea. I offer a pair of quotations: "The task of *seelsorge* is to empower people to embrace paradox." And, "It is the restoration of soul, I believe, that will enhance the recovery of paradox in human life." To be sure, Anderson is interested also in diversity and community, regarding which he also thinks "the soul's paradox . . . will articulate an anthropological vision that is deep enough and broad enough to encompass the diversity of human life today."

When he does address the question of what the term *soul* may mean, he indicates that it is "a metaphor for meaning and memory in our time." Several times he emphasizes this metaphorical character, seeming to hold it to be a virtue, unless he assumes the metaphorical character of all language—a point beyond the scope of this essay, except to say that some language is intended to be more precise than some other.

Although I readily admit that the term *soul* has a rich connotation of meaning for us, and that, as a metaphor that can be employed to make and emphasize certain points, especially those related to the depth of being of the person, it is always going to be needed, I am not ready to accept his proposal. This hesitancy may have to do with a certain difference in outlook between us as heirs of Luther and Calvin, a difference evident at times during our years of teaching together. (Lest too much be made of this, I want to point out that, in proposing to debate ninety-five theses, Luther was not at that time a proponent of ambiguity and paradox, but rather of clarity. The two-kingdom, paradoxical Luther came later.) For Anderson, paradox is apparently something to be sought; for me it is something to be accepted when unavoidable.

The incarnation, to take an exemplary instance, is a paradox, if one accepts the premises about the distinction between the divine and the human underlying the Chalcedonian formula. However, to take an instance he cites, being a victim and being responsible is not necessarily paradoxical, for we devote our helping efforts to freeing persons from the bondage of past victimization and to clearing up the ways in which it still determines their lives, and identifying in what ways they are relatively free from it. I think this is an instance of the resort to paradox when none exists.

I believe that the idea of soul is too laden with the baggage of body/soul dualism and its consequent denigration of both body and person to bring it back as a central denotative concept. Anderson himself seems to be well aware of this problem, for he devotes several pages to what is apparently a defense against this charge by asserting that it is an antidote to dualism—a point difficult for me to see. Although I agree that the term *soul* has a certain moral weightiness, if we make the paradoxical soul the center of a pastoral diagnostic scheme, we do not help the practitioner who must always choose, as difficult as that may sometimes be, between alternative understandings as a basis of action. Again, I agree that we must recognize paradox when we bump into it and respect mystery when we find it. However, seeking it is not an endeavor in which I want to engage.

CHRISTIE COZAD NEUGER has provided us with an insightfully reflective and theologically challenging essay in her "Gender: Women and Identity." It is the kind of feminist piece that tends to make many men both irritated and protective of the woman who wrote it and hence unable to say much of anything about it. Hence, I will try to be as analytical as possible and thus to avoid being an instance of patronizing patriarchalism being discussed (among other aspects of patriarchalism) in the essay.

There is much that I can easily applaud. Neuger seems to me to be right on target in saying that the key problem in women's identity formation is in the mixed messages received by girls and women from the culture that places them in a double bind. (She calls these paradoxes, a term I reserve for truly knotty problems like the determinism/freedom question. These double-binding messages are contradictory in their impact, but their origins can be traced to differing need systems within the culture.) I think that these messages are also received by boys—for instance, to be both macho and organized—but that these are not as severe in their impact on many boys.

She is also correct, in my estimation, in stressing the relational character of all human beings: "It is a human issue to be related and in community, not a woman's issue." Her skepticism that the notion of embodiment can be a general salvatory concept is well founded, even though acceptance of the body will have to be a part of any corrective proposal, I believe. Access to symbols and symbol construction is indeed important for women, even though deliberate myth making will, I think, always be a precarious enterprise, with unintended outcomes littering the cultural landscape. I think of the French Revolution.

The analyses of developmental problems provided by Ballou and Gabalac on the one hand and by Kaschak on the other are quite suggestive and point to significant issues in girls' development that can be addressed. The need for psycho/spiritual separation from the father as a general prescription strikes me as a remedy with a probably high price, although I can understand the reasoning that led to its proposal.

I dispute the contention that Neuger and other feminists make that "fact and truth are created by those who have the most invested in the explanations." Fact and truth may indeed be distorted by those with vested interests, and interpretations certainly are. But if fact and truth are invented by interested parties, the feminists, too, can only spin self-serving yarns. Truth is hard to find, but the search must go on.

I also find the rather extreme environmentalist position taken in which culturally constructed gender is viewed as more powerful than biology to be out of balance. Without biological sexuality, gender has no base. What we see is an amalgam of the two, in which culture, to be sure, plays a very significant role.

As a pastoral theologian, I found the clinical evidence for women's mirroring themselves in the eyes of God ("indeterminate male eyes"?) in a disturbing way to be the most intriguing aspect of the study, and that this negative imaging of themselves could be changed if God were designated female. Does Neuger intend here that we should stress the gender of the deity as female when presenting the notion of God to girls? Should we state that God is only female? Mainly female? Should we say that God has no gender, but for our weakness we need to think of God as having gender? What of the role of gender in our theologizing? Does our God no longer have a punitive superego, internalized better in the past by girls than by boys? If not, what kinds of sanctions for human behavior, if any, does God use now?

These are some important questions that, it seems to me, are implicated in Neuger's discussion, although we could not expect her to address them all in a short essay.

MUSINGS AND FURTHER DIRECTIONS

What follows will first be mainly in the "musings" category—additional reflections on some points made by the contributors. Those elements that might be seen as further directions are chiefly indications of some paths I seem to be interested in following myself and are not intended as prescriptive, or even necessarily suggestive, for others in the field of pastoral theology. The very last comment about relationships to institutions in which pastoral theology is carried on as an academic discipline might be said to have a prescriptive flavor.

Musings

It seems to me that there were three concerns shared by two or more contributors to this volume: (1) the addition of the concept of "soul" to the model of human being employed, or the use of soul as a central concept in another model, (2) the need for a more inclusive and diverse experiential base for theological anthropology and pastoral theology, and (3) the call for a new emphasis on the corporate or community dimensions of pastoral care and pastoral theology. Although these themes were, no doubt, shaped to some extent by the contributors' perceptions that they were addressing deficits in one of the models that I have put forward at various times (or different versions of the same model, as Hunter would have it—I am not sure myself how much the earlier salvation/health model informs the later self/spirit model, though it undoubtedly does to some extent), I believe that they also represent rather widespread agenda among pastoral theologians and pastoral caregivers.

Beginning in the mid-1970s, I became convinced that in order to move forward with integrity, the field of pastoral theology needed to find a way of speaking theologically about human beings, but without giving up the practical gains it had achieved through the use of dynamic psychology. The model of human being used in *Salvation and Health* was essentially a psychoanalytic ego psychology model that was linked to a Whiteheadian universe by means of the idea of participation. It was not a model with a definite structural/functional theological anthropology component as such, although the goals of human life were theologically determined—the link to the later self/spirit model, where goals were not in focus, but rather assumed.

In this model, much of what had been described as participatory was linked to the human spirit and its vectors, whereas maintenance and development were viewed as functions of primarily the self. Thus the ancient concept of spirit was joined to the relatively modern one of self in a union that is yet to be proved enduring. Indeed, many would say, although none of the contributors did say, even if they thought it, that such linkage of ancient and modern constructs should not be attempted in principle—that they belong to different worlds that cannot be joined.

Three contributors, Capps, Loder, and Anderson, made differing proposals, but all involved the restoration of soul to a significant place in anthropology—in Anderson's proposal the central place. Without rehearsing the discussion I presented in connection with each one, I can say here that they all seem to accept the idea that we do need some ancient constructs, explicitly or implicitly linked to modern ones. I rejoice in their interest in this kind of model building and hope for its continuation and enlargement.

I have expressed reservations, which I will not repeat here, about the use of soul as a central denotative construct, but I think that I understand why it has appeal, and respect the efforts being made to rehabilitate it. I believe and expect that those using it will be careful regarding the dualistic abuses of the past. I am aware that spirit is also subject to confusion and abuse, and that all such ancient meaning laden ideas come with baggage.

In my own work, I hope for clarity for diagnosis and indications for action, and metaphor and paradox for reflective moments. I never expect to find the Virgin Mary's self magnifying the Lord (Luke 1:46); her soul will always do so. Neither would I look forward to encountering the self of the 104th psalmist being urged to bless the Lord (Ps. 104:1). Poetry is poetry, and we need it for what may be called paradiagnosis—those processes on the margins of focal awareness that are nevertheless crucial to it—as well as for personal faith and meaning. Perhaps this point is similar to Polanyi's tacit elements in knowledge cited by Loder.

I will continue to use the term *self* for communication purposes and also because of its richness as a depository of much of the lore of modern, and especially dynamic, psychology. I note that when the translators of the New Revised Standard Version of the Bible needed a denotative term, they retained *self* in Paul's crucial description of the war in his members, "For I delight in the law of God in my inmost self" (Rom. 7:22). I have some company.

The second issue to which I will point, of concern to Cobb, Justes, Emerson, and with regard to women, to Gardner, is that the experiential base of pastoral theology be multicultural and reflective of gender and racial/ethnic differences. I am offering a cautious concurrence. I agree that data from other cultures are needed, and especially from the mostly underrepresented constituencies in our own society—African Americans, women, Hispanics, and Native Americans. I am glad to say that both African Americans and women are now becoming better represented, even if we still have distances to go before both are perceived in the field as full conversation partners—with women being very close to this status, though sometimes not in their own self-perception.

I am cautious about endorsing pluralism for its own sake or for the sake alone of the presumed or actual enrichment as such that it brings. I own that I have a values test, shaped in Reformed theology, modified by process theology, informed by dynamic psychology and ethics spawned in the enlightenment. (Yes, I admit to having such enlightenment values as human rights and human reason, even though I am aware that both can be carried to extremes.) I do not accept slavery, torture, foot-binding, indentured servitude, or patriarchy, but there are some societies that either endorse or tolerate one or more of these. The point here is that multicultural sources alone are an insufficient criterion for pastoral theology. Pluralism must be coupled with hard thinking about the range of acceptable values embodied in these sources, and this does mean discriminating, though not prejudicial discrimination.

Also, I believe that, for sake of communication, we need to have some concepts in the field that have relatively stable meanings. Pluralism leads to word coinage, some of which is inevitable and even helpful in moderation (I indulge myself), but a plethora of overnight new constructs impedes communication, especially if they have esoteric roots and are known only to a few. Ours is a fragile discipline only beginning to take shape. It is easily overwhelmed.

The corporate, or community, dimension of anthropology, and by implication pastoral theology, was lifted up in different ways by Hunter, Childs, Emerson, and Justes. Hunter's concern was mainly that we incorporate a systems theory outlook into our anthropology (a concern supported by many pastoral theologians; see Larry K. Graham's *Care of Persons, Care of Worlds: A Psychosystems Approach to Pastoral Care and Counseling*),[17] whereas Childs emphasized the role of the caregiving community in defining the quality and quantity of life, and decision making about them. He also alluded to the increasing role of public policy in influencing both quality and quantity of life. As I write this, the President of the United States is preparing to offer to the Congress his proposals regarding a comprehensive health care plan, certainly bringing the public policy dimension home to us all. Emerson's concern, as we have already noted, is to lift up the community emphasis in East Asian culture for what it can teach us. Justes cited in particular the values of learning shared in community.

Although I am supportive in principle of a community emphasis, and indeed offered one, albeit too limited, in *Salvation and Health*, I am not optimistic that we can find a unified theory of human beings that does justice to both community and individual, and particularly to their interaction. To my mind, systems theory has always seemed a partial and sometimes misleading approach if taken as a guide to the whole human arena, made up, as systems theory is, of bits and pieces of theory gleaned from biology, the social sciences, and clinical observation. Although it has undeniable utility in dealing with families, the limits of this utility are sometimes ignored by enthusiastic proponents and indeed are hard to discern in some instances. But if individual lives have been damaged, then the limits have been exceeded.

At the other end of the scale of community, in which ever larger dimensions of the polis come into play, systems theory seems progressively weaker in discriminating among various types and levels regarding their power to affect lives. We are aware, for instance, of the large number of variables that must be taken into account in trying to assess the potency of even the relatively low-level community represented by a church congregation.

Earlier in this essay I alluded to the concept of the artificial person, which still seems to be the implicit theoretical construct in much thinking about the individual and his or her agents. It seems questionable whether we are well served by a 300-year-old concept that treats corporate entities, whether family or the state, as quasi-individuals of which the person is a part, having yielded agency to them. A model that can better discern the actual relationships of individuals and the various communities of which he or she is in some sense a part is badly needed, and may be at hand. But I am not aware of it.

In the meantime we need to continue to identify those points at which the community, in its several dimensions, most directly affects individuals, both positively and negatively. We need also to begin to identify those ways in which we, as pastoral theologians and caregivers, can begin to influence the communities in which we live and work.

Further Directions

I continue to think that communication with integrity within and beyond the field of pastoral theology is the most important single issue in the field. We still do not have shared language and models adequate for this purpose. Unless these are developed in the near future, I fear that our still nascent discipline may founder, for common interest is dependent upon common language and models that seem useful and pertinent, even though complete agreement is neither necessary nor desirable.

This is not to say that I think no progress has been made along these lines. As indicated above, those contributors who focused on the anthropological model question seemed to accept the principle of linking ancient and modern constructs, even though they did not agree on which constructs or how they should be linked. Still, I would say that, with the exception of Anderson, who seemed to focus almost exclusively on the question of the rehabilitation of the concept of soul, all used some kind of spirit/self (ego) linkage. All seemed determined to take theology very seriously as a contributing discipline.

There seemed to be no consensus about a clearly defined self theory, even though it seems to me that the various meanings employed were not very different from one another. Perhaps through more "conversation" about the self, a greater degree of consensus can be reached.

Although Browning was the only contributor to make direct use of hermeneutics in his essay, Patton, Gerkin, and Capps have also made significant contributions toward developing an approach to pastoral theology in the hermeneutical mode.[18] It may well be that "conversation," based upon the hermeneutics of Ricoeur and Gadamer, will be the vehicle through which a greater consensus about self, spirit, soul, and their mutual relations can be developed. If that can be the mode, I wish the hermeneuts well and hope to join the conversation, even though I have not paid my dues as a hermeneut and do not carry a card.

Turning now to a second point, I hope that we can better bring our resources to bear on questions of good and evil, and I intend to keep working on this broad range of issues. I believe that our field may have something of considerable importance to say about ethics as well as something to learn from ethics. (Here I recall earlier extended conversations with Browning about the relationship of pastoral theology to ethics.) The discussion of forgiveness and vindictiveness alluded to earlier in my response to Patton's essay is one important potential source of contribution to the understanding of good and evil. Although it is not yet clear to me exactly what we can contribute to the realm of public policy, I believe that we do have reflections on pastoral experience, particularly with the elderly, that can be of importance. I hope to keep working in this area as well, and I expect and hope to be joined by many others, some of whom, of course, are already there.

Finally, I think that pastoral theologians need to think more carefully about a matter to which they have hitherto given little thought, at least in the public realm. This is the question of the relationship of pastoral theology to the institutions in which it operates—theological seminaries, hospitals, counseling centers, parishes, and university-related divinity schools. These are the elements of the corporate domain most readily at hand, and moreover, they are the ones most influential in the lives of pastoral theologians and their discipline.

This is especially so because all the humanities and social sciences seem to be heading into a period of unusual self-professed subjectivity and denial of anything resembling the pursuit of truth, following the French pied pipers Foucault and Derrida. This trend started in English departments, according to Louis Menand, and spread from there. Menand, himself an editor and professor of English, finds this trend to be appalling and undermining the principal justification of academic freedom—the pursuit of truth. "[T]he line separating 'knowledge' from 'ideology' has become increasingly hard to draw for many people in the humanities and social sciences these days."[19]

This trend is evident also in theological education. For some, hermeneutics suggests that interpretation is everything, text is forever obscured, data foggy, theory (theology) inherently compromised. I am aware that not all hermeneuts take this position. With my colleagues who have identified themselves with hermeneutics, I believe that truth must be sought through conversation, and to some extent emerges from it. Nevertheless, it has an ineluctable "deposit" character, too. We need both understandings of truth—as deposit and as emergent—to get a full picture.

I believe that pastoral theology must present itself as seeking the truth through reflection on practice in light of its ongoing theory, and correcting and amplifying theory in light of that. As indicated earlier, I think that we have actually discovered some truths about forgiveness through this method, even though much remains to be discovered. A writer in *Pastoral Psychology* put it as follows in 1976 in an editorial entitled "Truth and Pastoral Theology":

> I would like to ask you to reflect with me on the deeper implications of our failure to identify ourselves primarily as truth seekers. Then I would like to challenge you to begin to look within your

own pastoral practice for experiences that not only validate others' formulations of truth but also serve to critique them and the methods by which they were achieved.[20]

The writer was Peggy Ann Way, hardly a hopeless reactionary. It is important for pastoral theologians to claim to be seeking truth, and actually to be seeking it, in a day of confusion about the validity of that endeavor. For sooner or later, I believe, the academics and their constituents will discover that the English departments were like the "fox who had no tail" and persuaded others to cut theirs off. Literary criticism has always had a weak case for the claim to be seeking truth, according to Menand,[21] and its time of enhanced status for not seeking it will end, I think, when those in other disciplines who could seek it find that they too quickly have accepted a presumably postmodern notion that it could not be found (actually a much older notion).

Even if other disciplines do not arrive at this conclusion, pastoral theologians need to hold to their heritage of truth seeking through reflection on practice in light of tradition. In this way they will maintain and enhance their own relationships with the institutions in which they serve, and also will enhance the mission and strength of these institutions with their constituencies by increasing credibility. The way forward in this case is by holding to the best of the past and finding new and creative ways to use it. Let us embrace all the elements of truth seeking to which we are heir, and we will continue to discover more of the truth and to encounter it in conversation.

NOTES

1. James N. Lapsley, *Salvation and Health: The Interlocking Processes of Life* (Philadelphia: Westminster Press, 1972), 22.

2. Ibid., 122.

3. Elizabeth Wolgast, *Ethics of an Artificial Person* (Stanford, Calif.: Stanford University Press, 1992).

4. Ibid., 53.

5. John B. Cobb, Jr., *A Christian Natural Theology* (Philadelphia: Westminster Press, 1965).

6. "Multiculturalism in Vienna: The Future of Human Rights," *The Christian Century* 110, no. 20 (June 30–July 7, 1993): 660–62.

7. David E. Scharff, *The Sexual Relationship: An Object Relations View*

of Sex and the Family (London: Routledge & Kegan Paul, 1988), 220. Scharff cites H. Segal, *Introduction to the Work of Melanie Klein* (London: Hogarth Press, 1973).

8. James Emerson, *The Dynamics of Forgiveness* (Philadelphia: Westminster Press, 1964).

9. Robert N. Bellah and Chris Adams, "Individualism and the Arts," *The Christian Century* 110, no. 21 (July 14–21, 1993): 703.

10. See James N. Lapsley, "Reflections on the Electric Circus," *Journal of Pastoral Care* 23, no. 1 (March 1969): 9–12.

11. Bruno Bettelheim, *Freud and Man's Soul* (New York: Alfred Knopf, 1983), 15.

12. See, for example, Seward Hiltner, "Paul Tillich and Pastoral Psychology," *Pastoral Psychology* 16, no. 159 (December 1965): 8.

13. See, for example, Susan Brooks Thistlethwaite and Mary Potter Engel, eds., *Lift Every Voice* (San Francisco: Harper & Row, 1990).

14. B. F. Westcott, *The Epistle to the Hebrews* (Grand Rapids: Wm. B. Eerdmans, 1952), 101.

15. John Patton, *Is Human Forgiveness Possible?* (Nashville: Abingdon Press, 1985).

16. Doris Donnelly, "Forgiveness and Recidivism," *Pastoral Psychology* 33, no. 1 (Fall 1984): 15–24.

17. Larry K. Graham, *Care of Persons, Care of Worlds: A Psychosystems Approach to Pastoral Care and Counseling* (Nashville: Abingdon Press, 1992).

18. John Patton, "Clinical Hermeneutics: Soft Focus in Pastoral Counseling and Theology," *Journal of Pastoral Care* 35 (1981): 157–68; Charles V. Gerkin, *The Living Human Document: Revisioning Pastoral Counseling in a Hermeneutical Mode* (Nashville: Abingdon Press, 1984); Donald Capps, *Pastoral Care and Hermeneutics* (Philadelphia: Fortress Press, 1984).

19. Louis Menand, "The Future of Academic Freedom," *Academe* 79, no. 3 (May–June 1993): 12.

20. Peggy Ann Way, "Truth and Pastoral Theology," *Pastoral Psychology* 24, no. 4 (Summer 1976): 263.

21. Menand, "The Future of Academic Freedom," 15.

Contributors

HERBERT ANDERSON is a Lutheran pastor and Professor of Pastoral Theology at Catholic Theological Union in Chicago. He is currently at work on a five-volume series on Family Living in Pastoral Perspective. The volume topics are *Leaving Home*, *Becoming Married*, *Regarding Children*, *Promising Again*, and *Living Alone*. He was a teaching colleague of James Lapsley at Princeton Theological Seminary from 1969–75.

DONALD CAPPS is William Harte Felmeth Professor of Pastoral Theology at Princeton Theological Seminary. He holds the B.D. and S.T.M. degrees from Yale Divinity School, the Ph.D. from the University of Chicago, and the Th.D. (hon.) from Uppsala, Sweden. He is past-President of the Society for the Scientific Study of Religion and is author of several books, including *Reframing: A New Method in Pastoral Care*, *The Depleted Self*, and *The Poet's Gift: Toward the Renewal of Pastoral Care*.

DON S. BROWNING is Alexander Campbell Professor of Ethics and Social Sciences at the Divinity School of the University of Chicago. He is the author of several books, including *A Fundamental Practical Theology: Descriptive and Strategic Proposals*.

BRIAN H. CHILDS (coeditor) is Professor of Pastoral Theology and Counseling at Columbia Theological Seminary in Decatur, Georgia. A former student of James Lapsley and Seward Hiltner at Princeton, he is the author with John Patton of *Christian Marriage and Family, Caring for Our Generations*, and *Short-Term Pastoral Counseling: A Guide*. He is Book Review Editor of *Pastoral Psychology*. Through the National Endowment for the Humanities, he recently finished a fellowship with the Institute for Medicine and the Humanities in Hiram, Ohio.

JOHN B. COBB, JR., retired in 1990 from the School of Theology at Claremont. He continues part-time at Claremont Graduate School, where he is a director of the Center for Process Studies. His books include *Christ in a Pluralistic Age*, *Can Christ Become Good News Again?*, *Sustainability*, *Praying for Jennifer*, *Becoming a Thinking Christian*, and *Theology and Pastoral Care*.

JAMES G. EMERSON, JR., is Pastor Emeritus, Calvary Presbyterian Church in San Francisco; he is Chair of the Editorial Board of *Pastoral Psychology* and a mission volunteer in education and Consultant in Asia (Presbyterian Church, U.S.A.). The author of *The Dynamics of Forgiveness: Divorce, the Church, Remarriage*; and *Suffering*, he is a former lecturer at Princeton Theological Seminary and San Francisco Theological Seminary.

FREDA A. GARDNER is Thomas W. Synnott Professor of Christian Education, Emerita, at Princeton Theological Seminary. She is a graduate of the State University of New York and the Presbyterian School of Christian Education. An elder in the Presbyterian Church (U.S.A.), she was a colleague of James Lapsley at Princeton for thirty years.

CHARLES V. GERKIN is Franklin N. Parker Professor of Pastoral Theology, Emeritus, at Candler School of Theology, Emory University, Atlanta. In his active career, he was also a certified supervisor with the Association for Clinical Pastoral Education and a *Diplomate* in the American Association of Pastoral Counselors. He was founder and first Executive Director of the Georgia Association for Pastoral Care, and he is the author of *Crisis Experience in Modern Life*, *The Living Human Document*, *Widening the Horizons*, and *Prophetic Pastoral Practice*.

RODNEY J. HUNTER is Professor of Pastoral Theology at Emory University's Candler School of Theology in Atlanta. A former student of James Lapsley and Seward Hiltner at Princeton Theological Seminary, he has authored numerous articles on pastoral theology and was general editor of the *Dictionary of Pastoral Care and Counseling*. A member of Cherokee Presbytery, he is an active participant in Central Presbyterian Church in Atlanta and is a member of the Board of Governors of the Georgia Association of Pastoral Care.

EMMA J. JUSTES is a graduate of Colgate Rochester Divinity School. She received her Ph.D. from Princeton Theological Seminary under the guidance of James Lapsley. She is an ordained American Baptist minister, and her interests in study and teaching include work on issues related to women, human sexuality, aging, and race/culture. She currently teaches at Northern Baptist Theological Seminary in Lombard, Illinois, and lives in Skokie with her two sons, Kito and Micah.

JAMES N. LAPSLEY is Egner Professor of Pastoral Theology, Emeritus, Princeton Theological Seminary; he retired in 1992. He was Academic Dean at Princeton from 1984–89 and is a Presbyterian minister. Born in Clarksville, Tennessee, he is the author of *Salvation and Health*, and *Renewal in Late Life through Pastoral Counseling*, and he edited *The Concept of Willing*. He is the author of several articles and chapters in books in the area of pastoral care and pastoral theology, including especially material on theoretical topics. He was a member of the Board of the Council for Clinical Training, a member of the counseling staff of Trinity Counseling Service (Princeton), and is the past Chair of the Editorial Board of *Pastoral Psychology*. He is the father of two adult children, and he lives with his second wife, Helen, in Sun City, Arizona.

JAMES E. LODER received his Ph.D. from Harvard University in 1962. Prior to this time, he spent one year as a Danforth Fellow at the Menninger Foundation where, as a colleague of James Lapsley, he studied theology and psychiatric theory. He joined the Princeton Theological Seminary faculty in 1962, where he and Lapsley were colleagues for approximately thirty years. He is currently Mary D. Synnott Professor of the Philosophy of Christian Education at Princeton.

LISTON O. MILLS is Oberlin Alumni Professor of Pastoral Theology and Counseling at Vanderbilt University Divinity School. The editor of *Perspectives on Death*, he was also Associate Editor of the *Dictionary of Pastoral Care and Counseling* and is past-Editor of *Pas-*

toral Psychology. He is a certified supervisor with the Association for Clinical Pastoral Education and supervises at the Veteran's Medical Center in Nashville.

CHRISTIE COZAD NEUGER teaches at United Theological Seminary of the Twin Cities in Minneapolis. Prior to going to Minnesota, she taught with James Lapsley at Princeton Theological Seminary. She is coeditor of the *Journal of Pastoral Theology*.

JOHN H. PATTON is Professor of Pastoral Theology at Columbia Theological Seminary. Prior to becoming a full-time professor, he was active in clinical and administrative dimensions of pastoral care and counseling. He is a certified supervisor with the Association for Clinical Pastoral Education and is a *Diplomate* and past-President of the American Association of Pastoral Counselors. The author of *Is Human Forgiveness Possible?* and, most recently, *Pastoral Care in Context*, he was Man of the Year in *Pastoral Psychology* in 1979.

DAVID W. WAANDERS (coeditor) is Professor of Pastoral Care and Director of the Th.M. Program in Pastoral Counseling at New Brunswick Theological Seminary in New Jersey. An ordained pastor in the Reformed Church in America, he completed his Ph.D. at Princeton Theological Seminary with James Lapsley and Seward Hiltner. In addition to his teaching, he is a clinical staff member at Trinity Counseling Service (Princeton).